Period Rooms
in The Metropolitan Museum of Art

Period Rooms

in The Metropolitan Museum of Art

Amelia Peck

James Parker

William Rieder

Olga Raggio

Mary B. Shepard

Annie-Christine Daskalakis Mathews

Daniëlle O. Kisluk-Grosheide

Wolfram Koeppe

Joan R. Mertens

Alfreda Murck and Wen C. Fong

Photography by Karin L. Willis

The Metropolitan Museum of Art, New York

Harry N. Abrams, Inc., Publishers, New York

Produced by The Metropolitan Museum of Art

John P. O'Neill, Editor in Chief
Barbara Burn, Executive Editor
Nai Chang, Designer
Gwen Roginsky and Chris Zichello, Production

Library of Congress Cataloging-in-Publication Data

Period rooms in the Metropolitan Museum of Art / Amelia Peck ... [et al.].
p.   cm.
Includes bibliographical references and index.
ISBN 0-87099-805-6 (MMA). — ISBN 0-8109-3744-1 (Abrams)
1. Interior decoration—Themes, motives. 2. Furniture—Styles.
3. Interior architecture—Themes, motives.
4. Metropolitan Museum of Art (New York, N.Y.)
I. Peck, Amelia. II. Metropolitan Museum of Art (New York, N.Y.)
NK2110.P47   1996
747.2' 074747' 1—DC20   96–15562

The color photographs in this book were taken by Karin L. Willis
of the Photograph Studio, The Metropolitan Museum of Art,
except for those in the chapters on the Gubbio studiolo,
which were taken by Bruce Schwarz of the Photograph Studio,
and on the Astor Court, which were taken
by various staff members of the Photograph Studio.

Frontispiece:
The Boscoreale Bedroom, about 40–30 B.C. (Rogers Fund, 1903,03.14.13)

PRINTED AND BOUND BY ARNOLDO MONDADORI EDITORE S.P.A., VERONA, ITALY

Table of Contents

NEAR AND FAR EAST

Period Rooms
in The Metropolitan Museum of Art

Introduction

BY PHILIPPE DE MONTEBELLO

DIRECTOR

One of the most popular attractions at the Metropolitan Museum—and ironically one that is not without controversy—is our collection of period rooms. Virtually everyone who visits the Museum's American Wing finds there the opportunity to experience a sense of the way our forebears lived. Visitors walking through the Wrightsman rooms—from the shopfront of 3 quai de Bourbon past the Varengeville and Cabris rooms to the Tessé salon that once overlooked the Seine—can survey a century of French interiors and decoration at their highest level. In 1995 critics applauded the faithful reinterpretation of our English rooms, and most recently we were gratified by the tremendous response to our reinstallation of the newly restored *studiolo* from Gubbio, surely the most impressive example of Italian Renaissance illusionistic intarsia in this country. Tucked away in the Museum's galleries are a Roman bedroom, once buried by the eruption of Mount Vesuvius, a Syrian reception room of 1707 from a house in Damascus, and a fully furnished living room, of 1912–15, from a Frank Lloyd Wright house at Wayzata, Minnesota. The Cloisters, in upper Manhattan, provides a harmonious setting for the arcades from medieval French cloisters, including Saint-Michel-de-Cuxa, complete with perennial and herb gardens based on those of the Middle Ages.

It is clear when one visits the Museum why these spaces are evocative and appealing. What may not be clear is why their very existence is the subject of debate. Some scholars and experts in the field of decorative arts do not agree on their appropriateness in an art-museum setting, their purpose, and their degree of authenticity. Some would prefer to have such rooms confined to historic houses, where they may be seen in their original architectural context. But others feel that the careful combination of architectural elements rescued from condemned buildings with contemporaneous works of decorative art and furniture serves a number of important functions, not the least of which is preservation.

The Metropolitan's rooms run the gamut from the completely authentic to the mostly interpretive. The Frank Lloyd Wright room contains furniture, lamps, and windows created under the supervision of the architect himself, and they are arranged according to Wright's plan. At the other extreme is the Cloisters' Campin room, which has an authentic medieval

Spanish ceiling but is otherwise designed and furnished—albeit with original works of art—in harmony with the interior represented in the famous Annunciation triptych by Robert Campin installed there.

What of the rooms that fall somewhere in between? Does the re-creation of a missing section of molding or the repainting of a peeling wood panel make a room less authentic? Maintenance was an important part of any room in situ, and so by reproducing moldings, replacing worn upholstery, or repairing a damaged piece of furniture are we deceiving the Museum visitor, or is it an acceptable way to ensure the legibility of a work of art? Surely it is valid to restore architectural ornament to what we believe was its original appearance, just as archaeologists have restrung countless ancient beads (which would be meaningless otherwise) according to depictions on ancient paintings and sculptures. By appropriately furnishing a room with fine contemporary pieces, are we falsifying the presentation or providing the best possible context? The fact is we have selected both options at the Metropolitan, for countless pieces of furniture and decorative arts are also shown as individual exhibits. In short, we believe in the relative merits of both approaches.

The tradition of period rooms in America is usually associated with institutions that thrived during the 1920s, when entire buildings were created and filled with rooms in such styles as "Early American," "Colonial," and "Federal." Winterthur, Colonial Williamsburg, the Brooklyn Museum, and the Metropolitan with its American Wing (which opened in 1924) all participated with great enthusiasm. As scholarship became more sophisticated, questions of authenticity were posed about rooms that had been "enhanced" where the original was in less than perfect condition. Also, the beginnings of the activist historic-preservation movement made people aware that it was preferable to save buildings intact rather than to remove rooms. At this point, the period-room movement went into a quiet phase, which lasted for nearly thirty years, from the 1950s to the 1980s, when curators and art historians began to reevaluate the importance of period rooms and in many cases revised not only their thinking but also the rooms themselves.

Long before the 1920s the Metropolitan Museum began collecting period rooms. In 1903 we acquired the recently excavated bedroom from a villa near Pompeii, and three years later we purchased a seventeenth-century wood-paneled chamber from the Swiss town of Flims and an eighteenth-century bedroom from the Palazzo Sagredo in Venice. This charming room, with its plaster ceiling thickly decorated with a swarm of cherubs, was not on exhibition until 1926 (it was moved to its present location in 1954), and then certain changes were made to accommodate it in the available space in the Museum. James Parker, the curator who installed most of the Wrightsman rooms, discovered in preparing the chapter on the Sagredo bedroom that the windows were originally on the opposite wall but were changed to allow natural light from windows in the existing Museum building.

Adaptations occur commonly with period rooms, a fact that leads many scholars to dismiss their value. Some of ours, for example, are composites of two or more; some that were originally used as parlors are now furnished as bedrooms. The Sagredo bedchamber once had a dressing room attached, but it was left behind in the palazzo (where it remains today) because of space considerations. The authors of this book are quick to point out such adjustments, often providing as well the original intention of the installing curator.

It is not surprising that the first curators working on our period rooms were often as influenced by their own time as by the period they were attempting to re-create. Amelia Peck, associate curator of American Decorative Arts, explains that in the case of our Powel room, the Colonial Revival, a movement begun in the 1870s and at its peak in the 1920s, informed many of our installations of pre-Revolutionary date. When the enlarged American Wing reopened in 1980, curators decided to acknowledge this earlier interpretation and keep the Powel room in its Colonial Revival mode rather than make it more authentic to the eighteenth century.

Several of our rooms were installed principally as galleries to display suites of furniture selected from the Museum's holdings and combined in the setting to express a particular style, rather than to reinvent the original room. Clearly, curators must be responsible for making these exhibits as historically accurate as possible, but it is not always easy. Our Shaker retiring room, for example, contains one bed rather than four, as the original would have had; the Metropolitan does not own four Shaker beds, and it was decided that it would be more beneficial to the Museum visitor if the room was filled with other types of authentic Shaker objects than reproduction furniture. Whatever may be said about the nature of the regroupings, at the Metropolitan the visitor is never faced with reproductions and may always be certain that all the pieces on view in these rooms are original. It is only their context, their arrangement, that may be a curator's interpretive re-creation.

Some scholars believe that putting a piece of furniture in a period room detracts from its value as an individual work of art and that great pieces should be viewed outside of any contextual setting, as indeed many are in other galleries here. On the other hand, it cannot be denied that period rooms afford the viewer a chance to experience the furnishings as related to each other in time, place, and style in a way that isolating them cannot. This opportunity for broader insight is part of what makes the Metropolitan's period rooms so popular with the public.

In the first room to enter the collection, the Roman *cubiculum* (bedroom) from Boscoreale, the floor and the furnishings, which are of a slightly later date, are completely incidental to the remarkable wall paintings, but the space still manages to convey a sense of the lifestyle of a wealthy Roman at his country estate. The Nur al-Din room in the Islamic galleries—the oldest surviving Syrian room in existence—makes one feel, if only briefly, like a guest of the owner. Visitors to the Cuxa cloister invariably lower their voices as if they feel the presence of monks making their way to vespers, and the Astor court is as much a retreat for the harried New Yorker as its inspiration was for the Chinese scholar who first built it.

In spite of the range of the Metropolitan's period rooms, one still cannot survey the entire history of interior design through them, except perhaps in the American Wing. We have no Russian or German rooms; no Japanese or Indian examples, although a Jain temple dome gives some sense of the rich architecture of this particular culture. There is no room from the continents of Africa or South America, yet a painted bark ceiling from Papua New Guinea is installed in such a way that one can envision the original Kwoma ceremonial house from which it came, and painted wood models from a Middle Kingdom tomb of the early twentieth century B.C. offer a glimpse of the environment in which the ancient Egyptians conducted their daily lives. To make up for the gaps, we are exceptionally rich in French Rococo and Louis XVI interiors and in the Neoclassical designs of Robert Adam, not only those of his native England but also examples representing his influence in America.

It is possible, however, to survey the history of period-room design at the Metropolitan, for we have been involved in that branch of museology for nearly one hundred years. A fascinating though little-appreciated refinement in such installations is the contribution of lighting designers; behind every drapery and window are hidden lights and paper reflectors manipulated to suggest the luminous qualities of sun, candle, fire, and oil lamp.

Over the years the intentions of our curators may have varied to some degree—from re-creating a "period feeling" to restoring an original interior in every detail—but the current curatorial staff has no inclination to deny the work of their predecessors. Just as we acknowledge in a gallery label the reattribution of a painting by Goya, we explain straightforwardly to our period-room visitors (and to readers of this book) exactly what they are seeing and how it got that way.

When we are fortunate enough to have the funding and the expertise and knowledge beyond that of our predecessors, however, we are happy—indeed bound—to review and revise existing installations. The most recent example, the Gubbio studiolo, underwent a restoration that lasted about a decade and enabled our conservators, thoroughly familiar with the complex Renaissance technique of intarsia inlay, to bring back the room to an appearance far closer to the original than did the last restoration dating from 1937. As we preserve our rooms and the objects in them, we also find ourselves bringing back to life the methods by which they were produced, an exercise that affords us new insights into their creation and into the minds of the artists who made them.

Even a swift perusal of this book will make it evident that the

Museum's period rooms are the product of many hands—not only those who designed, built, and lived in them but also those who saved, restored, and installed them here. Some of our rooms went through several lives: the Vélez Blanco patio, originally constructed in sixteenth-century Spain, was reshaped to fit into the brownstone of financier George Blumenthal and then refitted for two different locations at the Met before coming to rest in its present site outside the Watson Library. The beautiful *boiserie* (wood paneling) from the Paar Palace in Vienna was removed from the original building before it was demolished in 1937 and sold to a Parisian decorator, who dispersed the panels far and wide. When a London house that incorporated some of the panels was slated for destruction some twenty years later, the decorator bought them back and eventually sold them to Mr. and Mrs. Charles Wrightsman, whose incredible generosity to the Metropolitan Museum over the years has made our elaborate suite of eighteenth-century period rooms one of the most admired in the world. The rooms are filled with outstanding pieces of French furniture given by the Wrightsmans and by other donors.

In the chapters that follow, you will read the names of many of the donors and curators responsible for the Museum's rooms. We should also remember that each installation is a collaborative effort, requiring the talent and hard work of those whose names we will never read: the craftsmen who painstakingly carried out the original designs and fulfilled the wishes of their patrons; the conservators who rescued, repaired, and restored the elements to their former brilliance; and the technicians who put the rooms in place, built the structures that support them, painted the walls, and hung the draperies. We also owe our gratitude to the authors of the essays in this book, to Karin Willis, whose photographs make the rooms look as inviting on the page as they are in actuality, to Nai Chang for his handsome design, and to Barbara Burn, who shaped the book, with the help of John O'Neill and Joan Holt.

Continental
Europe

The Boscoreale Bedroom

NEAR POMPEII ◆ ABOUT 40–30 B.C.

The region surrounding the Bay of Naples was favored by Romans of the late Republic and early Empire for their country retreats. Initially, these were working farms, but as increasingly large sums were spent to create comfortable, even sumptuous living quarters, the farmhouses served more and more as a setting for the social and intellectual pursuits of their owners. When Mount Vesuvius erupted in A.D. 79, the volcanic ash buried not only Pompeii and Herculaneum but also a considerable number of other sites, including Boscoreale, an area about a mile north of Pompeii, where several such villas were situated.

The complex to which the Museum's *cubiculum*, or bedroom, belongs seems to have been built shortly after the middle of the first century B.C. Although the owner responsible for the wall paintings has not been identified, the name of one of his successors in the first century A.D., Publius Fannius Synistor, is used to identify the villa. The original house was organized around a central atrium, a columned courtyard, open to the sky, where rainwater was collected in a pool. The atrium provided light and air to the adjacent rooms. In Fannius's villa, the bedroom—identified as M by the excavators—was located at the northwest, preceded by a small vestibule.

OPPOSITE:
The *cubiculum* (bedroom) from Boscoreale is the most significant well-preserved Roman chamber with fresco painting in the western hemisphere. The original entrance, on the south wall, has been maintained in the Museum's reconstruction. The couch, footstool, and mosaic were not integral to the room but are appropriate in evoking its appearance in antiquity. The ceiling is modern.

BELOW:
The isometric view presents the known portions of the villa in elevation as well as in plan. In addition to the cubiculum M, parts of rooms L, H, and F and the peristyle are preserved in the Museum. The view is useful in showing the sizes of private spaces in relation to those of more public areas. It also indicates the light sources for each space, a feature always incorporated into the painted decoration.

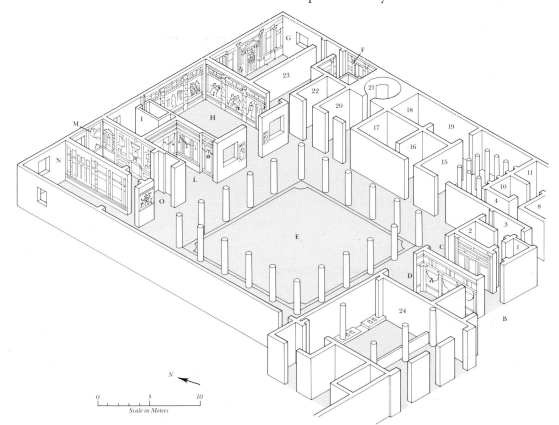

OPPOSITE ABOVE:
The rear wall is articulated by two painted columns—all of one and the lower part of the second—as well as the window. The ends of the wall show rocky embankments covered with foliage. At the top of each stands an arbor, at the bottom a fountain, and birds are everywhere. In between there is a parapet painted with a landscape and supporting a glass bowl full of fruit.

OPPOSITE BELOW:
Detail of the northwestern corner of the cubiculum. The decorative program presents a succession of progressively more open spaces. The concentration of architectural elements diminishes toward the back wall, with its painted garden and a window that very likely opened onto a natural landscape.

It is provided with its own window, which suggests that the view was significant; of demonstrable consequence for the painted decoration is this source of light.

The villa of P. Fannius Synistor was discovered in 1900 and initially published in 1901. Following common practice at the time, the frescoes on the walls were cut out, framed in wood, and divided between local authorities and art dealers. The panels that remained in Italy are now in the National Archaeological Museum in Naples. The rest were acquired by the dealers Canessa in Paris, from whom the Metropolitan Museum purchased its group. The remaining panels are dispersed among the Louvre and museums in Amiens, Bayonne, Beaulieu-sur-Mer, Brussels, Mariemont (Belgium), and Amsterdam.

Since all four sides of the cubiculum in New York are preserved, it has been displayed consistently as a period room. The ceiling is a modern reconstruction based upon similar cubicula, and the ancient mosaic floor is one of several in the Museum from a building discovered at Montebello, just north of Rome, in 1892. The center of the mosaic shows two figures, one standing and the other seated, flanking a vessel proper to the cult of the goddess Isis. The Egyptianizing theme occurs as well in some features of the walls, but the floor is datable to about a century and a half later, to the first half of the second century A.D. Although not inappropriate to this evocation of a Roman bedchamber, it is not strictly accurate.

In a similar vein, the couch and footstool are pertinent to the room but not contemporaneous. Acquired through the bequest of J. Pierpont Morgan in 1917, these furnishings, datable to the first century A.D., consist of wooden frames overlaid with appliqués of bone and glass. It is worth mentioning that, although Museum displays strive for historical accuracy, the reality of a living space more often than not involves an accumulation of elements that are neither of the same date nor from the same source. In our day and culture, we tend to appreciate furnishings that are older than the walls. In the cubiculum as currently presented, the walls are the oldest constituent.

The decoration of the cubiculum creates an extraordinary illusion of space for what is, in fact, a small room. The side walls are bilaterally symmetrical. Nearest to the entrance, on the left and right, are three vertical scenes separated by red columns ornately embellished with gilded foliage. The nearest scenes show relatively urban clusters of houses and porticoes. The next scenes offer views of precincts shielded by gates and walls that permit only glimpses of what lies beyond: lofty pylonlike structures enclosing images of Hecate on the west (left) wall and another goddess on the east. The third scene, again of "high-rise" buildings and verandas, makes these triptychs symmetrical not only between each side of the room but also within each wall. It is significant to note that it is only when one stands in front of the central section with the pylons that the perspective and orthogonals achieve their desired effect.

ABOVE & OPPOSITE ABOVE:
The decoration of the long walls of the cubiculum corresponds from side to side: the west wall is illustrated above on this page, the east wall on the page opposite. The pilasters running from the floor to the cornice serve a significant function by differentiating the room's entrance—with the triptychs of massed buildings flanking a courtyard and pylon—from the spaces directly around the couch.

RIGHT:
Detail of the southwestern townscape (the first one on the left side beyond the entrance). Although the Romans built houses with multiple stories, these townscapes represent highly evocative inventions. They combine functionally disparate elements heightening the illusion of tangibility and plausibility by the amount of meticulous detail. Of special note in these scenes is the pervasive silence—no birds or water, as in the garden scene on the end wall.

Detail of the northeastern panel (the farthest back on the right wall). The viewer faces a courtyard surrounded by a colonnade with a small circular structure in the center. While access to the precinct is prevented by barriers of different heights and a curtain behind, the vistas offer considerable depth and air. This space contrasts with the central panels of the triptychs, which are even more closed and provide only glimpses of statuary and pylonlike gates.

The distinctiveness of this "introductory" portion of the room is emphasized by the painted pilasters that rise from floor to cornice level and acquire additional assertiveness from the series of square bosses, each of which casts a shadow. These superb trompe-l'oeil pilasters delimit the far end of the room, which is quite different in character. The side walls terminate in vistas of a circular building within a columned courtyard, while the back wall presents a garden with arbors above grottoes and fountains, as well as birds among vines. Basically horizontal in format and symmetrical in composition, the wall is interrupted by the window and by another pair of embellished red columns connected by a low parapet. On top of this red ledge stands a glass bowl with fruit, an early still life; below it is a landscape executed entirely in tonalities of yellow.

The cubiculum from Boscoreale is a most extraordinary creation because virtually every detail has both a decorative and an iconographical aspect. The technique employed is that of true fresco, in which the pigment becomes an integral part of the plaster wall and thus enables the colors to retain their vibrancy. The illusion of spaciousness depends significantly on the masterful deployment of architectural elements, especially the juxtaposition of restricted and open vistas. At the same time the repeated portrayals of closed doors, high walls, and secret gardens signal quite unmistakably that access to the world depicted in the frescoes is severely limited. Similarly, the progression in subject matter—from the cityscapes nearest the entrance to the garden farthest away—is visually effective. It is evident, however, that the courtyards with their *tempietti*, sculptures, portals, and such details as the masks and shields also carry meanings whose correct interpretation continues to occasion scholarly debate.

JOAN R. MERTENS

OPPOSITE:
The right half of the end wall of the cubiculum

BELOW:
Glassmaking was an art that the Romans refined and developed. This bowl represents a type known from actual examples, and the transparency and sheen of the medium itself may account for the popularity of glass objects in wall paintings. Within the larger program of the Boscoreale cubiculum, this beautiful detail epitomizes the reciprocal relation between the creations of man and nature— a major theme of the decoration.

23

The Cuxa Cloister

CATALONIA ♦ ABOUT 1130–40

Commanding dramatic views of the Mount Canigou foothills in the eastern Pyrenees, the medieval monastery of Saint-Michel-de-Cuxa is situated on the northern border of the medieval region of Catalonia, now the French Roussillon. The monastery at Cuxa (pronounced COO-sha) was founded in the mid-ninth century, initially as a small settlement of Benedictine monks dependent on the monastery of Saint-André-d'Exalada, and was expanded in 878 by their brethren from Exalada, who were forced to flee when the River Têt flooded. It is perhaps Cuxa's beginnings as an outpost of Exalada that informs its name: *cuixà* literally means thigh or leg in Catalan, a word that could refer to this branch, figuratively an appendage, of the mother house. The new monastery prospered, and from the second half of the tenth century the abbots undertook a steady campaign of building improvement, expansion, and construction. By the early twelfth century, the monastery (now known as Saint-Michel-de-Cuxa because of its dedication to Saint Michael, the warrior archangel of heaven) had established itself as a leader in the religious and artistic life of the region.

OPPOSITE:
The garth garden of the Cuxa cloister in lush full bloom at The Cloisters. The imposing tower, positioned to the northeast, recalls the south transept tower still standing at Cuxa.

Cuxa capitals and arcades before World War I at George Grey Barnard's museum in upper Manhattan. Barnard respected their original plein-air setting by situating the cloister elements in a garden adjoining his museum.

Aerial view of the Cuxa garth showing the intersecting walkways and the central fountain. Each quadrant is planted with a fruit tree, a feature typical of monastic gardens. Clockwise from the upper left are a crab apple, a cornelian cherry (a European member of the dogwood family), a hawthorn, and a pear.

OPPOSITE:
View of the garth looking north from the cloister walkway. The fountain is framed by purple asters, Russian sage, rue, and spirea, while sweet alyssum, lamb's-ears, and coreopsis spill over the raised planting beds and onto the path.

At the center of the monastic complex, to the north of the monastery church, was an imposing cloister—the covered walkway surrounding a garth, or open garden area, with its central fountain—that served as a conduit to other important monastic buildings (the church, the chapter house in which daily meetings were held, the dormitory, and the refectory, where the brethren took their meals). As such, a cloister was both passageway and processional walkway, a place for meditation and for reading aloud. At once serene and bustling, the cloister also served the monks' very practical needs as the site for doing laundry, washing, and shaving. Lauded as the first sculpted cloister in Catalonia (completed about 1140), Cuxa was also the region's largest, measuring roughly 156 by 128 feet. Excavations indicate the cloister was irregularly quadrilateral in shape, with some documentation suggesting that the eastern side was marked by pairs of double columns and capitals, while the remaining three sides were composed of single-column arcades.

As a result of the damage wrought in the seventeenth century by warring Spanish and French forces, the monastery entered into a period of decline. In 1654 the complex was sacked by troops loyal to a local count, and five years later it was ceded to the French crown. In 1790, soon after the French Revolution and the state's seizure of ecclesiastical foundations, the monks left Cuxa. The deserted buildings deteriorated rapidly; the church roof collapsed in 1835, and the north transept tower crashed to the ground four years later.

With the monastery buildings sold, the cloister was dismantled and its parts offered piecemeal throughout the nineteenth century and in the first years of the twentieth to local buyers and establishments. Some elements were used as building materials, such as those fashioned into a bathhouse portico in the nearby town of Prades. Others were integrated into the public fountain of the village of Codalet, and many were reused in local buildings. One capital ended up supporting a cash register in a tobacco shop, and several others found their way into the collection of Pierre Yon Vernière, a local magistrate, who by 1875 had installed them in his garden at Aniane, near Montpellier.

George Grey Barnard, an American sculptor living in France from 1903 to 1913, acquired many of these carvings; he later installed them in his museum of medieval art, called the Cloisters, opened in 1914 in northern Manhattan's Washington Heights. Governed by a romantic sensibility and possessed of a keen artistic eye, Barnard was a passionate advocate of medieval art and aspired, through his museum, to instruct the American public in the beauty and wonder of what he termed "the patient Gothic chisel." This he hoped to achieve by exhibiting art in an environment suggestive of its original context. Accordingly, Barnard respected their plein-air monastic placement and installed the Cuxa elements as an ensemble in an outdoor garden adjacent to his museum.

The Metropolitan Museum of Art purchased the Barnard Cloisters in 1925 through the generosity of John D. Rockefeller Jr., and its collection became the foundation for a new Museum structure that opened thirteen years later in what is now Fort Tryon Park in upper Manhattan. Following Barnard's pioneering principle of contextual installations, this branch of the Museum, now known as The Cloisters, was constructed in a building style evocative of medieval precedents, combining monastic and castle architectural

Capital with a masklike face supported by a patterned column and framed by volutes

The western walk of the Cuxa cloister at The Cloisters. Such protected walks were an integral part of medieval cloister design, sheltering its many activities.

forms with original elements into an integrated whole. (A curator associated with the Museum later recalled that the intention of this design was to create installations that allowed "the objects to speak for themselves, inviolate, as far as possible, from time and handling and changing taste.")

Of the four reconstituted cloisters that were integrated into the new complex, Cuxa became the central focus. Museum curators, in arranging the stonework, strove to be as historically accurate as possible. To that end, the installation was based on evidence offered by its surviving elements as well as on studies of the original site and documentation, which included a late-eighteenth-century plan of the monastery. As reconstructed, the Cuxa cloister measures only a little over half (89 x 78 feet) its original size, and the walks are twelve feet wide instead of fifteen. The surviving south transept tower from Cuxa's monastery church inspired the Museum's tower (designed for offices), which now overlooks the cloister in much the same way as its model did. Similarly, a twelfth-century French chapter house from the abbey of Notre-Dame-de-Pontaut was installed next to the western cloister walk, recalling a common placement of chapter houses in medieval monastic plans.

In building the cloister, original portions were kept together whenever possible. When additional stone was needed to complete the masonry fabric, blocks of the distinctive pink-veined marble were cut from the quarries between Ria and Villefranche that had supplied the stone for Cuxa in the twelfth century. The resulting structure gives the impression of the original whole; Museum labels indicate the medieval elements. Architectural details, such as the floor tiles and plaster walls, as well as the beamed-and-planked oak ceiling with its terracotta roof and supporting stone corbels, were also closely modeled on prototypes found at Cuxa and elsewhere in the region.

The enclosed cloister garth was divided into four quadrants with a central fountain placed at the intersection of the two walkways. An octagonal fountain made from the same pink marble used at Cuxa but originating from the nearby monastery of Saint-Genis-les-Fontaines was acquired in 1926 for this purpose. (A fountain from the smaller infirmary cloister at Cuxa later entered the collection of the Philadelphia Museum of Art.) Although cloister-garth designs are well known from medieval plans and surviving examples, surprisingly little information has come down to us regarding how such gardens were planted. The Cuxa garth, as a result, serves as the main ornamental garden at The Cloisters, providing color and blooms from spring through autumn. Interspersed with modern hybrids are plants typical of medieval herb gardens, such as rue, lavender, betony, and red valerian.

The cloister arcades themselves are distinguished by over thirty capitals of remarkable uniformity in size but tremendous variety in their carvings. Because the capitals were not acquired on site but were gleaned from diverse venues following their dispersion, a few installed in the Museum's cloister have recently been determined to have formed part of other sculptural programs at the monastery and perhaps elsewhere in the French Pyrenees. They nevertheless illustrate a sculptural style identified with Cuxa, harmonized by the warm beauty of the pink marble used by its sculptors. Some capitals are fashioned in the simplest block forms, while others are carved with palmette designs, vine patterns, or stout acanthus leaves surmounted by volutes and masklike human heads in a lively interpretation of a Corinthian capital. Figurative capitals show twin lions with a single head (a special breed for the corners of capitals), some of them rearing and gnashing their teeth, while others devour humans or seem to gnaw on their own forelegs. Brawny, impassive men are depicted holding up imposing apes that squat at the capital corners. The meaning of such carvings remains enigmatic; they may be interpretations of Eastern motifs, derived from textile designs or manuscript illuminations.

Many of the Cuxa elements remaining in France have been returned to the monastery, again an active house of Benedictine monks. The Museum, too, has loaned appropriate architectural fragments not included in its cloister reconstruction to Cuxa. In its guise as a modern museum installation, the Cuxa cloister maintains many of its original medieval functions. It is still a walkway, connecting different gallery spaces, as well as a place of contemplation and renewal. Recorded liturgical chants are played in the cloister at various times of day. In this way the Cuxa cloister embodies Rockefeller's aspirations for The Cloisters, to serve as an "uplifting [place] of beauty . . . surrounded by nature at her best."

MARY B. SHEPARD

Capital showing a man, nude to the waist, supporting two simian creatures. This fantastic medieval interpretation of a Corinthian capital retains the classical scrolling volutes, but the acanthus leaves have been transformed into rather ribald "monkeys" while the impassive stare of the man replaces the surmounting rosette.

The Campin Room

NORTHERN EUROPE ◆ 15TH–16TH CENTURY

The acquisition of the famed triptych of *The Annunciation* by the painter Robert Campin of Tournai represented the fulfillment of the Museum's long-standing desire to establish at The Cloisters a gallery devoted to the arts of the late-medieval domestic household. Traditionally known as the Mérode Altarpiece, after the family that owned the painting during the nineteenth century, the triptych illustrates the moment when the archangel Gabriel tells the Virgin Mary that she has been chosen by God to be the mother of Christ. The painting's patron, Ingelbrecht of Mechelan, and his wife gaze upon the event from one of the side panels, while Joseph, working in his carpenter's shop, occupies the other wing.

Campin's fascination with the natural and domestic world dominates his telling of the sacred story. The artist carefully renders even the smallest details in an innovative technique combining translucent oil overlay on water-base opaque pigments. The resulting optical effects enhance Campin's inter-pretation of the Virgin's private chamber as an affluent fifteenth-century interior filled with household appointments and goods similar to those Ingelbrecht would have known and to the furnishings of the Campin room itself. Benches, like the elaborately carved example with lion finials and an attached footboard with paw-shaped feet, were the most common type of seating used in the Middle Ages. Trestle tables were also extremely popular since they could be easily dismantled, leaving the center of the room free. Trestles with round, or in this case polygonal, boards had been in use since the twelfth century. The fine maiolica pitcher, a ware imported from Italy, the brass can-dlestick and double-spouted laver (a basin used for washing hands), and the finely wrought-iron candle sconces and fireplace andirons were all expensive household implements, which readily signaled the wealth and taste of their owners. The construction and design of the chamber, with its massive fire-place and the wood beamed ceiling, were also potent indicators of the owner's wealthy status. Glazed-tile floors were generally reserved for only the most prosperous of homes. The Lowlands were renowned for the production of such tiles, which found a ready market throughout Europe. Windows, such as the ones depicted behind the Virgin, were often glazed, usually in fixed frames. Normally only the bottom portion was hinged to open and possibly fitted with lattice screens — like the one here — to provide privacy. Many objects similar to these are exhibited throughout the Campin room, enveloping

OPPOSITE:
View of the Campin room in its current installation at The Cloisters. As was typical of late-medieval households where rooms had multiple uses, the furniture is shown pushed against the walls. Chests and stools, like those shown here, were widely used. The iron birdcage, on the other hand, is the only one known to have survived from the Middle Ages.

33

The Annunciation triptych by
Robert Campin (Netherlandish,
ca. 1378–1444), painted about 1425
in Bruges, is today the focal point
of a gallery installed with furniture
and household objects similar to
those in the painting.

the Museum visitor in the ambiance of a fifteenth-century environment.
Despite this close interplay between Campin's *Annunciation* and the Museum's
installation, which suggests that the room's function as a domestic interior
derived from the painting, it was, in fact, the painting that perfectly embodied
the Museum's expressed intention for the room.

As early as 1929, with the acquisition of an impressive wood-beamed
ceiling of the fifteenth century, the Museum sought to create a harmonious
exhibition space for late-medieval works of art that originally functioned in a
domestic setting. The ceiling, constructed of red pine and decorated with
layers of gesso and paint, originally came from a small Spanish palace at
Illescas, located halfway between Madrid and Toledo. Essentially square in its
dimensions, the ceiling is composed of 216 panels transversed on the long
axis by three great beams, which separate the ceiling into four almost equal
parts. The three master beams are supported by huge consoles, while the
small cross beams support planks running parallel to the larger beams and
carry small rectangular painted panels inserted between the rafters. Such
massive members were required in medieval ceilings to support the floor of

the level immediately above it. The surrounding frieze is composed of two registers, which are separated by a ropelike molding. According to tradition, the ceiling was once part of a chamber occupied by the French king Francis I while he was held prisoner by Emperor Charles V from 1525 to 1526. Recent examination and conservation of the ceiling have revealed that most of the painted decoration is post-medieval in date.

Noting the popularity of period-room installations among American museums of the day, Joseph Breck, then the Metropolitan's assistant director, installed the Spanish ceiling in a small gallery located in the first-floor European decorative arts galleries of the Museum's main building on Fifth Avenue. Breck intended the ceiling to give a "somewhat domestic character" to the gallery with "the rich polychromy of the ceiling [providing] an effective contrast to the white plaster walls against which are exhibited tapestries, sculpture, and furniture of various nationalities, dating from the fourteenth to the early sixteenth century."

This installation, by Breck's own acknowledgment, was not a permanent one. When the decision was made to replace George Grey Barnard's Cloisters

museum (which the Metropolitan took over in 1925) with a new structure located in what is now Manhattan's Fort Tryon Park, the Spanish ceiling was transferred from the main building to The Cloisters, where it became the focus of an intimate gallery built to its dimensions. Christened the Spanish room, after the ceiling, the space maintained Breck's original idea for the gallery. Its initial appearance was sparse, with only a high-backed chair and an early-fifteenth-century tapestry on exhibition. The room was lit by three modern double-lancet windows designed after a window in the episcopal palace in Barcelona later destroyed during the Spanish Revolution. Three fifteenth-century sandstone capitals, decorated with stiff palmette patterns typical of Catalonia, were integrated into each window at the juncture of the central mullion and the cusped lancet tracery. In a guidebook published at the opening of The Cloisters, James Rorimer (who succeeded Breck as curator in charge) advised visitors that the appearance of the room was only temporary: "It is hoped," he cautioned, "that eventually furnishings of the period will be found to complete the installation."

By 1951, when a revised edition of the Cloisters guidebook was published, the room had been sparingly equipped with a few key examples of furniture and objects typical of late-medieval households, including chests, benches, stools, chairs, and even an iron brazier. The resulting character of the room was not specifically Spanish in nature but rather suggested the surroundings one might encounter in a prosperous urban home in northern Europe, where tables and stools, a few chairs, and several chests sufficed to meet a wealthy family's needs.

View of the Spanish room after the acquisition of pieces of furniture and the nine-branch bronze chandelier.

Late-medieval furniture was constructed to be both multifunctional as well as portable. As there were no built-in closets in a medieval home, chests were the most essential pieces of furniture. They were used for storage (both at home and on the road) but could also double as seating or as tables. Chairs, emblems of authority since antiquity, were few in number and were reserved for the head of the household and prominent guests. Rorimer included two representative examples in the gallery. One, shown against the wall, is a wrought-iron French curule dating from the late fourteenth or early fifteenth century. Designed as a folding chair with diagonally crossing arms and legs and a leather or fabric seat, the curule was ideally suited for travel or easy transport. The three-legged wooden chair with semicircular seat and back, shown behind the walnut-and-oak table, dates to the second half of the fifteenth century. Such chairs were favored in the Middle Ages, as their tripod design made them particularly stable, even on the most irregular of floors.

The splendid bronze chandelier was the most important addition to the room. Created in the Lowlands, the chandelier would once have lit a room for a family of some means, since candles were a luxury in the Middle

Ages. It was fashioned with great care, the pieces cast separately and each of the nine branches given an assembly mark corresponding to a mark on the central shaft. The entire surface was tooled, and the rough spots on the bronze were smoothed before it was polished to a high gleam.

The installation, five years later, of the newly acquired Annunciation triptych changed the focus of the room from the ceiling to the painting and eventually led to the room's current name, the Campin room. Furniture was rearranged and selected examples of ceramics and metalwork of the types of objects represented in the painting were added. The third edition of the guidebook touted the room as having "been furnished as a domestic interior such as one sees in late medieval paintings." Subsequent changes drew inspiration directly from the painting. New leaded-glass casements were made for the three double-lancet windows, and five German heraldic stained-glass roundels were glazed into their transoms to emulate the patrons' arms displayed in the window behind the Virgin. Later, the room's heavy velvet curtains were removed, and wooden shutters opening into the interior like those in the painting were fitted to the lancets.

The relationship ultimately established between the painting as a work of art and the Campin room as a Museum gallery was consistent with the fundamentally contextual nature of The Cloisters. As an object of private devotion, the painting would have been integrated into the furnishings of the owner's private quarters, possibly attached to a wall or set atop a cabinet. Its hinged wings could be opened and closed according to the daily cadence of private prayers or following the traditions of the Christian calendar. As such, the ability of the painting's owners to empathize with and to visualize the sacred story (an important goal in late-medieval piety) was further enhanced by the artist's rendering of contemporary, everyday objects in recounting the narrative—in furnishing the Virgin's chamber, in revealing the bustling city outside Joseph's window, or in depicting the ordered garden where the patrons keep watch.

Although Campin clearly delighted in representing things of the real world with an emphasis on their form and texture, he was essentially guided in his choice of household objects by the symbolic needs of the story. The brass laver signifies Mary's purity, as does the Madonna lily in the maiolica pitcher. Thus the Virgin's room is not necessarily a faithful portrait of a fifteenth-century room but rather a compilation of familiar parts arranged to further the narrative. Similarly, the Museum gallery does not replicate the actual appointments of a specific private chamber of the period, nor does it reproduce the grouping represented in the painting. Rather, gallery space and art unite to evoke the intimate qualities of a room in which an affluent family of the late Middle Ages might have lived and worshiped.

MARY B. SHEPARD

LEFT:
This heraldic stained-glass roundel dates to about 1500 and was most likely made in the middle region of the Rhine River. The coat of arms, showing a sprightly row of daisies and possibly daffodils, remains unidentified. Comparable examples suggest this roundel was once part of a set.

ABOVE:
The high-backed bench, or settle, currently on view in the Campin room was made in the South Lowlands during the 15th century. Derived from benches like the one depicted in the Annunciation triptych, such settles were frequently designed with hinged seats, which allowed the lower compartment also to function as a chest. Its linenfold decoration, a prevalent motif of the time, is thought to emulate rows of pleated linen. Period textiles, like this tapestry from the South Lowlands (1460–80) showing the Annunciation, are regularly rotated to prevent damage from excess exposure to light and other environmental factors.

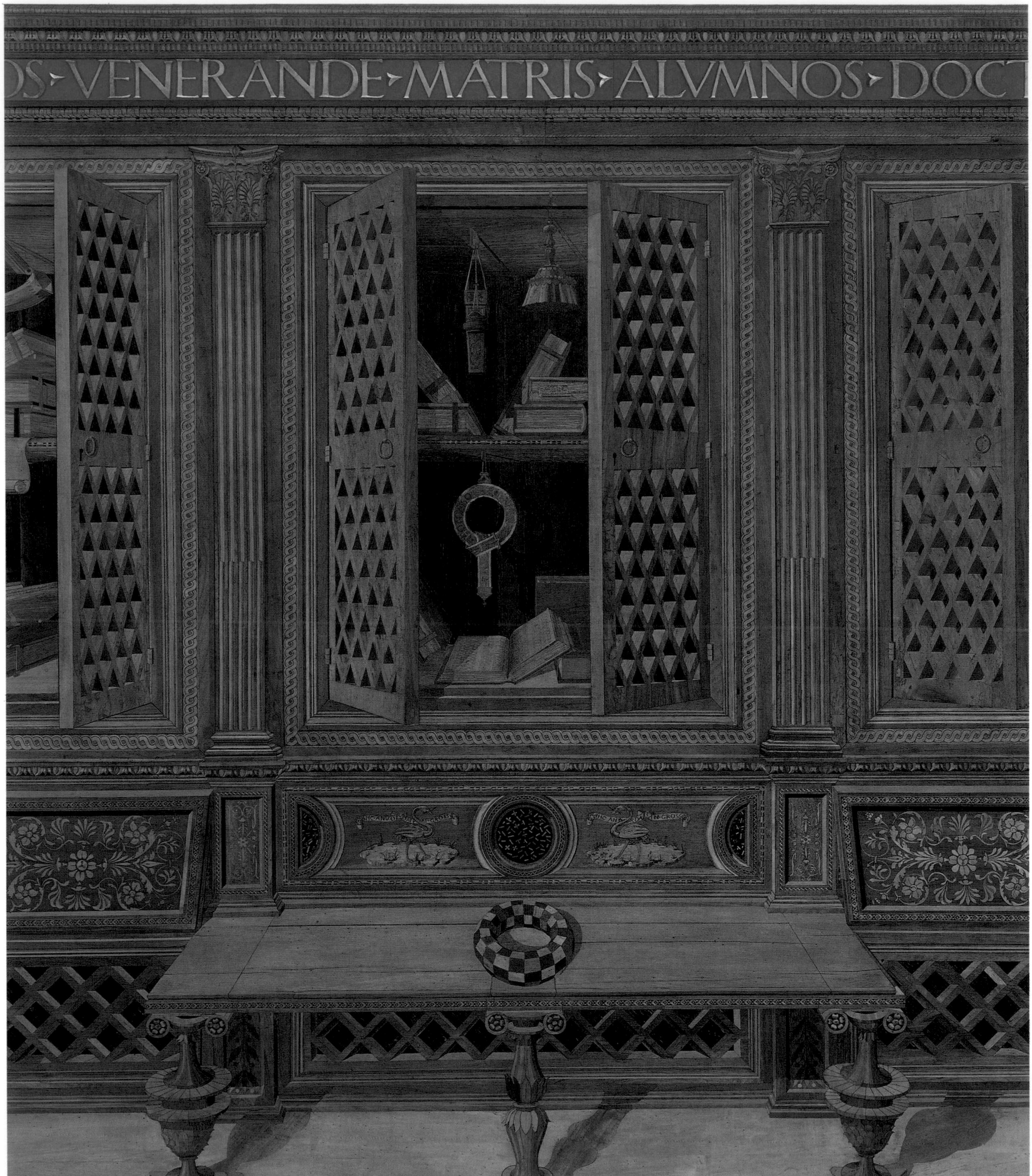
OS · VENERANDE · MATRIS · ALVMNOS · DOC

The Gubbio Studiolo

GUBBIO ◆ ABOUT 1478–82

In the fifteenth century in a mountainous region of Italy in the northern part of the Marches, the small state of Montefeltro was part of the Papal States, which recognized the pope as their feudal lord. The city of Urbino was their capital, and Gubbio, strategically placed close to the high valley of the Tiber and the plain stretching south toward Rome, defined the southern-most border. From 1444 the ruler of this state was Federico da Montefeltro (1422–1482), the tenth count of Urbino, one of the most admired military leaders of his day, famous for his humanistic knowledge and his understanding of architecture, mathematics, and all the arts. Early military successes and a reputation for fairness and loyalty, as well as shrewd diplomatic skill and sheer good luck, propelled Federico to the center of Italian political life, where he found the support of Cosimo de' Medici and the humanist pope Nicholas V.

During the relatively short periods between campaigns, the count resided in his ancestral Urbino home, which he planned to make into one of the most brilliant Italian courts of his day. He decided to build a large palace in the Renaissance style next to the old residence and determined to secure

The middle cabinet on the long wall of the Gubbio *studiolo*. Rendered in the celebrated Florentine Renaissance technique of perspective intarsia are, on the top shelf, a quill case, inkwell, brush, and books; hanging from the shelf is the Order of the Garter, awarded in 1474 to Federico da Montefeltro, who commissioned the room. Below, on the bench, is a *mazzocchio*, a wooden ring around which cloth was wrapped to make fashionable men's headgear.

The ducal palace at Gubbio. Originally built in the 14th century and redesigned by Francesco di Giorgio Martini, about 1476–80.

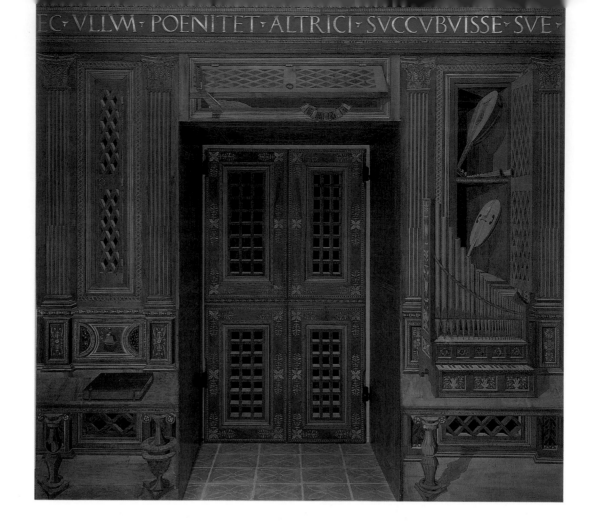

Entrance wall of the studiolo

the services of the best artists in Italy. During a period of grief following the deaths of his beloved wife and of his close friend the architect and humanist Leon Battista Alberti, work on the palace came to a halt. In 1474, however, Federico received a number of honors, including the title of duke of Urbino and the prestigious English Order of the Garter, and his household took on the character of a true princely court. He hired the Sienese painter, sculptor, architect, and engineer Francesco di Giorgio Martini (1439–1501) to complete the palace, including a small study retreat, the celebrated *studiolo*, which can to this day be admired at Urbino. Conceived as a tiny chamber, totally enclosed by continuous wooden illusionistic wainscoting executed in Florence in the intarsia technique, the Urbino studiolo immediately became famous as one of the marvels of the ducal palace. Its success undoubtedly encouraged the duke to plan the construction of another one in his new palace at Gubbio.

Federico did not own his new palace at Gubbio, which had been the town's old civic center; it was not until 1480 that the city fathers formally granted Federico ownership in recognition of the "great expense and magnificent, splendid, and sumptuous works of construction and decoration" he had lavished upon it. About 1476 Francesco di Giorgio began to transform the building into a Renaissance palace. The wing on the southeast was designed to house a small chapel, a spiral staircase, and the duke's private studiolo, accessible from a narrow gallery, which was probably intended as a library.

As at Urbino, the wainscoting of the Gubbio studiolo was made of a series of illusionistic intarsia panels depicting latticed cupboards holding a variety of books, scientific and musical instruments, and other objects. The twelve consecutive sections surround the room on all sides. Although as early as 1673 the studiolo lost the paintings that were originally installed above the wainscoting, the coffered ceilings and wood paneling remained undisturbed for the next two hundred years. In 1874 all the wooden parts were removed to a villa at Frascati, near Rome, where they remained until 1937, when they were sold to a German dealer. They were acquired by the Metropolitan Museum in 1939 and installed in 1941 as a separate room in the old Italian Renaissance Galleries. Today, a long campaign of study and conservation has allowed us to carry out a new and much-improved presentation based on the evidence gathered at the ducal palace itself.

The first impression experienced by the visitor is that of having entered a total environment, a space unified by the warm tone of the woods, the aggressive geometry of its intricately designed panels, and the subtly controlled lighting from its three windows. The panels are divided by illusory fluted pilasters capped by composite capitals, which support an entablature and flank cabinets with latticed doors variously ajar. Below the cabinets is a continuous fictive bench supported by balusters, with some of the seats raised to show their underside decoration of flat ornamental inlay.

Two different techniques were used to achieve the variety of effects called for by the complexity of the design: a traditional type of wood inlay

The studiolo in Venice in 1938, when it was owned by a German dealer

Detail of the studiolo's main ceiling after its restoration at the Metropolitan Museum

Long wall of the studiolo. Below the cabinets, which hold a variety of musical instruments, books, and memorabilia, are a frieze of emblems and devices and a bench on balusters, which cast shadows that correspond to the original light sources in the room.

to form the decorative borders, ornamental panels, and flat designs such as emblems and devices, and the celebrated Florentine technique of perspective intarsia, created in the wake of the fifteenth-century rediscovery of the principles of linear perspective. The latter technique, with its marvelous possibilities, became a component of several small private studies commissioned by Italian humanist rulers.

The viewer who stands in the center of the Gubbio studiolo can immediately grasp the coherent perspectival design of its paneling. As one's eye is drawn to the side facing the window, the wall's overall design appears clearly focused on the Order of the Garter hanging in the middle of the central cabinet. Close to the Garter's circlet is the vanishing point where the orthogonals established by the benches converge. On all four walls the horizon line is maintained a little below the central shelf of the cabinet, with the vanishing point at the center of each panel, always determined by the converging orthogonals of the cabinets or of the objects on the benches. The viewer has the impression of being surrounded by four converging perspectives, an impression reinforced by the carefully calculated arrangement of objects and books inside the cabinets.

At Gubbio one senses the presence of a mind chiefly preoccupied with the geometric nature of objects, especially books, whose abstract blocks are stacked to establish secondary planes within the cabinets. Astonishing as the perspectival treatment is, perhaps even more impressive is the importance given to the play of light and shadow that seems to be everywhere, achieving a homogeneity governed by correspondence with the sources of the original light in the room. Shadows are thrown by the balusters supporting the bench, as well as by some of the large objects on the bench, such as the lectern. Inside the cabinets, the play of light and shadow makes the objects—inkwell and brush, tuning key, brass candlestick—virtually come to life.

Federico's high regard for arithmetic and geometry is well known; in a letter he stated that in his view, being based on scientific truth, they were "the most important of the Liberal Arts, as well as the very foundation of architecture." This statement is a key to our understanding of the special

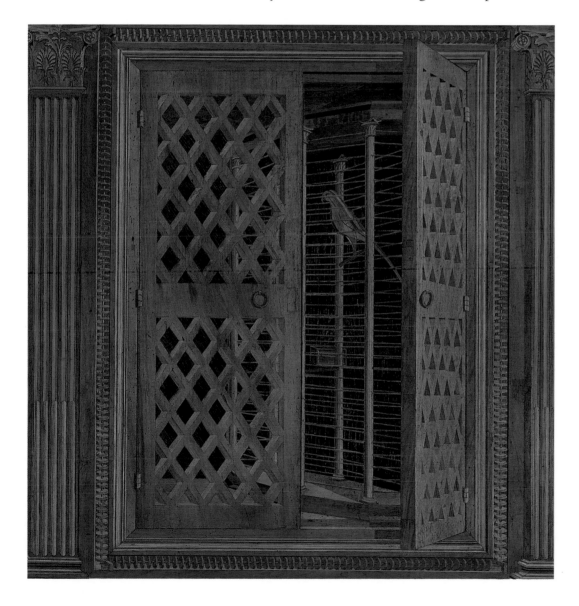

Parrot in a cage in a window-niche panel of the studiolo. In the 15th century exotic birds were extremely rare and prized possessions, kept only by popes, kings, princes, and the wealthiest merchants. This status symbol is charmingly rendered in colored woods with green feathers and a red beak.

climate of mathematical humanism that characterized the court of Urbino and is reflected in the decorative program of the Gubbio studiolo in such details as the armillary sphere, the quadrant, a plumb bob and set square, a cittern, and a pair of dividers—all related to measurement and proportion. In the fifteenth century the theory of musical ratios and the studies of linear perspective and architectural proportions were seen as expressive of the same mathematical truth, an interrelationship admirably expressed here in the meaningful choice of objects depicted, such as the organ, fiddle, lute, cornetti, rebec, harp, and hunting horn. Pieces of armor evoke the pageantry of courtly tournaments, and Federico's personal emblems or devices are repeated throughout—an ostrich, a horse bit and brush, as well as an olive tree, the traditional symbol of peace.

It is believed that the room's original series of paintings depicted the liberal arts and hung over panels devoted to the same subjects: Grammar, Dialectic, Rhetoric, Geometry, Astronomy, Music, and Arithmetic. The visual unity of the ensemble must have been enhanced by the continuous line of green-velvet carpet in the paintings.

The duke of Urbino died in 1482, before the completion of the studiolo, which was finished by Francesco di Giorgio as the duke had wished. Francesco had entrusted the woodworking to the prominent Florentine master Giuliano da Maiano (1432–1490), who had a large workshop in Florence. The work on the paneling had started in about 1478 and was nearly complete by the duke's death. Only today, thanks to the process of conservation and a careful historical analysis, have we succeeded in recapturing the original aspect and the many facets of the studiolo, which can now be enjoyed as one of the most perfect creations of the Italian Renaissance.

OLGA RAGGIO

OPPOSITE:
Armillary sphere, books, and, hanging from the shelf, a horary quadrant

Coat of arms of Federico da Montefeltro inlaid in the soffit of the entrance doorway

The Vélez Blanco Patio

SPAIN • 1506–15

Vélez Blanco is a small mountain village, not far inland from the port of Almeria on the southeastern coast of Spain. Lying between the fertile plain of Murcia and the ancient Moorish kingdom of Granada, Vélez Blanco was once the seat of the feudal lords of the region, the powerful Fajardo family, whose early-sixteenth-century castle still dominates the town. Here the Fajardos lived until the end of the seventeenth century, when the family died out. Thereafter, the castle was only occasionally inhabited, and in the nineteenth century, following the French invasion and the decades of political and social upheaval that overtook the country, it was almost completely abandoned. In 1904 its magnificent ensemble of arcades, columns, and window and door enframements was removed by an interior decorator, J. Goldberg of Paris, and transported to that city. Together with these elements went other large pieces of Renaissance carving from the castle, such as the wooden ceiling, or *artesonado*, of one of the salons and two doors.

There was no better moment for the sale of this ensemble. In the United States the fashion for Renaissance architecture—promoted by such professionals as Stanford White and Charles F. McKim—was at its peak. The marbles were offered first to Archer M. Huntington, whose interest in Spain led to the founding of the Hispanic Society of America. The patio from

The patio as installed in the George Blumenthal house on Park Avenue in New York City

LEFT:
The Fajardo castle at Vélez Blanco (1506–15), which was erected on the remains of an old Moorish fortress, stands on an outcrop of rock dominating a vast plain.

OPPOSITE:
The Vélez Blanco patio, looking northeast from the gallery, where today Spanish sculptures and decorative arts of the 16th and 17th centuries are displayed

The doorway leading into the patio. At the right, inside a fruit wreath, is the coat of arms of Don Pedro Fajardo, for whom the castle was built. This carving was originally on the wall of the castle's main tower.

Vélez Blanco was to be considered for use in the society's new building. Negotiations fell through, however, and shortly before 1913, George Blumenthal, later president of the Metropolitan, purchased the marbles for the house he was constructing on Park Avenue. There they were combined with a number of additions to create a sumptuous inner hall, in which a second-floor gallery ran on three sides and a coffered ceiling was made from the artesonado.

At his death in 1941, Blumenthal bequeathed his entire house to the Metropolitan. Four years later the house was torn down, and the nearly two thousand marble blocks of the patio were dismantled, carefully numbered, and moved to the Museum. Almost twenty years went by before space was made available for their installation as part of a new wing, completed in 1964, to house the Thomas J. Watson Library.

To rebuild the patio as faithfully as possible was a difficult task. Although the castle was commonly acknowledged as an important landmark in the history of the Spanish Renaissance, there was little precise information about its original appearance. Located in a remote corner of the country, it had largely escaped the attention of travelers and historians. A few photographs taken of two sides of the patio before dismantling and the dealer's watercolor sketch of an ideal reconstruction were the only records of it. The Museum still lacked indispensable facts, such as the actual number of arches on the longest side, so new photographs, measurements, and plans to aid in the reconstruction were secured on a trip to Vélez Blanco in 1959. These new materials, along with the old photographs and the sketch, provided ample information about the original arrangement.

Along the south, short side ran a double gallery of five arches. Here, at one end of the ground floor, was the patio's main entrance. Nearby was a marble staircase to the second floor, where a sumptuous marble portal once led to the castle's two great reception halls. To the east a plain wall ended in a second-story gallery of six arches that corresponded to the arches on the castle's exterior. Thus, they formed not a simple *paseador*, open only to the outside, but a wide covered loggia, where one could look both into the patio and toward the vista of the great plain of Vélez. Across from this wall was a facade containing three pairs of superimposed windows with rich marble enframements. Close to this facade was a simple hexagonal marble well, used to reach the large reservoir built, in the Moorish fashion, underneath the courtyard. The fourth, or north, side of the court was closed by the main tower, its severe wall broken only by a high small window. Below the window was a large shield encircled by a heavy fruit wreath carved with the coat of arms of Don Pedro Fajardo, the marqués of Vélez, for whom the castle was built.

Some modifications to the patio had to be made to fit the new space in the Museum. The slightly irregular original plan was changed to a perfect rectangle, and the architectural elements of the two long sides were exchanged, so that the three vertical pairs of windows could be placed on the blank wall of the preexisting Museum building. The orientation of the stairway was changed, and one doorway was transposed from the second to the first floor. On the side once occupied by the tower we placed another door from Vélez Blanco, together with an Italian balcony and an Italian portal, both almost contemporary with the patio. Other changes were necessary to meet new construction requirements, such as thicker and stronger floors to replace the wooden floors and ceilings of the castle. Some of the color once supplied by the ceilings and by a dado of luster tiles that lined the sides of the staircase

The double gallery of five arches each on the east side of the patio. At the left is the doorway, and at the right a marble staircase leads to the second floor, where, in the castle, the grand reception rooms were located. Beneath the cornice is part of the inscription citing the castle's builder, his titles, and the dates of construction.

was restored with the use of an extraordinary ensemble of sixteenth-century enameled Sevillian tiles on the ceiling of the second-floor gallery.

A regrettable loss is that of a balustrade that ran along three sides of the patio above the heavy marble entablature, which consists of an inscribed frieze surmounted by a classical egg-and-dart cornice from which protrude several large Gothic gargoyles. The dealer's sketch shows a balustrade with carved piers on top of this cornice, and old photographs taken in 1881 show the balustrade and the cornice toppled to the ground. This pictorial evidence has been corroborated by a local historian, who described the patio as originally having a "parapet" above the cornice. The only elements of the balustrade known to have survived are four carved piers that were adapted into the Blumenthal house as pilasters for the staircase and are so used in the Museum installation.

One of the conspicuous features of the patio is the Latin inscription carved in handsome Roman capital letters immediately beneath the cornice, which reads in translation: "Pedro Fajardo, first marqués of Vélez and fifth governor of the kingdom of Murcia of his lineage, erected this castle as the

castle of his title. This work was started in the year 1506 after the birth of Christ and finished in the year 1515."

One of the highest-ranking noblemen in Spain, Don Pedro Fajardo y Chacón (1477/78–after 1541) was raised and educated in the immediate entourage of the monarchs. As a boy, he had been among a choice group of the sons of Spain's greatest families selected by the queen to receive a humanistic education from Pietro Martire, a brilliant young Italian scholar, who had been brought to the court in 1488. At an academy for young nobles, under Martire's guidance, Don Pedro learned to enjoy the classics and to express himself in beautiful, fluent Latin, a skill of which he was so proud that, after leaving the academy in 1500, he continued to use it for correspondence.

When his father died in 1503, Don Pedro established his residence at Murcia, the capital of his lands. This region, which he ruled partly as a representative of the crown and partly as the most powerful feudal lord in the province, was often raided by the Moors entrenched in the kingdom of Granada. Ten years after their surrender of Granada in 1492, Moorish rebellions against the Spanish nobles were still frequent; the last was brilliantly suppressed with the help of Don Pedro, who saved the king, Ferdinand II of Castile and Aragon (1452–1516), from being captured. Despite his distinguished conduct, Don Pedro had great difficulties with royal authority.

The north side of the patio is reminiscent of 15th-century Venetian palace design, with two tiers of window frames laid out like embroidered hangings, tied together by a plain horizontal molding.

A capital of the first-floor arcade, showing the Fajardo coat of arms and a bird with raised wings

The monarchs exercised firm restraint on the ambitions of the unruly feudal nobility, and less than three weeks after the death of his father, Don Pedro had to agree to return to the crown the strategic port of Cartagena, which his grandfather had received from King Henry IV of Castile in 1466. In exchange Don Pedro was given a group of Moorish towns on the plain of Vélez and some surrounding lands. The most important of these was the fortified town of Veled-Albiad, or Vélez Blanco, the seat of a Moorish stronghold that had surrendered to King Ferdinand in 1488. Six months after receiving the lands, Queen Isabella I exiled Don Pedro from Murcia for his high-handed conduct of military affairs there and suspended his governorship. After her death in 1504, his sentence was revoked by Isabella's daughter, Joanna I.

Local historians record that Don Pedro arrived at Vélez Blanco in 1505 and began to erect his own castle on the foundations of the old Moorish fortress. He probably envisaged a castle-palace similar to those built by Spanish nobles one generation earlier in Castile—that of Manzanares el Real near Madrid or that of Cuéllar near Segovia.

Don Pedro's architect is not known, but typically Spanish motifs, such as the many coats of arms applied to the facade, and structural details such as the hexagonal pilasters of the paseador with the decorative bands of pellets, segmental arches, and flat timber ceilings with exposed beams in the patio galleries, clearly indicate the work of a Spanish master trained in the tradition of late Gothic architecture. The patio itself, so closely related to the rest of the castle, was certainly planned by this Spanish architect, who may also have worked on the Fajardo family chapel in the cathedral of Murcia: the patio is similar to the chapel in its very original combination of late Gothic and Hispano-Moresque traits.

The patio's original irregular plan is at variance not only with the Renaissance style of its marbles but also with many patios of contemporary Castilian palaces, which, whether late Gothic or Renaissance, are normally nearly square and consist of two stories of arcades on four sides, with a central doorway connecting to the outside. At Vélez Blanco the elongated plan, windowed wall, and arcaded portico at one short end and the side entrance were features comparable to those of the typical Moorish patios of Andalusia, which are usually rectangular, with a side entrance, to avoid a direct view of the patio from the vestibule, in keeping with the Arab desire for privacy.

The Italian character of Vélez Blanco's carvings was probably not due to the architect but was most likely the result of Fajardo's desire to surround himself with an architectural environment evocative of the antique world and of the splendors of the great Italian palaces of the day. Fajardo's choice was almost surely inspired by the nearby palace of La Calahorra, built from 1509 to 1512 by Don Rodrigo de Vivar y Mendoza, a relative of Fajardo's wife.

Inside this austere Castilian structure was a courtyard in Lombard style with marble work by carvers from Lombardy and Liguria, executed under the direction of the Lombard architect-sculptor Michele Carlone. Certain resemblances between some of the decorations at Vélez Blanco and those at La Calahorra indicate a common design source and perhaps even the work of the same carvers. Since the Vélez Blanco marbles were probably made during the last three or four years of its construction, which was completed in 1515, they were probably started just as the work at La Calahorra was ending in 1512.

Large Gothic gargoyles project from the classical cornice.

The architectural and sculptural motifs employed throughout the Museum's patio reflect the most refined and capricious phase of Italian early Renaissance style, which flourished in the last two decades of the fifteenth century and in the years immediately following 1500. An analytical style, it was composed of motifs either invented or, more often, borrowed from ancient monuments, combined with naturalistic and antiquarian details—foliage, birds, monsters, medals, vases. This rich type of decoration reached its most accomplished expression in some of the famous North Italian buildings of the time: first in the palace of the duke of Montefeltro at Urbino and later in the Lombardesque churches and palaces of Venice, Verona, and Vicenza, and still later in the palaces of Ferrara. Reminiscent of Venice, for instance, are the three sets of window frames laid out like embroidered hangings and tied together by a plain horizontal molding, as well as the combination of rounded windows on the top story with square ones below. Other North Italian examples are recalled by the high lintels with paired decorative panels surmounting the arched windows.

The Vélez Blanco capitals are exquisite examples of the delightful variety and classical discipline achieved by Italian architect-sculptors of the late quattrocento. Some are elegant but sober variations on the Roman Corinthian and composite types that we find from Brunelleschi down to Giuliano da Sangallo, but more frequent are the playful, nonclassical kind that delighted Lombard designers. For instance, normal volutes are replaced by rams' heads and human faces or by paired dolphins drinking out of a vase. Traditional acanthus leaves are enlivened by grinning, big-eared masks or fluttering birds or tiny shields with the Fajardo arms, all treated with the cheerful, unconventional imagination expressed in capitals of many North Italian buildings, especially in Ferrara.

A triumph of the designer's skill is the treatment of the pilasters of the windows, with their narrow, difficult proportions, within which are arranged hanging designs or ascending garlands. Among the most attractive are the helmets, suits of armor, panoplies of shields, swords and daggers, trumpets, flutes, cymbals and drums—motifs frequently used in contemporary North Italian and Tuscan monuments.

An abundance of fantastic animals is a striking feature in the Vélez Blanco carvings. Monsters and crossbreeds of the North Italian repertory—

Heraldic animals on a second-floor spandrel

goats with leafy bodies and serpents' tails, griffins, dragons, and sphinxes—all are treated with a lively, almost aggressive imagination. Some are harbingers of the new taste for grotesque decoration stimulated by the recently discovered frescoes of Nero's Golden House in Rome. In contrast to such exuberant animal life, there is little use of human figures, only some timid putti in the spandrels of the upper-floor gallery and two winged half-women on a window panel.

For all their richness of effect, the carvings are based on relatively few motifs and compositions. This remarkable unity of design indicates that they were derived from one source, probably a sketch or pattern book containing a number of isolated elements—details of classical armor, candelabra, friezes, and capitals, some possibly taken from ancient monuments in Rome, others from Renaissance sources.

One day, we hope, the discovery of documents concerning the castle of Vélez Blanco will solve some of the mysteries surrounding the creation of the patio. What matters most, however, is that the Metropolitan has been able to reconstruct an extraordinary monument that transcends national boundaries and represents a beguiling aspect of the early Renaissance both in Spain and in Italy.

OLGA RAGGIO

Details of window pilasters. At the left is a "candelabra" design, conceived as an imaginary plant rising from a vase on a central stem. At the right is a hanging garland made of pieces of armor.

decorated in the Baroque style. The coat of arms of Johann Gaudenz and his wife, Amalie Dorothea von Schorsch (d. 1717)—an arrow for the Gaudenz family and a tower for the von Schorsch family—and the date of the building's foundation, 1682, are displayed above the main portal. The same coat of arms decorates the center of the elaborate ceiling of the most important room in the house, the *Reiche Stube* ("Rich Chamber"), which served as the main reception room. Now installed in the Metropolitan Museum, the geometric ceiling panels and wainscoting of this room were originally located at the right end of the second-floor corridor in the Schlössli. In Johann Gaudenz's day the visitor was led through a simple ground-floor hall and a modestly decorated barrel-vaulted staircase into a wide rib-vaulted corridor before entering the ornate reception room. Even in this remote Alpine region, the unidentified architect followed strict tradition in the arrangement of public space, where unembellished secondary halls and corridors led up to the first major room in the building. Here the visitor would be impressed by the pictorial and symbolic richness of the decoration, a metaphor for the earthly wealth and spiritual strength of its owner.

The four walls of the reception room, which measures about twenty-three by twenty-one feet with a ceiling height of eleven feet, are covered with panels of mainly local woods—walnut, maple, lindenwood, pine, and sycamore—inlaid and carved in relief. Flat panels, in which applied scroll-work frames two-dimensional marquetry wall niches, alternate with caryatid figures standing on acanthus-volute pilasters, interrupted by three recessed windows and the doorway. The entablature, with acanthus volutes and putti in the middle section and a dentate cornice, supports the frieze above. Grotesque herm figures hold up the ceiling, some of them dressed in Turkish costumes reminding inhabitants of the danger of a Turkish invasion, an ever-present fear during the period when the room was designed.

The frieze panels are decorated with grotesque scrollwork and mythological animals. The depictions of these fantastic goats, horses, lions, and other beasts derive from medieval bestiary illuminations that were especially popular in this mountainous region, although the number of animals with two horns is unusually high, perhaps an allusion to the Old and New Testaments. The unicorn, often used to represent Christ, is here characterized with the wings of Pegasus fighting with a multitailed lionlike beast in a depiction of the combatant forces of good and evil. The panel to the right above the entrance shows a pelican opening its breast with its bill, a reference to the myth in which a pelican sacrifices its blood to revive its starving young. This has been interpreted as a symbol of Christ the Redeemer and the

The *Reiche Stube* ("Rich Chamber") features a ceramic stove original to the room.

Detail of the frieze showing a panel in which a unicorn confronts a multitailed lionlike beast

Eucharist. In contrast to this Christian vocabulary, the spread-winged eagle prominently placed in the center panel of the double window wall represents the worldly power of the Holy Roman Empire.

The doorway of the room is of particular interest. The frieze illustrated here shows two heraldic lions holding a tower with two crossed arrows, symbolizing the union of the Capol and von Schorsch families. In the broken pediment a nude female figure reclines in an ornate cartouche over a frieze picturing a dinner party surrounded by cupids that evoke the pleasures of life, worldly ostentation, and frivolity. The figure in the cartouche has lost the attribute she once held in her right hand; she may have been Vanitas looking into a mirror, a reminder that "all is vanity" and that these pleasurable activities will one day come to an end. This interpretation is supported by the surrounding ornamentation, which is carved in the so-called Auricular style. Formed like the lobes of an ear, hence its name, this type of ornament was used to convey the idea of vanity during the Baroque period. The variation applied here with its masklike profile is based on the designs of Friedrich Unteutsch (ca. 1600–1670), whose most important pattern book, *Neues Zieratenbuch*, was published about 1650.

Lest the visitor be overwhelmed by this rather negative pictorial program, the nude figure of Fortune appears on the inside of the door to help ensure the happiness of all who stay at the Schlössli. Inlaid in colored woods and surrounded by a complicated architectural frame, Fortune is clearly distinguished from the other subjects in the room. This panel is executed in relief intarsia, a technique preferred by the cabinetmakers of Eger, a town in Bohemia, where in the second half of the seventeenth and the early eighteenth century relief intarsia was fashionable and very much in demand. The craftsmen of Eger produced cabinets, game boards, and narrative panels

The central panel on the inside of the room's door, possibly made by a member of the Haberstumpf family from the town of Eger, is decorated with the figure of Fortune.

The room is furnished with a draw-top table with an inserted slate top and 17th- and 18th-century backed stools, called *stabelle*, a form very typical of the Alpine region.

in large numbers and exported them throughout Central Europe. It is very likely that Johann Gaudenz himself bought this exceptionally large panel on one of his trips. A close look reveals that parts of the panel's original frame were cut away to fit the space in the center of the door and to make room for the engraved and pieced rim-lock box.

Some minor restorations and replacements were made during the installation of the paneling in New York, and the original location of two walls was switched. In Flims the double-window wall was positioned on the left beyond the entrance, but this section now forms the opposite side of the portal wall. The wall facing the entrance originally held the paneling with only one window niche and three panel sections, the central one concealing a hidden door. The floor plan on page 66 shows that this secret door was the only access to a small alcovelike chamber in the tower of the castle. The real purpose of the chamber is not documented, but the decorative plasterwork featuring naked putti and the existence of a secret door are rich with possibility.

It is believed that the woodwork in the Swiss room was made by a craftsman known as Master Thaddäus Acker of Feldkirch, who, according to

an archival note in the parish register of the neighboring town of Sagans, was "at present joiner with Provincial Judge Gaudenz of Capol." No other carving has been ascribed to this individual.

The room is now furnished with objects from the Museum's collection, including seventeenth- and early-eighteenth-century furniture and late-sixteenth-century stained-glass panels from Switzerland and Germany. The imposing ceramic stove, however, is original to the room. Its material—tin-glazed cream-colored earthenware tiles painted blue, yellow, green, and manganese brown—contrasts sharply with the dark brown woodwork. Located in the corner to the right of the entrance, the towering hexagonal stove dominates the room. Made about 1684–85 in Winterthur, the center for pottery-making in Switzerland, the stove is painted on all sides with narrative scenes from the Old and New Testaments. In the lower section the faience painter followed the designs of Tobias Stimmer (1539–1584) published in Basel in 1576, while scenes on the upper frieze were inspired by the etchings of Christoph Murer (1558–1614) published in Strassbourg in 1625. The painter has added the biblical citation and interpretive texts to each scene, presumably for

Room from Flims, Swiss, after 1682, wall with one window niche and the concealed door that originally led to a secret tower chamber

their uplifting educational and moral value. The text in the cartouche beneath the scene of Samson and the Lion (Judges, 14: 5–7) reads in translation: "As Samson's lion gave honey after his death, so Christ's death brings us sweet life." The corner tiles depict Christ as Salvator Mundi and the Apostles, whereas the panels on the back contain the Christian virtues of Hope, Justice, Truth, Tolerance, and Faith, which surround a narrow pilaster tile picturing an elegantly dressed man identified in an inscription as *Hauptmann* (captain), perhaps an allusion to the military rank of Johann Gaudenz. It has been suggested that the workshop of David II Pfau (1644–1702) may have designed and produced the stove with the help of his cousin Hans Heinrich III Pfau. Similar stoves from David Pfau's workshop can be seen in the town halls of Winterthur and Zurich, as well as in the Musée d'Art et d'Histoire in Geneva.

Johann Gaudenz died without direct heirs and the Schlössli was left to Marie von Capol, the daughter of his brother. She married Hercules Dietegen von Salis-Seewis, a member of another prominent Swiss family, in whose possession it remained until 1858. In that year the structure was acquired by Johann Parli of Flims, and he passed it on to Captain Mattli-Bavier. Since 1948 the building has been maintained by the town of Flims, which uses the castle as a rectory and for municipal offices. The room and the stove, however, were apparently removed in 1883 and sold to a Mrs. von Sprengel from Munich, presumably an art dealer. Documents indicate that it was bequeathed two years later to the Kunstgewerbemuseum in Berlin by a German collector and philanthropist named Dr. Rybeck. As the Berlin museum already owned two similar rooms, the paneling, along with the stove, was offered in 1905 to The Metropolitan Museum of Art. Letters in the Museum's archives, written by European art historians at this time, point out that the decoration of the panels was considered rather "brittle and boring" and that "this period is not desirable." These remarks were made when Late Baroque art, especially its regional interpretation outside Italy and France, was not very fashionable.

In the floor plan of the Schlössli's second story, the connection between the Museum's room, at the lower left, and a tiny secret chamber in the tower is clearly marked.

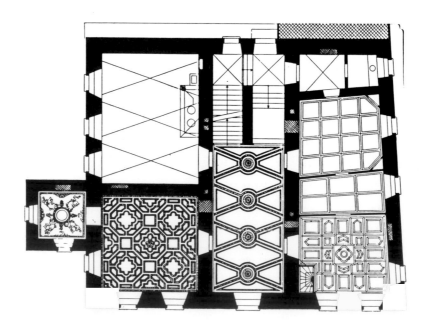

Detail of the ceramic stove showing Samson with a lion, based on a biblical illustration by Christoph Murer

Flims was far away from the cultural centers of the late seventeenth century, and the room has no pretensions to high style. Nevertheless, it is an important example of the interior decoration commissioned by Swiss nobility and is exceptional in the complex program of its decoration, which includes several unusual features, such as the Auricular ornament and the Eger relief intarsia on the door, to say nothing of the fact that the room is virtually complete, with its original wainscoting, ceiling, doorway, and ceramic stove.

WOLFRAM KOEPPE

The Sagredo Bedroom

VENICE ◆ 1718

The Palazzo Sagredo stands on a stretch of the Grand Canal's north bank, above the Rialto Bridge. Its facade, somewhat remodeled, dates in part from the thirteenth century; its exterior Byzantine ornament has been supplemented by fourteenth-century elements, such as the series of four Gothic window surrounds on the third floor, the palazzo's *piano nobile* (principal floor).

One of several palaces owned by the Morosini, a renowned Venetian family, it was bought in the early part of the eighteenth century (1704–14) by Zaccaria Sagredo (1659–1729). The offspring of a family that had come to Venice from Dalmatia in the ninth century, Zaccaria was a nephew of Niccolò Sagredo (1606–1676), who, toward the end of his life, was elected doge, or chief magistrate, of Venice. Zaccaria did not seek political office but led a secluded existence and devoted his energies to forming a celebrated collection of paintings, drawings, and prints (he is believed to have been one of the early patrons of the Venetian painters Tiepolo, Piazzetta, and Canaletto). After his acquisition of the palace that would bear his family name, part of his art collection must have been displayed in the six large reception rooms on the piano nobile, their windows giving onto the Grand Canal and the Campo Santa Sofia.

OPPOSITE:
Bed alcove from the Palazzo Sagredo in Venice. The gilded limewood headboard for the bed, covered with red and gold silk brocade, was made in Venice about 1725–35; the gilded walnut armchair covered in red velvet is also Venetian, about 1750.

This view of the Palazzo Sagredo from the Grand Canal was etched in 1880 by James Abbott McNeill Whistler. A wing of the palace extends along a side of the Campo Santa Sofia at the right; on the left the Palazzo Pesaro abuts a jetty that is now a *vaporetto* stop named for the Ca' d'Oro Palace, visible at the far left. The Museum's two rooms were originally at the back of the palace overlooking an interior courtyard. The artist published this print in transposed form, but for the purposes of this illustration, the image has been flopped to correspond to the scene as Whistler saw it and as the visitor may see it today.

Three of the winged children in the ceiling over the entrance to the alcove support a shield bearing the interlaced initials Z and S, the monogram of Zaccaria Sagredo, who commissioned the redecoration of the interiors of the palace.

Lying off the interior courtyard, behind one of these salons, and adjoining the main staircase was a series of three small rooms consisting of a dressing room, an anteroom, and a bed alcove. The entrance wall to the bed alcove is surmounted by a swirl of winged babies holding a shield with the monogram of Zaccaria Sagredo: the initials Z and S interlaced. This bed alcove and the anteroom preceding it were purchased by the Museum in 1906—one of the earliest instances of the acquisition of period-room elements by an American museum.

A sense of movement, characteristic of the Italian Baroque style, is exemplified by the winged children who frolic on the ceilings of these two rooms amid fringed and tasseled folds of drapery, against a ground of low-relief strapwork decoration, all executed in stucco. The pine-paneled walls are carved with relatively subdued classical and Baroque motifs, painted and gilded; the plain surfaces of this paneling are covered with a gold-and-green brocatelle of the period, a replacement for the original material, which has been lost. The inlaid wooden platform under the bed is original, while the terrazzo floor of the anteroom is modern. The oil painting on canvas representing Dawn, set into the center of the ceiling in the anteroom, is by the artist Gaspare Diziani (1689–1767), from Belluno.

A chief attraction of the two rooms is the ceiling, where twenty-nine almost three-dimensional figures, some of whom bear military attributes, seem to be trying to fly from their attachments. These freehand stucco sculptures were modeled by the sculptor before they were fixed to the enclosing wood framework with iron clamps. Stylistically, they are related to configurations of flying angelic children produced in about 1687 in the Sicilian workshops of the virtuosic sculptor-*stuccatore* Giacomo Serpotta (1656–1732). Clusters of these figures, prototypes of those at the Museum, are spread over church walls in Palermo; they represent cherubim, an order of heavenly

ABOVE:
Two winged children play with a flag, shield, and helmet, while a third holds up the fringe of a tasseled canopy. This painted-and-gilded stucco decoration is located in the bed alcove to the left of the bed.

LEFT:
An oil painting, *Dawn* (ca. 1720), by Gaspare Diziani, is set into the anteroom ceiling.

OPPOSITE:
In the anteroom stands a Venetian console table, which together with its mate, was made about 1720 for the Palazzo Sagredo; the Sagredo coat of arms is carved on each apron. The wall mirror above, also one of a pair, is set with two gilt-bronze candle branches and dates to about 1735. A casement window is shown at the left; another such window, in the same relative position, is in the bed alcove. Both windows were originally on the opposite wall, judging from their former site in the palace, but the side walls were interchanged when the room was installed in the Museum in 1925–26 to allow the diffusion of natural light from an interior well. This arrangement was perpetuated when the rooms were moved to another location in the Museum in 1953–54 and electric light replaced daylight.

beings, not to be confused with similar-appearing cupids, the winged symbols of earthly love.

The name of the architect who designed Zaccaria Sagredo's interior decorations is not known, but the names of two stucco workers are incised on the ceiling of a room, the so-called Saletta delle Armi, on the floor above the bedroom, together with the date 1718. On the basis of these signatures, Abbondio Statio (1675–1757) and his pupil Carpofaro Mazzetti (ca. 1684–1748), both born and trained as *stuccatori* in the Lugano region of Switzerland, have been credited with the work of the Museum's bedroom, as well as of the dozen or so ceilings and rooms that still remain in the palace. Stucco ornament elsewhere in Venice—in the Albrizzi, Merati, Loredan, and Zenobio palaces—is also attributed to Statio and Mazzetti.

The stuccowork must have been in progress when the date 1718 was inscribed on the cornice; it was the year that Zaccaria Sagredo became sixty-one years of age. In spite of the playful and witty mode manifested in the decoration of his bedroom, the space itself was probably not intended for informal activity or even the pleasures of sleep. It would have been more likely that the room's function was mainly official, that it constituted Sagredo's state bedroom, where, like other noblemen all over Europe, he would lie abed in the relatively late morning granting audiences to local tradesmen, clergymen, city officials, visiting dignitaries, or his artist friends. The anteroom in front of the bed alcove may also have served as a room for Sagredo's regular attendants—secretaries, housekeepers, valets, hairdressers, cooks, and other servants—awaiting instructions.

The theory of an official bedroom gains substance from the existence of two narrow staircases that lead from the alcove to the lower-ceilinged floor above, where the owner's actual sleeping quarters may have been located; the doors to the two staircases opened from the alcove, to the right of the bed and from the rear wall of a stucco dressing room adjoining the anteroom. This smaller dressing room was behind the present location of the visitors' entrance, its two windows in alignment with the two other windows of the apartment. Approximately half as wide as the anteroom, it formed the third unit in a conventional sequence found in such apartments at the time: bed alcove, antechamber or waiting room, and dressing room. When Museum officials were negotiating the Sagredo purchase in 1906, they decided that the dressing room might be superfluous, taking up space unnecessarily, and that because of its awkward proportions, it might detract from the visual effect of the other two chambers shown together. Thus, the dressing room was left behind and has remained in its original location at the palace.

The anteroom and alcove were dismantled in 1907, the woodwork easily disassembled, and the stucco decoration sawed into large sections for packing and shipment. The Museum lost no time in acquiring the first pieces of furniture for the new installation. The Venetian dealer and restorer

A plasterer working on the palace decoration incised the date 1718 and his name, Abbondio Statio, above the cornice of one of the rooms on an upper floor. He was assisted by Carpofaro Mazzetti, another Swiss-trained *stuccatore*, who also signed his name on this lavishly decorated ceiling. They have been credited with modeling all the stuccowork of the Museum's two rooms, as well as much other ornament that survives in the palace.

Antonio Correr, who was acting as an agent for the Sagredo family when he sold the rooms, had also sold the Museum in the same year (1906) a pair of onyx-topped, painted-and-gilded wood console tables. These early-eighteenth-century pieces, each carved on its apron with the Sagredo coat of arms, were part of the palace's furniture and are now exhibited in the Museum's anteroom.

In 1913 the Palazzo Sagredo was bequeathed by a Sagredo descendant to the Venetian patriarchate (archbishopric); it was resold back into private hands in 1936. In the meantime, this forty-room palace had been in part rented to a school, the Istituto Ravà, which vacated the premises in the 1930s. In November 1987 most of its remaining contents were auctioned off. The building, protected by what then corresponded to landmark status, was bought by a consortium of Milanese businessmen, who intend to renovate it for practical use.

In New York no space was available for the installation of the two rooms for twenty years (this long delay between acquisition and exhibition has been more the rule than the exception for period rooms and testifies to the Museum's difficulty in finding space, usually allocated in new wings, to accommodate them). At last a suitable area was found at the far end of the Fifth Avenue south wing, the last section of the long facade to be completed. The Sagredo room was then slotted in among ten new galleries for European decorative arts, which opened April 6, 1926, on the second floor of Wing K, where its two windows gave onto an interior light well.

The impending opening had revived the search for suitable furniture. In June 1925 Joseph Breck, curator of decorative arts, made a trip to Venice, where he was able to buy several pieces from Antonio Correr. These included a pair of mirrors with elegantly shaped gilded-wood frames, purportedly from the Palazzo Gradenigo, Venice, now hanging on the entrance wall above the already acquired console tables; another rectangular framed mirror, with a scrolling crest from the Palazzo Sagredo, on the left wall above a carved walnut sofa; and the imposing carved-and-gilded limewood headboard for a bed, dating to 1725–35, slightly later than the bedroom, reputedly from the collection of the conte Giovanelli, Venice. The rooms were furnished in time for their first presentation in their new location at the Metropolitan, which, as occasionally happens with period elements in museums, was not destined to be their last.

Between the years 1949 and 1954 a massive renovation and reallocation of space took place at the Metropolitan. The area affected was mainly within one of the older parts of the building, constructed between 1884 and 1894. No fewer than forty-nine galleries of European seventeenth- to eighteenth-century decorative arts and period rooms opened in 1954 on the first floor and in the basement of this space. An area was set aside for Italian seventeenth- and eighteenth-century objects on the first floor near what is now the Armor Hall. To exhibit the Sagredo room properly alongside other objects related to it, its transfer was decided upon. Once again, in 1953, the stucco ceiling was sawed into large sections and reassembled, together with the other elements, in the new location. At the same time, peripheral areas on the first floor were utilized for installation (or, in two cases, reinstallation) of the Museum's other holdings of seventeenth- and eighteenth-century European period rooms. This suite, which opened on November 11, 1954, was expanded to hold a number of the other rooms described in this book, some of which were acquired after 1954 and were therefore added to the sequence.

Together these rooms form an impressive ensemble, starting with the early-seventeenth-century Sagredo anteroom and bed alcove, a magnificent vestige of Italian Baroque interior decoration.

JAMES PARKER

The Varengeville Room

PARIS ◆ 1736–52

The introduction of a system of radiating and interconnecting avenues known as the *grands boulevards* was to lead to radical changes in the appearance of the city of Paris. The program was inaugurated early in the Second Empire (1852–70) under the supervision of Baron Georges-Eugène Haussmann (1809–1891). Haussmann, Napoleon III's prefect of the Seine from 1853 to 1870, suggested to the emperor a scheme for a broad new avenue on the Left Bank, to be driven through the Faubourg Saint-Germain, the "noble Faubourg," as he referred to it. Demolition operations to clear ground for the present boulevard Saint-Germain began in 1855, but progress was very slow. By 1877 a widened artery had advanced seven hundred yards along the rue Saint-Dominique, sweeping away whatever obstacles stood in its path, including some fine eighteenth-century buildings for which the quarter was justly famous. Among the obstructions suffering damage was the Hôtel de Varengeville, a private residence that originally stood on the old rue Saint-Dominique. The hôtel, which had remained relatively undisturbed for more than 170 years, lost its front elevation as well as half of its two courtyards with their stables and kitchen. Its address, moreover, changed from no. 16 rue Saint-Dominique to no. 217 boulevard Saint-Germain. (The principal quarters

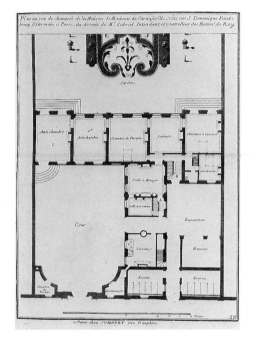

ABOVE:
Plan of the first floor of the Hôtel de Varengeville. It is not known which room originally contained the paneling now in the Museum.

LEFT:
Garden elevation of the building at no. 217 boulevard Saint-Germain that was originally the Hôtel de Varengeville. The interior has been much altered, and the top floor was added after 1877.

OPPOSITE:
A view of the chimneypiece wall from the Hôtel de Varengeville. The gilded beechwood armchair in the foreground is part of a set signed by Nicolas-Quinibert Foliot.

Hôtel Pillet-Will, rue du faubourg St-Honoré Nº 31. Vue d'ensemble du Grand Salon.

of the remaining building are now occupied by a club, La Maison de l'Amérique Latine.)

The Museum's gold-and-white paneled room came from the back of the house, which was left undamaged by the relentless advance of the boulevard. Although the room's precise site in the interior of the Hôtel de Varengeville is not identifiable, it may have been on the ground floor behind the garden elevation. In spite of a top floor added after 1877, the house preserves some of the eighteenth-century aura that it must have had when it was built in 1704.

Its architect was Jacques Gabriel (1667–1742), a member of a family of architects—his son, Jacques Ange (1698–1782), was even more famous than his father. Jacques began his career as an assistant to Louis XIV's great architect Jules Hardouin-Mansart (1646–1708) and became late in life, in 1734, royal architect to the young Louis XV (1710–1774). His best-known works are the place Royale in Bordeaux, two other large squares in Rennes and Dijon with some of their public buildings, the remodeling of the royal château La Muette in the Bois de Boulogne (destroyed), the early Louis XV

ABOVE:
Before coming to the Museum, the *boiserie* from the Hôtel de Varengeville was installed at the Hôtel Pillet-Will in Paris, together with door frames and overdoors from another source. The paneling was auctioned off at this site in 1963. This view dates from the 1890s.

LEFT:
Almost all the panels on the chimneypiece wall, including the rounded corner panels, were originally installed at the Hôtel de Varengeville. The two long panels flanking the mirror on the end wall are modern and were added to make the room larger in order to accommodate the Savonnerie carpet and additional pieces of furniture. The *fleur-de-pêche* marble chimneypiece (not original) dates to about 1740, the period of the old woodwork.

work at Versailles, the Rococo wing of Fontainebleau (where he was assisted by his son Jacques Ange), a number of bridges over French rivers (notably the bridge across the Loire at Blois, which is still usable), the cathedrals of Orléans and La Rochelle, as well as other town houses in Paris.

Jacques Gabriel built the Hôtel de Varengeville for Charlotte-Angélique Courtin, the widowed marquise de Varengeville, who at her death in 1732 left it to her daughter Jeanne Angélique Roque. In 1709, at the age of nineteen, Mlle de Varengeville had married Hector, duc de Villars (1653–1734), a great military commander under Louis XIV. Mme de Villars and her husband lived in the magnificent newly built Hôtel de Villars on the rue de Grenelle; so she first rented out her mother's house and then sold it in 1736 to Marie-Marguerite d'Allègre, comtesse de Ruppelmonde, who owned it until her death in 1752. It was probably during this period that the original paneling for the Museum's room was commissioned.

The hôtel then passed by inheritance to the Guerchy family, who owned it until 1837, renting it out on several occasions; further remodeling may have been carried out during these years. Between 1886 and 1891 the paneling of the room was removed from the Hôtel de Varengeville and sold by Mme Jean-Martin Charcot (the wife of a well-known neurologist who had bought the hôtel in 1884) to the comte Frédéric-Alexis-Louis Pillet-Will, a regent of the Bank of France. Pillet-Will planned to install the woodwork in a residence he was having built for himself on the site made available by the demolition in 1887 of an eighteenth-century building, the Hôtel Marbeuf. Thus, the Hôtel Pillet-Will rose at 31 rue du Faubourg Saint-Honoré, on the Right Bank of the Seine, not far from the place de la Concorde; it was here that the doors and panels from the old hôtel on the Left Bank were incorporated with other extraneous elements to form the grand salon of a new hôtel.

In early 1963 an auction was held and parts of the salon were sold in situ; shortly thereafter the *boiseries* from the Hôtel de Varengeville were reunited, bought by Mr. and Mrs. Charles Wrightsman and presented to the Museum. Four years later the Hôtel Pillet-Will, in its turn, fell to the wrecking ball; it was replaced by a contemporary aluminum-and-glass building commissioned by the Japanese government.

This 1759 writing table, commissioned by Louis XV for his study at Versailles, now stands on a Savonnerie carpet, part of a series designed by Charles Le Brun for the Grande Galerie of the Louvre. The table remained at Versailles until 1786, when it was replaced by a marquetry version commissioned by Louis XVI. The two portraits flanking the chimneypiece, which depict the marquise d'Argence (left) and the duchesse d'Orléans, were painted by Jean Marc Nattier (1685–1766).

The details of the carving of the Museum's boiseries recall the Rococo work of the designer-architect-sculptor Nicolas Pineau (1684–1754). Early in his career he spent fourteen years in Russia, where he collaborated with a team of French craftsmen to embellish Peter the Great's city of Saint Petersburg. After Pineau returned to France in 1730, he worked for a number of well-known architects, designing and even carving woodwork for Paris mansions. The fantastic storklike birds carved at the sides of the mirror crests and on the wide panels in the Museum's room are reminiscent of the Rococo-style work that Pineau produced from 1730 until his death.

The present installation, intended to provide an effective setting for furniture, incorporates the elements recovered from the Hôtel Pillet-Will;

ABOVE:
Louis XV was well informed about the scientific developments of his day and is likely to have owned a microscope comparable to this example. It is inscribed "Passemant au Louvre," which refers to Claude-Siméon Passemant, instrument maker to the king.

RIGHT:
One of a pair of corner cabinets in the Varengeville room, with incised coromandel-lacquer decoration on the doors. These lacquer panels were cut from Chinese screens and adapted by French craftsmen to the cabinets, which are made of oak veneered with ebony, in about 1745–49.

since nothing is known about the original sequence of these panels, their present arrangement is entirely arbitrary and is supplemented by panels carved in Paris in 1963–64 in order to give the room its present dimensions. There was no model or original document upon which the plaster cornice could be based, so the design for its molded ornament was improvised in the style of the period; the gilded-plaster ceiling rosette was based on an engraved design by Pineau published in 1727. The *fleur-de-pêche* marble chimneypiece, given to the Museum by J. Pierpont Morgan in 1906, is roughly contemporary with the old woodwork, as is the flooring, which consists of oak squares of the type called *parquet de Versailles*.

The chief attraction of the room, its extraordinary gilded wood carving, can be assigned stylistically to the developing phase of the Rococo, which barely precedes the extreme asymmetry that marked the style between 1736 and 1752. The series of panels on the chimneypiece wall, almost all old, display original, highly decorative carvings that epitomize the Rococo style and incorporate some of its characteristic motifs: C-scrolls, S-scrolls, fantastic birds, palmettes, foliage sprays, and bats' wings. This conventional form of ornament can be compared with the more symbolic and representational ornament of the trophies, rounded on the back wall to form corners and recesses and flat on the side and entrance walls. These motifs, which hang from carved, tasseled bowknots, represent allegories and allude to abstract concepts and qualities.

There are also four allegories of the Seasons (to the right and left of the main entrance to the room): Spring with garlands and a cornucopia of flowers crossed with a torch; Autumn with panpipes, grape leaves, and a wine pitcher superimposed on a satyr's thyrsus; Winter with indoor amusements represented by a jester's gear—a tambourine, castanets, and an actor's mask—wreathed with ivy and holly; Summer with a parasol, beehive, rake, scythe, and a sickle against wheat stalks. The subjects alluded to in the other original trophies are Military Fame, Princely Glory, Truthfulness, Music, Poetry, Commerce, and Gardening. (Some of these trophies can be easily identified among the narrow, curved panels on the back of the chimneypiece wall.) The pair of double doors at the sides also exhibits four comparable but much smaller trophies carved close to eye level on the central framed panel of each door. The two modern carved overdoors were made in Paris in 1969 and added to the Museum's room just before its opening on November 21, 1969. They frame two paintings on canvas dated 1753 from the workshop of François Boucher (1703–1770) depicting allegories (Lyric Poetry on the right and Autumn on the left).

Some of the Museum's most extraordinary Louis XV objects are in this room. These include the scarlet-and-gold japanned writing table placed on a magnificent wool Savonnerie carpet dated 1680. The desk, its front and sides painted in gold with chinoiserie ornament, bears an inventory number,

This fantastic bird perched at the top of a mirror frame, part of the original paneling, is made of carved, painted, and gilded oak.

2131, painted under its central section. The number corresponds to a written description in the royal furniture registry and identifies it as the example delivered on December 29, 1759, by the royal cabinetmaker Gilles Joubert (1689–1775) for Louis XV's study at Versailles. On the right side of the desk stands a splendid tripod microscope of gilt-bronze and blue-green sharkskin, or shagreen, dating to about 1760. It is signed by Claude-Siméon Passemant (1702–1769), the scientific instrument maker to Louis XV. The owner of this splendid microscope could, at the same time, indulge an interest in scientific knowledge while gratifying a taste for beautiful objects.

Other works of art in the room include a pair of gilded beechwood armchairs, part of a large set ordered in Paris by the Danish ambassador to France in 1753. These commodious armchairs, signed by the chairmaker Nicolas-Quinibert Foliot (1706–1776), are covered with their original Beauvais tapestry. In the fireplace of the chimneypiece stands a gilt-bronze andiron set with a reclining figure of Pluto, god of Hell (suitable for a fireplace), dated about 1753; the matching andiron supports a figure of Proserpine, Pluto's wife. Placed above their heads, on the mantelpiece shelf, is a pair of beautiful Japanese porcelain potpourri bowls, mounted in French gilt bronze. Against the near corners of the room is a pair of incised Chinese coromandel-lacquer corner cabinets, datable to 1745–49 on the evidence of marks stamped into their gilt-bronze mounts; each is signed in the wood on top with the initials B.V.R.B. for a cabinetmaker of Dutch origin, Bernard Vanrisamburgh II (active ca. 1730–64). In the eighteenth century his furniture was acquired by Louis XV and the French court. The vogue has lasted, and pieces by him are still prized and sought after by present-day collectors.

JAMES PARKER

OPPOSITE:
On the shelf of the marble chimneypiece sits a 17th-century Japanese porcelain potpourri bowl (one of a pair) mounted in French gilt-bronze, about 1750. On the hearth below is a gilt-bronze andiron on which the figure of Pluto, god of the fiery underworld, is seated. His spouse, Proserpine, is seated on the matching andiron. These are attributed to Antoine Le Lièvre (active 1738–53); a similar pair is in the Louvre.

RIGHT:
This gilded beechwood chair, one of a pair in the room, is part of a set of 12 armchairs and two settees, covered with the original wool-and-silk Beauvais tapestry. The seats and backs of the armchairs are woven with animal and bird subjects after Jean-Baptiste Oudry (1686–1755). The set was ordered in 1753 in Paris by Baron Johann Ernst Bernstorff, a Dutch ambassador to the court of Versailles, for the tapestry room at his palace in Copenhagen.

The Paar Room

VIENNA ◆ 1765–72

When it was constructed about 1630, the magnificent Paar Palace in Vienna served as an impressive residence for its owner and also as his place of business. A large quadrilateral structure with a central courtyard, the Baroque palace was built on the Wollzeile, an ancient street that extended from Saint Stephen's Cathedral to the medieval city walls. The owner was Baron Johann Christoph von Paar (d. 1636), who held the appointment of Imperial Hereditary Postmaster of Austria, an immensely lucrative position that enabled him to build the palace. Paar flaunted his new wealth on the ornate facade but assured his livelihood by installing a fully equipped post office

OPPOSITE:
The end wall in the Museum's room from the Paar Palace, about 1770. The marquetry writing table and the filing cabinet (or bookcase) were made by Joseph Baumhauer, master cabinetmaker, about 1749–72.

LEFT:
One of a pair of sandstone portals to the Paar Palace surmounted by the imperial double-headed eagle bearing a shield with the Paar coat of arms

The Paar Palace in 1900. When it was erected, the building housed a post office at the back. The 18th-century reception rooms lay behind the tall windows on the third floor. The Museum's paneling comes from two rooms in the family living quarters behind the reception rooms, which were aligned along the sides of a large central courtyard. The building was razed in 1938 and replaced by a modern apartment house.

with a coach house and stables at the back of the building. His descendants continued to exercise the function of hereditary postmaster until 1813, when the Austrian Post Office was nationalized and the then-current Prince Paar renounced his extra title.

Paar family members were made counts in the seventeenth century, and in 1769 Count Wenzel Johann Joseph von Paar was elevated to the rank of prince by Empress Maria Theresa. The next year he was delegated by the empress to organize a mounted escort to conduct her fourteen-year-old daughter, the Archduchess Maria Antonia, on a ceremonial trip to the German-French border on the Rhine near Strasbourg. There she would assume the name Marie Antoinette before proceeding to Versailles for her marriage to the French dauphin, who became Louis XVI when he succeeded his grandfather four years later.

It might have been anticipation of future honors that primed the then Count Wenzel to plan a complete renovation of his town palace's main floor in 1765. A French-born architect, Isidor Canevale (active 1760–88), and an Austrian sculptor, Johann Georg Leithner (active 1757–85), were commissioned to provide designs and execute wood carvings for three of the large reception rooms behind the series of nine tall windows on the left side of the main facade, as well as for the more modest living quarters at the back of the palace on the same floor. This renovation program was completed in 1772. The splendid effect of the redecorated state rooms is conveyed in an account of 1792: "The palace of Prince Paar stands near the Stubentor and is splendidly furnished within. The principal bedroom is hung with a rich French fabric that cost ten ducats a yard, the canopied bed being hung with the same material. The chairs are covered with silver material, while the doors are inset with mirror glass. In a many-mirrored white-and-gold room hangs a rock-crystal chandelier that cost 16,000 gulden. There is, in addition, a smaller room with watercolor paintings of exotic flowers and fruit."

In the nineteenth century the Paar descendants began to neglect their Viennese palace, renting it for long periods to Russian aristocrats. By the end of World War I, already stripped of its furniture, it stood dark and deserted. The dismantling of the paneled rooms, which began in 1931, was completed when the Paar family sold the building to developers in 1937; it was then demolished and replaced by a nondescript apartment house.

Vestiges of three great *boiseries* on the Wollzeile front were salvaged, but without their magnificent ceilings, which were left behind to be demolished with the masonry. (From one of these rooms, a pair of doorways with overdoors painted in the manner of François Boucher was donated in 1931 by the Counts Paar to the Viennese Österreichisches Museum für Angewandte Kunst.) The boiseries in the remaining two rooms, each with sets of mirrored double doors, were perhaps the finest in the house. They were bought in 1938–39 by Antenor Patiño, heir to a Bolivian tin-mining fortune, and his brother-in-law Jorge Ortiz Linares, to embellish their recently acquired Paris residences. When Patiño moved to a new house in Paris in the early 1970s, he gave what remained of his boiseries from the *Paradezimmer,* or "Parade Room," of the Paar Palace to the Museu Nacional de Arte Antiga in Lisbon.

In the last few years of the palace's existence, a decorating and dealing firm based in Paris had acquired the right to remove and sell its interior fittings. Thus, many of the palace's boiseries were transported to Paris to be used as stock or to sell to the company's clients. This was to affect not only the reception rooms already mentioned but also the boiseries of about a dozen other main-floor rooms whose windows opened onto the interior court and a back street. As these rooms constituted the living quarters, the boiseries were smaller, their carvings and gilding plainer. The firm's customers for the woodwork of these rooms were French, English, Belgian, and American. One of the earliest sales was to a well-known English collector, Sir Philip Sassoon, who in 1934 bought panels that had been assembled from two separate rooms formerly at the back of the residential wing of the palace and had them installed in his London house at 45 Park Lane. When this house was about to be demolished in the mid-1950s, the Parisian decorating firm reacquired its former boiseries and in 1963 sold them again, this time to Mr. and Mrs. Charles Wrightsman, who donated them to the Metropolitan in that year, together with the room from the Hôtel de Varengeville.

The panels are arranged arbitrarily here, like those of the Varengeville room. The wood carvings in soft pinewood (the Varengeville panels are of oak) can all be dated about 1770, with the exception of the French window surrounds on the far left wall and the adjacent doorway, which are modern. The blue color of the wood surfaces matches traces of blue paint discovered under layers of overpaint when the paneling was removed from 45 Park Lane.

The inventiveness and natural élan of the early Rococo style is tempered in this late manifestation. The inspiration for the design of the woodwork derives more from German than from French sources. Specifically, the scrolls and reverse curves of the double doors and overdoors recall configurations in much earlier ornament prints by the German-trained François de Cuvilliés (1695–1768). In France decor was more progressive, and a room furnishing of about 1770 very likely might have shown strong evidence of the emerging Neoclassical style.

The plaster cornice, cove molding, and ceiling rosette are based on photographs taken of the family living quarters as they had existed in the palace. Never installed in the Paar Palace, the *brèche d'Alep* marble chimneypiece is probably French of approximately the same date as the Austrian woodwork. The flooring consists of eighteenth-century oak *parquet de Versailles.*

The large and magnificent wool Savonnerie carpet in the Paar room is comparable to another, somewhat narrower Savonnerie carpet in the adjoining Varengeville room (see page 78). The borders of the two carpets are similar, as are the colors of the weaving, while some of the compartmentalized motifs—rinceaux, palm sprays, royal emblems, and flower garlands—appear in the decoration of each. These analogous motifs are due to the fact that both were part of a series of ninety-two carpets woven for the Grande Galerie of the Louvre between 1668 and 1685, a dating that makes them considerably older than the woodwork of the rooms in which they are shown in the Metropolitan Museum.

Charles Le Brun (1619–1690), named director of the arts and head of the royal furniture manufactory by Louis XIV, supplied designs for this series of knotted-and-cut wool-pile carpets that were a specialty of the Savonnerie factory, which was named for its site near Paris where an old soapworks (*savon* is "soap") had stood. In the seventeenth century the factory produced almost exclusively for the crown, and Louis XIV's former ownership of the carpet now in the Paar room is emphasized by the display of his emblems over its surface. These include the king's monogram of interlaced Ls (on the sides), fleur-de-lis motifs surmounted by royal crowns (near each end), and the central feature, a sunflower, which alludes to Louis XIV as the Sun King.

Among the pieces of French furniture now in the Paar room are no fewer than five examples by or attributed to Bernard Vanrisamburgh II (active ca. 1730–64; a pair of Chinese lacquer corner cabinets by this maker is in the Varengeville room). A Japanese lacquer *commode-en-console,* a rare form of furniture consisting of a console table fitted with a drawer, signed with the initials B.V.R.B., is attached to the wall on the right of the chimneypiece. Its irregular scrolling gilt-bronze mounts form a striking frame for the Japanese

At the ends of the Savonnerie carpet in the room are two reserves consisting of simulated bas-reliefs depicting personifications of Fortitude and Fame. Here Fame sits among military attributes blowing a trumpet. The carpet, 30 feet long by 15 feet wide, is one of a series designed by Charles Le Brun for the Grande Galerie of the Louvre. Another carpet from the same set is in the Varengeville room.

Tabletop veneered with tulipwood on oak, with marquetry inlay comprising scrolling bands of kingwood. Pieces of mother-of-pearl and slivers of horn stained red and blue compose the flowers, and green-stained horn was used to make the leaves. The top is enclosed on three sides by a pierced gilt-bronze gallery.

LEFT:
Detail of a console table, an unusual form that combines the drawer of a commode with the outline of a console table. The oak-and-pine structure is veneered with panels of gold-and-black Japanese lacquer, which may be 75 years older than the piece itself. The scene of houses and trees on the left side of the drawer is duplicated in reverse on the right side.

View of the end wall of the room, showing the chimneypiece wall at the right. Like the carpet, the magnificent 12-branch gilt-steel and rock-crystal chandelier dates to the period of Louis XIV, about 1710.

gold-and-black lacquer panels on the front and sides; the lacquer panels are datable to seventy-five years earlier than the console table that incorporates them. The near symmetry of the two raised-and-gilded lacquer scenes of houses and trees on the drawer front is unusual. Fragments of two door panels lacquered with these scenes in mirror image, taken from a pair of earlier Japanese cabinets, may have been used to produce this effect. Another dazzling table signed by Vanrisamburgh stands at the near side of the room. It is a small writing table or desk fitted with three retractable tablets that can be slipped out from under the top, providing an extended writing surface. Its marquetry consists of tulipwood veneered on oak and inset with mother-of-

pearl flowers and particles of horn stained blue, red, and green, forming flowers and leaves. In the eighteenth century, when they were freshly cut, marquetry woods were considerably brighter. Now they are often faded after several centuries of exposure to light. Stained wood is especially likely to discolor over a period of years, and a chemical reaction may have caused flowers originally stained blue to turn green. The brilliant, almost-new effect of the Museum's desktop is due to bright, unfading pigment applied over slivers of horn.

A gilded oak armchair, an apt counterpoint to the two extraordinary tables, stands on the carpet to the left of the chimneypiece. It was made in

The wood paneling in this room consists of elements from several rooms from the Paar Palace. The interior architecture was remodeled in 1765–72. This view looks toward the entrance to the Varengeville room.

On the wall opposite the chimney-piece hangs an oval portrait of a young woman reading, painted by Jean-Honoré Fragonard, about 1776. On the right is an early-18th-century French four-fold screen embroidered with bouquets. The doorway behind it is modern. The top of the small writing table is shown on page 91.

1749 for Louise-Elisabeth, duchess of Parma (the eldest and only married daughter of Louis XV), as part of a lot of furnishings she commissioned for the royal palace at Parma. Assistants in charge of sculpture at the workshop of the well-known woodworker, or *menuisier*, Nicolas-Quinibert Foliot (1706–1776), carved the various oak parts of the chair, which, in order to guard against damage, were not assembled before being shipped from Paris to Parma. Italian craftsmen then put the pieces together, applied the gilding, and even attached the upholstery. Amazingly, the Museum's chair covers are

the original crimson velvet (worn down to the nap), trimmed with its original silver-threaded gold galloon. Another armchair from the same set in the Hermitage Museum, St. Petersburg, must have served only on ceremonial occasions. It retains its worn red velvet covers ornamented with an extremely elaborate pattern of raised silver-threaded galloon, making the chair so uncomfortable as to be useless for seating.

JAMES PARKER

The chimneypiece is not original to the room but dates to the same period as the paneling. The two circular oil paintings are landscapes of about 1777 by Hubert Robert (1733–1808). The oak armchair at the left was commissioned by Louis XV's eldest daughter for the royal palace of Parma. It was most likely carved in Paris and shipped to Italy, where it was assembled, gilded, and upholstered.

The Tessé Room

PARIS ◆ 1768–72

The French term *quai*, like its English derivative "quay," originally applied to a kind of wharf for loading goods aboard ships or barges. Such was one function of the quais along the Seine River until their general use for commercial purposes dwindled during the nineteenth century. The quai Voltaire, on the Left Bank of the Seine, was so named in 1791 for the celebrated French author François Marie Arouet (known as Voltaire, 1694–1778). It is bounded on the west by the intersection of the rue du Bac, which leads off a seventeenth-century bridge, the Pont Royal, and on the east by the rue des Saints-Pères. At one time the quai overlooked the long southern facade of buildings comprising the royal palaces of the Louvre and the Tuileries on the opposite bank of the Seine, but that once spectacular view is now marred by traffic and parked cars along the quais.

The first recorded notice for a building on the present site of the Hôtel de Tessé is dated 1628. After the property had passed through a number of hands, the house was destroyed by a fire in 1760. In 1765 a widow, Marie Charlotte de Béthune-Charost (1713–1783), comtesse de Tessé, and her son comte René Mans de Froulay de Tessé (1736–1814) undertook the task of

OPPOSITE:
The armchairs flanking the marble chimneypiece are of carved-and-gilded mahogany covered in modern silk damask, part of a set signed by Louis Delanois (active 1761–92). Above the chairs is a pair of gilt-bronze wall lights made for Marie Antoinette, as were several other pieces of furniture now in the room. On the mantel are a French marble clock with bronze handles shaped like snakes and two covered vases of Sèvres porcelain.

LEFT:
The Hôtel de Tessé on the quai Voltaire, photographed about 1915. The building, which now contains residential apartments and shops, is highly visible, since it stands on the Left Bank of the Seine opposite the western extension of the Louvre. The Museum's room was behind three of the tall windows on the principal floor, the second, third, and fourth from the left.

The oak paneling in this room is exceptionally fine; it is the work of a little-known woodworker named Nicolas Huyot and was probably completed by 1772. The painting above the sofa on the right is a self-portrait by Rose-Adélaïde Ducreux (1761–1802); the double portrait on the far wall to the right depicts Jeanne Eglé Desbassayns de Richemont and her son, painted about 1803 and now attributed to Marie-Guillelmine Benoist (1768–1826). The commode in front of the large mirror is a companion piece to the drop-front desk on page 104. Like the mechanical table in the center of the room, the set was supplied for Marie Antoinette by the cabinetmaker Jean-Henri Riesener.

rebuilding. Their architect was Pierre Noël Rousset (1715–1793), and the edifice was under construction between 1766 and 1768. In the year of its completion Piganiol de la Force, a writer of guidebooks to Paris, commented: "M. Rousset, the skillful architect, has produced the design which is ingenious and in excellent taste." The shallowness of the lot obliged Rousset to design the hôtel's facade fronting on the street and the quai, rather than on an interior courtyard—"between courtyard and garden"—as was more generally the case. A handsome elevation, incorporating Ionic pilasters, was produced in what would later be known as the Louis XVI style (although at this date Louis XV still had six years to live!). The tall windows on the main floor are behind a balcony supporting a wrought-iron railing intended to facilitate the viewing of such diversions as the Seine might have to offer. The Museum's room was on this floor; its three windows are the second, third, and fourth from the left, that is, from the rue des Saints-Pères.

The room has been called a *grand salon,* or large reception room, since it was acquired (1942) and first exhibited (1954) at the Museum. Only very recently has documentation come to light proving this nomenclature to be wrong. After the death of the comtesse de Tessé in 1783, an inventory listing the prices of the hôtel's contents was drawn up in which the Museum's room is named the "salle du dais," literally the "room of the canopy." This means the interior was devoted to solemn receptions, rather as a throne room would have been in a royal palace. On these occasions Mme de Tessé, her son, or a family member may have been seated beneath the canopy. At the time the inventory was drawn up, this room contained twenty-nine chairs of varying types and sizes, most of them covered in crimson-colored material. The costliest item was the crimson damask canopy embroidered with gold thread, which was estimated at 200 livres. Although its dimensions were not recorded, this canopy is presumed to have hung across a good deal of the space between the doors on the wall opposite the windows. It was probably three-sided, like other canopies of the period, and must have projected into the room at some point below the cornice. Several chairs may have stood under the canopy, with others assembled around it. The placement of the two other pieces of furniture in the room—a six-fold screen and a small veneered bookcase—would have been adjusted to this chair arrangement.

A canopy of this kind was an explicit symbol of rank, and etiquette restricted its use to the king and the high nobility. Louis XIV is known to have owned thirty-nine royal canopies, and the kings of France continued to use them until the end of the regime. Although not of the highest rank, the comtesse de Tessé may have been acutely conscious of protocol and of the honors and distinctions due her and her husband's families. Evidence for this is contained in the 1783 inventory, where she is described as the widow of "the very high and powerful Monseigneur René Marie sire de Froullay, comte

de Tessé, marquis de Laverdin, grand d'Espagne [Spanish grandee]." The late comtesse's husband (1707–1742) held the rank of brigadier general and died in battle during the War of the Austrian Succession, and his grandfather had been honored by both Louis XIV and Philip V of Spain, from whom he received the coveted Order of the Golden Fleece.

The Museum's oak-paneled room was removed from the Hôtel de Tessé sometime before the donor bought it in 1931. The house was already designated a historic monument for its architectural features, a designation extended to its interior fittings in 1932–33 to forestall further sales.

The strictly organized but lavish wood carving has been applied principally to the three mirror surrounds and the four sets of double doors and their door frames. The mirrors are set as they originally were, against the two piers on the window wall, on the right-hand wall above the chimneypiece, and in a corresponding position against the left-hand wall. The four mirror frames, though differing in scale, received the same motifs. Their rounded tops are carved to suggest coffered arches in perspective, the crest surmounted by large floral wreaths from the sides of which emerge branches of laurel leaves and berries. The narrow sides of the mirror frames are carved with a series of hanging upside-down bouquets, tied with ribbon. A little-known woodworker, or *menuisier*, named Nicolas Huyot (1700–1791) was responsible for all such work in the room. He used his chisels on the doors to produce fine acanthus-leaf moldings and lintels supported by large-leaf consoles that end in four hanging clusters of laurel leaves and berries, which diminish in size as they descend between bead-and-reel moldings on the sides of the door frame. The white stucco tablets framed in the four overdoors are modeled with figures of dancing girls in low relief set against medallions flanked by larger-scaled figures of seated boys with garlands of flowers and fruit. These reliefs are attributed to Pierre Fixon (active 1748–88), known for the sculptures he executed at Notre-Dame Cathedral. The chimneypiece of Italian *bleu turquin* marble was supplied by a French sculptor–marble cutter named Jean Baptiste Antoine Lefranc. Its elegant gilt-bronze mounts were produced by members of two other closely associated guilds, those of the bronze casters and bronze gilders.

When the room first opened at the Museum in November 1954, it was located in a space now occupied by the Jack and Belle Linsky Galleries. For that installation the dimensions were based on measurements taken at the Hôtel de Tessé. In 1970 the room was dismantled and the paneling was shipped to Paris, where supplementary panels were fabricated to expand the room by about five feet in depth and two feet in width (across the window wall). This adaptation enlarged its capacity for the exhibition of furniture and created more space in the center. In Paris the *boiserie* was repainted its present gray-green color (when first exhibited it was solid gray, which was

Like the other three doorways in the Tessé room, this one, photographed about 1960, shows some of the finest wood carving in the room. The stucco reliefs in the overdoors are attributed to the sculptor Pierre Fixon, who may have kept master models in his workshop to facilitate the production of duplicates.

changed to white in 1956). The renovated room was reinstalled in proper
sequence among the Museum's French period rooms and reopened in
November 1972. The extraordinary original elements, the mirrors and doors,
fill the spaces that the architect Rousset had designed for them. The other
panels of different sizes, all carved with egg-and-dart molding, are mostly
modern, some probably replacements for lacunae left where textiles hung in
the eighteenth century. The three French windows, their gilt-bronze fittings,
and their painted wood reveals are all modern. The wood cornice is also
modern (the original plaster cornice and the ceiling rosette were left behind

in Paris). No gilt-bronze hardware was received with the four sets of double doors. These items, consisting of lock plates, doorknobs and bolts, hinges and hinge caps, were bought in 1954 from the Paris firm of Bricard et Cie.

Pride of place among the furnishings of the Tessé room belongs to furniture made for Queen Marie Antoinette, including a marquetry mechanical table and an upright secretary with its matching commode made by the cabinetmaker Jean-Henri Riesener (1734–1806). Of German origin, he was born in the town of Gladbeck, near Essen, in the Ruhr Valley, and by the age of twenty he was already living in Paris, where he found employment as an apprentice to another German-born cabinetmaker, Jean-François Oeben (1721–1763). (Riesener was to use his position to embark upon a brilliant career as an *ébéniste*, a cabinetmaker specializing in the production of veneered furniture. Ébénistes formed one of the main subdivisions of the Paris furniture-making guild, the other large contingent being the *menuisiers*. The word "ébéniste," coined about 1645, derived from the name for ebony, *ébène*, the wood most commonly used at the time for veneers.) In 1774, the year Louis XVI was crowned king, Riesener was appointed royal cabinetmaker, and in the next fifteen years he is said to have earned more than a million livres producing royal furniture, apart from his numerous private commissions. Riesener was able to maintain his status as the king's most favored cabinetmaker only until 1785, when an administrator who oversaw royal expenditures reported that his prices were "excessive, even ridiculous." This caused orders from Louis XVI and other members of the royal family to fall off drastically, but the queen was not deterred and continued to patronize Riesener until 1791.

The mechanical table standing in the center of the Tessé room has the distinction of being the earliest major piece of furniture Riesener carried out for Marie Antoinette. An inventory mark painted on its underside corresponds to an entry in the many-volumed ledger of royal furniture acquisitions. The text of this entry gives the date of the table's delivery, December 12, 1778, and the name of the cabinetmaker (which might otherwise not have been recorded since the piece is not signed) and specifies that it was purchased for the queen's use in her apartment at the Château de Versailles. The entry also describes the three main uses to which it may have been put: for eating, for dressing and coiffure, and for writing (or reading) in a seated or standing position. The table still converts easily to these uses. For eating, the hinged panels of the top are left in the closed position, and its height is adjusted by turning a crank on the side. As a makeup table, a mirror panel recessed below the marquetry in the center can be released by pressing a button on the front of the brass rim. Other buttons release hinged marquetry panels, part of the decoration of the tabletop that also serve as lids for six compartments intended to hold cosmetics and perfume, three on each side of the mirror. For writing when seated, these compartments must be kept closed to provide

RIGHT:

This drop-front desk, or upright secretary, like the matching commode at the end of the room (see p. 98), was supplied by Jean-Henri Riesener for Marie Antoinette. The interior of the desk, finely veneered in tulipwood banded with purplewood, contains a strongbox and a secret compartment. The queen's monogram—the initials M A interlaced—appears three times in the gilt-bronze frieze beneath the top of the desk.

BELOW:

Detail of the Japanese lacquer on the doors of the desk and of its gilt-bronze apron mount. Although as a leading cabinetmaker, Riesener was allowed to make mounts in his own workshops, he likely provided drawings to outside workers and supervised the results. This flawlessly cast and gilded mount consists of a floral wreath juxtaposed with horns of plenty. The means of attachment for the mounts were carefully concealed by the workmen in Riesener's shop who were responsible for fastening them.

a surface, while the raised mirror panel can be rotated on a horizontal axis to form a lectern, which when disengaged and laid flat becomes part of the surface of the table. For writing or reading in a standing position, the top can be cranked up a full 19½ inches on steel shafts in the four corners.

A German-born mechanic named Jean-Tobie Mercklein collaborated with Riesener on these mechanical fittings. His bill reveals the table was intended for "la couche de la Reine": the queen's lying-in. On December 19, just one week after she received it, Marie Antoinette gave birth to her first child, Marie Thérèse Charlotte, later duchesse d'Angoulême (1778–1851). Royal childbirths were tradition-bound ceremonies, and as etiquette required that casual day visitors to the palace be admitted upon request, Marie Antoinette gave birth in the queen's state bedroom before a crowd of strangers. Like a new toy concealing surprises, the table may have provided a moment's diversion and respite after a painful and upsetting experience. At the Museum the table relies on visual effects: its restrained lines and elegant latticework marquetry, characteristic of Riesener's workshop, and its fine gilt-bronze castings, such as the handle plate chased with roses and laurel sprays.

Five years after the table's production, the same workshop delivered to the queen two of the most splendid pieces of French furniture ever created: a drop-front desk, or upright secretary, and its matching commode, veneered with ebony and faced with seventeenth-century Japanese black-and-gold lacquer panels. Marie Antoinette had a penchant for Japanese lacquer and owned about eighty small bibelots of this material, which she kept at Versailles. The earliest complete description of this furniture, in an inventory of the queen's *cabinet intérieur* at Saint-Cloud, mentions their lavish gilt-bronze ornament, singling out the tripartite friezes below the marble tops, each length chased with Marie Antoinette's monogram intertwined with roses and jasmine, as well as the astonishing apron mounts of juxtaposed beribboned horns of plenty spilling over with flowers and fruit, coins and crowns, dazzling allegories of riches and plenty. There are no traces of nail or screw heads to detract from the integral effect of the ormolu, a refinement developed by French ébénistes in the 1760s. The method followed was to solder threaded pins to the backs of the ormolu pieces, pass them through holes in the oak backing, and secure them on the inside of the piece with bolts.

JAMES PARKER

The Cabris Room

GRASSE ◆ 1775–72

This small handsome room exemplifies an early, robust phase of the Louis XVI style, a style that was to be treated in a highly refined and more sophisticated manner later in the century. It is here expressed in the purest Neoclassical forms and in motifs of straightforward simplicity. The elements carved in relief in the *boiserie* forming the walls of the room are further embellished by largely original gilding of extraordinary quality.

The paneling was made for a house in the French town of Grasse, which became a flourishing provincial center in the eighteenth century, its prosperity based on the manufacture of perfumes and leather gloves (perfumery is still an important industry there). Grasse is in the southeastern corner of France, about twelve miles inland from Cannes.

One of the leading Provençal families, already known in the fourteenth century, was named Clapiers de Collongues. This family produced many branches, and, in the late seventeenth century, one member took the title marquis de Cabris, the name of an ancient castle near Grasse (destroyed in the Revolution) that was part of its domain. Jean Paul de Clapiers (1749–1813) was the third marquis de Cabris, a title that became extinct at his

ABOVE:
These panels are on the reverse side of the pair of doors to the left of the mirrored back wall in the present room and thus are not usually visible.

LEFT:
Garden facade of the former *nouvel hôtel de Cabris*, now the Musée d'Art et d'Histoire de Provence in Grasse, photographed in 1967. The Museum's room lay behind the first two windows to the left of the central projection on the second floor.

OPPOSITE:
One of four sets of double doors in the Cabris room. The door panels are carved with smoking incense burners and flaming torches set against crossed laurel branches.

death. In 1769 he married Louise de Mirabeau (1752–1807); the marriage had been prearranged by members of both families. His wife was a sister of Honoré Gabriel Riquetti, comte de Mirabeau (1749–1791), later a well-known orator and controversial figure associated with the French Revolution.

When Jean Paul de Clapiers became the third marquis in 1771, he opted to spend part of his inheritance on the construction of a town house in Grasse (to be called the *nouvel hôtel de Cabris*), adjacent to his mother's seventeenth-century house (the *ancien hôtel de Cabris*). The architect he chose for this project, Giovanni Orello, was a little-known Milanese-born resident of Grasse. The construction work, lasting from 1772 until 1774, resulted in a handsome, Italianate-looking building. For the decoration of the interior of the house, furniture and wood paneling had to be ordered in Paris, because, unlike Bordeaux (see p. 127), Grasse was too small to support a local wood-working industry. All these articles had to be carefully wrapped and crated in Paris and then transported to Grasse by water and overland. By 1776 the original estimated expenditure of 100,000 livres for the building had doubled; another 80,000 livres was spent on furniture, and a grandiose scheme for a black-and-gold marble "salon à l'italienne" was abandoned, presumably for lack of funds.

A short time later, matters began to go seriously wrong for the young married couple. In 1777 the marquis de Cabris gave unmistakable signs of the congenital madness that had afflicted his family. On January 11, 1778, a local court pronounced him legally insane, incompetent to manage his own affairs, and he was placed under the guardianship of his mother. The following month his wife was banished by her father to a convent at Sisteron, in a

This 12-branch chandelier includes figures of nymphs whose bodies end in leaf scrolls; their arms serve as supports for candle branches. The chandelier, of about 1785, is made of blued steel and gilt bronze; it is attributed to François Rémond.

remote region of Provence. Angered because his daughter had taken the side of her mother, from whom he was separated, the old marquis de Mirabeau used a peremptory legal device, the *lettre de cachet*, to confine her to a convent-prison for three years. These calamities put an abrupt stop to the improvements being carried out in the *nouvel hôtel de Cabris*. Its interiors had fallen into a state of disarray, as described in an inventory dated February 6, 1778: "An unimaginable disorder reigns in the house: furniture lying in a clutter on the floor; the doors standing open without keys; windowpanes broken, etc. . . . Everything suggestive of abandonment." Other items in this account particularize the unfinished state of these interiors: packing cases containing unused parts of marble chimneypieces and boxes full of slate tiles intended for stair-cases and metal attachments for hanging curtains, as well as chairs and sofas lacking upholstery, some of them still wrapped. One of the large rooms near the main entrance held nine crates, most still unopened, containing a lot of wall paneling described in the inventory as "carved, painted and gilded woodwork elements [*des bois*] provided for the *salon de compagnie* and its adjoining bedroom." Despite its brevity, this description covers the painted-and-gilded paneling of the Museum's salon, or reception room, which may not have been installed until ten years later.

Freed from her confinement at Sisteron in 1781, Mme de Cabris did not return to Grasse until 1788, after the death of her mother-in-law. It may very well have been at this time, between 1788 and 1790, that the boiserie of the Cabris room was unpacked and set up on the main floor of the house. In 1790, alerted by an uprising among her husband's tenant farmers, the marquise fled first to Paris and then to Italy, joining the ranks of French émigrés. She returned to France in 1796.

During the Revolution the main floor of the hôtel in Grasse was rented to accommodate a courtroom. In 1805, two years before her death, the marquise rented the second floor to a tenant who was allowed to buy much of the furniture ordered for the house thirty years earlier. Her mentally ill husband died in a Paris sanatorium in 1813, the same year his creditors forced his only heir, the comtesse de Navailles, to cancel all leases and sell the Hôtel de Cabris to the highest bidder. It was bought by two brothers named Bruery, natives of Grasse, who were perfume manufacturers. The building was still owned by the same family in 1910, when E. M. Hodgkins, an English dealer with premises in Paris, bought the small painted-and-gilded oak salon, which then was transported back to Paris. At the auction of Mr. Hodgkins's effects directed by the Hôtel Drouot on May 29, 1937, the boiserie was sold for 139,000 francs. Acquired by the international firm of Duveen Brothers, it was sold in 1957 to Mr. and Mrs. Charles Wrightsman, who installed the paneling in the dining room of their New York City apartment. It was given to the Museum in 1972.

Over the years, the Hôtel de Cabris lost the major part of its decorations and contents. The shell of the original building survives in the southern quarter of what is now the old town (*vieille ville*) of Grasse, near the public garden. In 1919 this building was leased to the Société Fragonard, an association formed for the purpose of establishing a new archaeological and ethnographic museum. When the museum was inaugurated in 1921, its holdings included a number of works by an artist born in Grasse, Jean-Honoré Fragonard (1732–1806). The name of the museum then was the Musée Fragonard, Musée d'Art et d'Histoire de Provence. In 1977 Fragonard's works were transferred to a nearby eighteenth-century building, which is now known as the Musée Fragonard; the former Hôtel de Cabris continues to house the local archaeological and historical museum.

A photograph taken of the paneling in Grasse shows a considerably shorter and narrower room: its width (the measurement of the window wall and the chimneypiece wall) was approximately five feet narrower than it is

The Savonnerie carpet dates to about 1660 and is the earliest of the Museum's carpets of this kind. It may have been used as a table cover or on the floor, as shown. The flowers, which are identifiable, form a wreath in the center and elsewhere are arranged in baskets and bowls.

now and the length correspondingly about seven feet shorter. This means that eight of the narrow, undecorated filler panels known as *pilastres* (two apiece on the side walls and four on the back walls) are new and have been added to provide more floor space and better sight lines for viewing the furniture. The other new woodwork elements make up the whole expanse of the entrance wall and the French window frames. After the change in dimensions, the plaster cornice was made over and a new ceiling rosette was added. A pair of framed rectangular wall mirrors surmounted by panels carved with olive wreaths and rose branches (shown opposite the windows) was lost sometime after the 1937 sale, but a single panel, one of three, has survived in the center of the wall opposite the entrance. There were originally five double doors and overdoors in what was a perceptibly smaller room. Only four double doors surmounted by overdoors have been used in the present installation. The door panels were carved with reliefs of smoking incense burners above motifs of lighted torches, and the background is filled with crossed branches of laurel. The decoration of the fifth pair of doors, which exists but is not exhibited, differs from the others: each of its panels is carved with a bow and a quiver full of arrows above a motif of crossed arrows hung with ribbon and set against wheat stalks. The four narrow, incurved corner panels display trophies of musical instruments hanging from bowknots on a background of laurel branches.

An ornate white-and-green marble chimneypiece, shown with this paneling in photographs taken about 1910, came with the room when Mr. and Mrs. Wrightsman bought it. They decided that this chimneypiece had

been added in the early nineteenth century and was therefore of too late a period to be used in their dining room. A substitute was found, a white marble chimneypiece datable to about 1775–78, from the Hôtel de Greffulhe, 8–10 rue d'Astorg, Paris.

Among the fine objects in the Cabris room is an extraordinary gilt-bronze and blued-steel twelve-branch chandelier, as well as a fire screen and a pair of side chairs made for Queen Marie Antoinette. All of these objects date from the mid-1780s.

The chandelier is exceptional for that period. It is not bedecked with the cut, faceted, and polished crystal drops that were frequently used as ornament and to reflect candlelight. Instead, it consists of metal parts: fine gilt-bronze decoration applied to a vase of blued steel. This ornamentation is attributed to the gilt-bronze maker François Rémond (1745/47–1812), who worked for the French court between 1784 and 1787. Pairs of gilt-bronze candle branches rise from the folded arms of two nymphlike figures, their

The marquetry table in the center can be closed to form a coffer on a stand. The top section is a separate unit with four short legs recessed into the corners of the lower section; this arrangement enables it to be removed and used as a bed tray. The center panel of the top can be raised to serve as a mirror or lectern. The table is signed by Martin Carlin and dates to 1775–80. The pair of small side chairs on either side of the table were supplied by chairmaker Georges Jacob in 1784 for Marie Antoinette's boudoir in the Tuileries palace.

The gilt-bronze and openwork ivory vase (one of a pair) on the table is a surviving example of a rare French decorative technique from the late 18th century, of which only about 20 objects survive. They are thought to have been made by a little-known ivory worker named Voisin le Jeune, who gave lessons in the technique to Louis XVI and members of his family. The gilt-brown motifs, moldings, and mounts are attributed to Pierre-Philippe Thomire (1751–1843). The French side table was once in the Anchikov Palace in St. Petersburg and dates to 1785–90. Of mahogany and gilt bronze, it is signed by Jean-Henri Riesener.

lower bodies ending in leaf scrolls, while two more pairs of branches spring from behind the curling horns of two satyr masks, which alternate with the nymph figures around the rim of the vase. A similar twelve-branch chandelier, set with three nymph figures and three satyr masks, is in the Musée Nissim de Camondo, Paris.

The gilded beechwood fire screen in front of the chimneypiece dates about ten years later than the paneling and consequently exemplifies a more developed and delicate phase of the Louis XVI style. Fine carving is displayed on the pairs of bracketed dolphins' heads upon which the fire screen rests, on its uprights in the form of bundles of sticks (an ornamental motif called a fasces) bound with spiral garlands of ivy, and on the moldings (above and below its silk panel) that consist of beaded ribbon spirals interspersed with pearls. Beneath the lower rail the fire screen bears the impressed mark "G.IACOB" for Georges Jacob (1739–1814), a *menuisier* who supplied the fire screen in 1786 for Marie Antoinette's use at the Château de Fontainebleau. Unfortunately, the original surface of burnished gilding complemented by silvering (used to enhance some of the carved details, such as the pearls) is missing; during the Empire period a uniform coat of lusterless gilding replaced it. The fire screen was part of a larger order for fourteen items, mainly chairs. The invoice was lost at the time of the Revolution (together with most of the records pertaining to Marie Antoinette's furniture purchases), but a document dated 1797 specifies that the original upholstery for the chairs and fire screen was white taffeta embroidered with flowers. The piece of eighteenth-century blue-gray silk brocaded with a pastoral vignette now on the fireplace panel is therefore not original.

As chance would have it, in 1977 the Museum was given a pair of gilded walnut side chairs, covered in modern pink moiré silk, made for the queen's boudoir in the Palais des Tuileries (recent research in France has uncovered this provenance). These chairs are also exhibited in the Cabris room. The points of resemblance between them and the set to which the fire screen belongs are the upright fasces used as back posts on the chairs, the spiral leaf garlands binding similar motifs on their seat rails, and the legs carved as quivers full of arrows. Neither of the side chairs bears Jacob's impressed mark, but eighteenth-century records confirm his authorship of the chair frames—but only of the bare frames themselves. The intricate work of carving these frames was the responsibility of a subdivision of the furniture-making confraternity, the wood-carvers (*sculpteurs sur bois*), who, unlike the *menuisiers,* were not in the habit of signing their products. The names of the *sculpteurs* are therefore often unknown, although the effect of a finished chair might depend largely on their skills. In this case the carvers were probably the workshop assistants of two brothers who were master wood-carvers: Jules Hugues Rousseau (1743–1806) and Jean Siméon Rousseau (1747–ca. 1822). The names of the two Rousseaus appear on a bill dated 1784 describing the carved details of the Museum's chairs. The brothers were responsible for supervising and contributing to the carving of some of the principal paneled rooms of the period at the Château de Versailles, including the library of Louis XVI in 1774 and Marie Antoinette's large private reception room in 1783.

JAMES PARKER

The Crillon Room

PARIS • 1777–80

The present place de la Concorde would be unrecognizable to an inhabitant of early-eighteenth-century Paris. Only the location of the routes leading off to the west, the Cours-la-Reine and the avenue des Champs-Élysées, which had been roughly laid out after 1616, might awaken a flicker of recognition in such an observer. A great deal of the land thereabouts was still undeveloped in 1722, when it became part of a new quarter of Paris, the Faubourg Saint-Honoré. Germain Brice, a writer of guidebooks, commented on the checkered appearance of the new district in 1725: "Because much open space remains in this quarter, it must be presumed that edifices will be built in due course for its embellishment, since of all the city suburbs, this is the dirtiest and most neglected." Expectations such as these were not to be unfulfilled. Some of the finest architecture in Paris was to adorn the Faubourg Saint-Honoré, mainly executed in the remaining years of the eighteenth century and in the early nineteenth century—buildings that still constitute a principal attraction of the district.

The land for the place Louis XV (the original name for the place de la Concorde), which consisted of a large rectangular plot extending to the Seine River on the south and the Tuileries Gardens on the east, was royal

OPPOSITE:
The back wall of the Crillon room. The door's upper panel is painted with a caduceus, a legendary staff belonging to the god Mercury that became a symbol of commerce, peace, and prosperity, as well as of medicine and health. The oval gold-and-grisaille painting below depicts the god of love holding a staff across his chest. These and other painted motifs derive from surviving fragments of Roman wall painting dating from the first century A.D. (see the Roman bedroom on page 16), which were first excavated at the end of the 15th century and became the basis for a style of interior decoration that was periodically readapted and revived, as shown here.

LEFT:
View of the place Louis XV (later place de la Concorde), looking north toward the two magnificent facades built in 1755–72 after designs by the royal architect Jacques Ange Gabriel. The Crillon room was installed in a town house at the extreme left behind the western facade; its windows overlooking a side street faced the site of the present American Embassy. This painting of about 1780 is attributed to Alexandre Jean Noël (1752–1834).

property. In 1748, after the city of Paris offered Louis XV the gift of a statue of himself, he approved the development of this land as a public square, in the center of which the sculpture would be placed. The over-life-size bronze of the king on horseback—by Edme Bouchardon (1698–1762), with a base by Jean-Baptiste Pigalle (1714–1785)—was completed in 1769. Although the statue was destroyed in 1792, its appearance is known from engravings and smaller bronze versions.

The focal point of the square was the north side, where an extraordinary ensemble of Neoclassical buildings was to take shape. The architect of the two palaces that closed the view behind the king's statue was Jacques Ange Gabriel (1698–1782), who was named royal architect to Louis XV in 1742, succeeding his father, Jacques Gabriel (1667–1742). Jacques Ange made provision for a street between the two main buildings, the present rue Royale, which, when planned, was to have led to the church of the Madeleine (built between 1764 and 1842).

Work on the two great Neoclassical facades fronting on the *place* began in 1755 and was completed in 1772. During construction the building to the right, or east, was designated as the Garde Meuble de la Couronne (Royal Furniture Warehouse). In 1792 it was expropriated by the Ministry of the Navy, which has occupied it continuously since then. The left-hand building near the Champs-Élysées was to be divided into four private residences, and bids for these properties were accepted in 1775. The land behind the facade was left vacant, so that the purchaser could build to suit his own taste, providing that the interior spaces corresponded with preexisting doors and windows. The first lot to be sold, the largest, was at the left-hand, or west, corner. It was bought by the architect-builder-entrepreneur Louis-François Trouard (1729–1794), who had no intention of occupying the house that he proceeded to design for the lot. It turned out to be a successful speculation, for in April 1776 he was able to rent the building, still unfinished, to a remarkable tenant, Louis Marie Augustin, duc d'Aumont (1709–1782). The fifth duke to bear this title, he had a reputation for keeping up with the times. In 1741 he had abandoned his family's antiquated town house in the Marais quarter for a more fashionable address, 29 quai Voltaire. His quest for novelty and visibility reached its peak when he moved into the place Louis XV.

Like many of his peers, the fifth duc d'Aumont spent a good deal of his early life in the army; he had retired with the rank of lieutenant general in about 1748. He devoted the remainder of his life to rather arduous duties as gentleman of the bedchamber to Louis XV (a close contemporary and boyhood friend), to managing widespread estates, and to forming a collection of French decorative arts, mainly contemporary, considered unique at the time.

The house that the duc d'Aumont had leased from Trouard was essentially a shell lacking almost all interior decoration. The missing decorations were commissioned from Pierre Adrien Pâris (1745–1819), a thirty-one-year-

One of the four dado panels that are located below the angled mirrors in the corners of the Crillon room

old pupil of Trouard, who was also a protégé of the duc d'Aumont. Born in Besançon, he migrated to Paris in 1760 to work as an architectural apprentice. He then undertook a three-year study of classical archaeology and Renaissance buildings at the French Academy in Rome. Shortly after his return to Paris, he started to work on the decor of the new Hôtel d'Aumont. The space he had to deal with was extensive, consisting of a suite of large and impressive formal rooms with windows overlooking the *place* and two wings at the back on either side. These included the duke's living quarters in the west wing and their windows, which looked out onto a tributary street called the rue des Champs-Élysées (now the rue Boissy d'Anglas).

Large numbers of architectural drawings bequeathed by Pâris to his native city are now at the Besançon Municipal Library. Among them are nine watercolors recording the interiors that Pâris, the architect, had designed for the duke. Two of these drawings show a small room painted with the decorative motifs similar to those of the small oak boudoir at the Museum. Part of its ornament consists of figures of diminutive animals—such as snails, mice, and shrews—perched on the scrolling rinceaux of the four dado panels decorated by an unknown artist following Pâris's sketches. These motifs are closely based on a series of ornamental paintings called grotesques carried out by Raphael and his assistants on the walls of the Vatican loggias in the early sixteenth century. Derived from prototypes of the Roman era, these grotesques would surely have been seen by Pâris during the three years he spent in Rome. The other fantastic motifs painted on the panels of the boudoir also reflect the influence of Raphael's grotesques.

At the duke's death in 1782, a nine-day sale of his collection was held at the Hôtel d'Aumont. The building then reverted to Trouard, who sold it definitively to Félix François Dorothée de Berton, comte de Crillon (1748–1827). The count's granddaughter Marie-Louise-Amélie de Crillon (1823–1904) married the third duc de Polignac, and she was the last member of the Crillon family to use as a private residence what was now named the

Hôtel de Crillon. After her death the original eighteenth-century decorations were almost totally destroyed—many of the *boiseries* were moved to another location in Paris—in preparation for the opening of a grand hotel on the site. In 1905 Mrs. George T. Bliss saw the boudoir in the west wing of the old building, which was about to be razed. She bought it and another small adjoining room for her family's town house in New York City. Her daughter, Susan Dwight Bliss, subsequently gave the beautiful polyhedral room to the Museum in 1944.

During the French Revolution the painted panels may have been whitewashed for their protection. They have been twice cleaned and restored at the Museum—in 1954 before the room opened to the public and again in 1977. The plaster cornice is a copy of the original, and the gilt-bronze door and window hardware were supplied by the Paris firm of Bricard et Cie in 1906. The flooring, which is old but not original, consists of oak squares called *parquet de Versailles*.

For the sale of the d'Aumont collection in 1782, an inventory was made of the furniture still in place in the hôtel. The description of the seating in the boudoir is remarkably evocative of the pieces in the room today. The inventory included a three-sided sofa ("à trois dossiers") in a mirrored niche and a pair of armchairs, probably part of a set with the sofa; all were painted white, and the carving was picked out with gilding. Also listed were four banquettes that must have been placed under the four angled mirrors in the corners. The only other piece in the boudoir was a small drop-leaf table, probably of mahogany and in the English style, for it is described as a "table anglaise." This would have been used for light, informal meals, possibly a French version of English tea.

Now on display in the Museum's room are a daybed, with matching rectangular headboard and footboard, which occupies the niche, and a *bergère* (a type of armchair with solid upholstery between the armrest and seat rail), which stands against an angled wall. The two uprights on the front of the daybed are exquisitely carved with busts of Egyptian maidens; these also appear on the armrest supports of the armchair. Egyptianizing decorative motifs had been introduced during an early phase of the Louis XVI style and had become fairly widespread by the 1780s. The bergère's fine carving includes a wreathed cartouche on its crest rail carved with the interlaced initials MA, the monogram of Marie Antoinette, who commissioned both pieces in 1788 from one of her favorite chairmakers, Jean Baptiste Sené (1748–1803).

Besides these two pieces, Sené's commission included another six items: four armchairs, a footstool, and a fire screen, all to be carved in walnut, painted white, and partially gilded. Of these only the fire screen has been identified with certainty. The Museum received it in 1966 as a gift, together with the daybed and armchair. At that time its panel was still covered on one

The Crillon room, looking toward the entrance and the gallery beyond. A marquetry mechanical table, smaller and less complex than the example in the Tessé room, can be seen at the right. Both tables were made for Marie Antoinette at Versailles. An oval reserve on the table top is filled with a marquetry trophy alluding to French supremacy in science, commerce, arts, and letters. The side chair, whose shield-shape back has been hollowed out vertically to provide comfort to the sitter, is signed BOVO, a little-known French chairmaker active in the mid-18th century. The room's shape is a modified octagon with a window on one side across from a recess containing a daybed.

side with its original colored-silk embroidery on linen, the needlepoint thought to have been carried out by Marie Antoinette herself. Unfortunately, since the Crillon room is not furnished with a chimneypiece, the fire screen cannot be exhibited with its former companion pieces.

Sené's contributions made up part of one of Marie Antoinette's principal decorative schemes at the end of her reign: the furnishing of her own apartment at the Château de Saint-Cloud outside Paris. In February 1785 she had purchased the château from her husband's cousin Louis-Philippe, duc d'Orléans (1725–1785). The building dated largely from the seventeenth century and was badly in need of repair. Between 1785 and 1788, sections were remodeled and reconstructed by the queen's habitual architect, Richard Mique (1728–1794), who had already executed commissions for her at Versailles and the Petit Trianon. At Saint-Cloud Marie Antoinette reserved the best space for her quarters, which occupied half of the south wing of the château, facing the courtyard. Louis XVI's state apartment had a less interesting view of the city of Paris, whose center was about six miles to the east. The enfilade of the queen's suite ended in a large reception room, or *cabinet*

Detail of a daybed (*sultanne*) that replaced the three-sided sofa described in a 1782 inventory of the duc d'Aumont; part of a larger set, which includes the armchair (*bergère*), also in the room (see p. 124), commissioned by Marie Antoinette for her dressing room at the Château de Saint-Cloud. The set was made by Jean Baptiste Claude Sené (1748–1803) in 1788.

LEFT:
Detail of the crest rail of the *bergère* showing the interlaced initials MA for Marie Antoinette. The exquisite carving is thought to have been done by Sené himself rather than by specialized wood-carvers under his supervision.

BELOW:
This small table, veneered in tulip-wood, sycamore, holly, and ebony on oak and decorated with Sèvres porcelain plaques, is shown with the writing drawer pulled out. The velvet-covered writing surface is hinged at the back and lifts to reveal a tulipwood recess beneath, similar to the compartment under the lid of the jewel coffer above. The woodwork is attributed to Martin Carlin (active 1766–85).

intérieur, which contained the magnificent black-lacquer upright secretary and commode by Riesener now in the Museum's Tessé room (see pages 99, 104). Adjacent to the reception room, with the queen's bedroom on the far side, was a smaller *cabinet de toilette*, for which the furniture ordered from Sené was delivered in 1788. Little time remained for the king and queen to savor the richness of these settings. Fate was closing in, and the last visit paid to their domain was in October 1790.

The château remained relatively untouched until the outbreak of the Franco-Prussian War. In September 1870 many of its contents were evacuated only a week before Prussian troops occupied the site and set fire to the buildings. The resulting ruins were allowed to remain for twenty years. Eventually, they were cleared away, and the location of the former château, its ground plan marked by lawns and yew trees, is now surrounded by the parc de Saint-Cloud.

The small combination jewel coffer and writing table is inlaid with thirteen Sèvres porcelain plaques painted with floral motifs and turquoise (*bleu-céleste*) borders, banded with gold on a white ground. The oval plaque in the center of the coffer lid is painted on the back with the Sèvres manufactory mark of interlaced L's enclosing a V (for the year 1774).

The cabinetwork is attributed to Martin Carlin on the evidence of similar examples bearing his signature. Like many other gifted cabinetmakers practicing in France, Carlin was German-born (in about 1730), a native of Freiburg im Breisgau, Baden-Württemberg. A master of the Paris furniture-making guild from 1766 until his death in 1785, he worked for the great entrepreneurial dealers Poirier,

Darnault, and Daguerre. With a knack for novelty, these merchants supervised the manufacture of new and exotic types of decor, which distinguished their furniture. These wares often incorporated Asian lacquers or examples of a technique called japanning, which imitates lacquer. Another decor they popularized was a combination of Sèvres porcelain, gilt bronze, and wood. Porcelain-inlaid furniture appealed mainly to the dealers' female clients, including great court ladies and royal mistresses. Mme de Pompadour (1721–1764) and Mme du Barry (1743–1793) owned examples of such pieces. They must have been drawn to the bright, enduring colors characteristic of Sèvres porcelain as well as to the charm of freshly colored vignettes of flowers painted on a white ground.

The unknown owner of the Museum's Sèvres-inlaid piece was probably a woman as well, one who would have stored her jewels in the coffer on top. This functioned as a strongbox, its interior veneered with plain tulipwood intended to contain cases of jewels or other valuables. The cabinetmaker added a small writing drawer below the coffer, its front also ornamented with a pair of Sèvres plaques.

The Metropolitan owns twenty-two pieces of French eighteenth-century furniture mounted with Sèvres porcelain plaques, the largest number in any public institution. Of these, seventeen pieces are shown together in the Museum's room from the Hôtel de Lauzun, including two similar jewel coffers on stands with green-bordered Sèvres plaques dating to 1768–75, the woodwork also attributable to Martin Carlin. The armchair and daybed in the Crillon boudoir closely match descriptions of the seating furniture in the 1782 inventory, forming an appropriate juxtaposition that benefits both the room and its contents.

JAMES PARKER

Another view of the Crillon room. A portable silver chamber candlestick is placed on the mechanical table at the left. It bears the marks of the maker, I S, who is not otherwise identified, and it dates to the first half of the 18th century. Hanging from the ceiling is a nine-branch chandelier, whose simulated candlelight is reflected in the large mirrors in the corners of the room, demonstrating how such mirrors would magnify by repetition the relatively weak light provided by 18th-century candles.

The Bordeaux Room

BORDEAUX ◆ 1785

Enlivening the solemnity of eighteenth-century interiors, round and oval rooms were found in both English and French domestic architecture. Reflecting the desire for a less formal lifestyle, small, curved rooms were particularly fashionable during the late eighteenth century. In fact, in his 1780 treatise on contemporary building and interior decoration, *Le Génie de l'architecture ou l'analogie de cet art avec nos sensations,* the French architect and theorist Nicolas le Camus de Mézières (1721–1789) referred to round rooms as being more lively and curved ones more voluptuous than those that were square or rectangular. They could be used as small bedchambers, boudoirs, or cabinets in the private apartments of mansions, where the presence of servants was not always welcome. A good example of such a small and intimate room is the Neoclassical interior of about 1785 from the cours d'Albret in Bordeaux, the latest in date of the Museum's French period rooms.

Due to a flourishing trade with the French colonies, Bordeaux, an important seaport on the Garonne River in southwest France, experienced an unprecedented economic and demographic growth during the second half of the eighteenth century. As a result, a number of ambitious projects to develop

OPPOSITE:
The wall niches in the Bordeaux room contain a pair of large plaster nymphs, possibly by Polly, an Italian sculptor and dealer in plaster decorations who was active in Paris about 1800.

LEFT:
Main facade of the Hôtel de Saint-Marc, Cours d'Albret, Bordeaux, which was built between 1782 and 1784 for Joseph Dufour by an unknown architect

RIGHT:
Jean-Paul-André des Rasins,
marquis de Saint-Marc, engraved
by Charles-Étienne Gaucher
(1740–1804) after a portrait by
Henri Pierre Danloux (1753–1809).
This engraving was used as a
frontispiece in *Les Oeuvres de Marquis
de Saint-Marc*.

BELOW:
Engraving from *Décorations Intérieures
Empruntées à des Edifices Français* by
César Daly (Paris, 1880), depicting
this room as "the salon of a private
house on the Cours d'Albret in
Bordeaux"

Jean-Paul-André de Saint-Marc.
Gravé par Gaucher, d'après Danloux.

and beautify the medieval city took place between 1740 and 1790 under the supervision of Louis Urbain Aubert de Tourny (1690–1761), the intendant of buildings between 1743 and 1757, and his successors. Among these projects was the creation of a new quarter, where a broad avenue, the Cours d'Albret—named after César Phébus d'Albret (d. 1676), marshal of France in 1654 and governor of the province of Guyenne in 1670—was laid out between 1745 and 1748, when trees were planted along the finished road. A series of elegant town houses, or hôtels, in the Neoclassical style was constructed in this district for wealthy merchants and aristocrats, who followed Parisian fashions in the decoration of their homes. One of these residences, now 91 Cours d'Albret, was built between 1782 and 1784 by an unknown architect for Joseph Dufour, *conseil du roi*. The rusticated facade of this mansion, facing the entrance court, is dominated by a semicircular Ionic portico crowned by a cupola; a peristyle resting on four Ionic columns embellishes the facade on the garden side. It is believed that the Museum's paneling came from this building, possibly from an ovoid room to the left of the portico on the court facade. The presence of a dumbwaiter in the kitchen directly below shows that this particular room could have been used for small dinner parties when the formal setting of the hôtel's official dining room, with its large windows overlooking the garden, was not required or appropriate.

The residence on the Cours d'Albret became known as Hôtel de Saint-Marc, after its second owner, Jean Paul André des Rasins (also spelled Razins), the marquis de Saint-Marc (1728–1818), who purchased it on June 6, 1787, from Dufour. Some of the furnishings, such as mirrors and tapestries, were also included in the sale.

An officer in the Régiment des Gardes Françaises, the marquis de Saint-Marc had retired in 1762 and then devoted himself to literature. He wrote scripts for the opera and the ballet, as well as poetry and educational pieces for children, so-called *demi-drames*. His complete works, *Les Oeuvres de Marquis de Saint-Marc*, were published in several editions between 1775 and 1809. The marquis died on October 11, 1818, and his widow, Catherine de Ségur, whom he had married in 1792, continued to live on the cours d'Albret until her death in 1847. The mansion was then inherited by their only surviving child, Marie de Saint-Marc, wife of Étienne-Henri-Stanislas de la Roze, who sold it in 1861 to the Hospices Civils de Bordeaux. The administration of the Centre Hospitalier Régional de Bordeaux is presently located in the building.

The Museum's *boiserie* must have been removed from Bordeaux between 1880—the year César Daly published an engraving of the room in his *Décorations intérieures empruntées à des Édifices français* as "a salon in a hôtel on the Cours d'Albret"—and 1931, when the paneling, the property of a dealer in Neuilly, was sold to Mrs. Herbert N. Straus. The boiserie, given to the Museum by Mrs. Straus in 1943, was installed in its present location in 1953–54. Measuring eighteen feet two inches in one direction and seventeen feet two inches in

The center of the parquet floor in the room is covered with a Beauvais tapestry carpet of 1787–90.

ABOVE:
The setting of this painting in the Museum's collection, *Le Souper interrompu* (The Interrupted Supper), is a room very similar to the Bordeaux room.

ABOVE RIGHT:
One of a pair of French gilt-bronze wall lights flanking the overmantel mirror, about 1780–90. These lights are decorated with vine swags and fruits and are suspended from a beribboned serpent.

the other, with a ceiling height of just over eighteen feet, the room is almost circular.

The finely carved pine paneling, which compares favorably with the high-quality Parisian work of the same period after which it was modeled, is exceptionally beautiful. The boiserie has been painted gray-green to match its original color, traces of which were found when layers of paint that had been added later were removed. The eight long and narrow panels, placed between the doors, mirrors, windows, and wall niches, display arabesques that consist of trophies representing various arts, hunting, and farming, combined with foliate ornament surrounding a vertical stem. Carved trophies are also found above the lintel of the double doors. One of them, showing a compass, a T square, and a basket overgrown with acanthus leaves (an allusion to the origin of the Corinthian capital), symbolizes Architecture. The other trophy, depicting various musical instruments, represents Music. The frames of the wall niches, the two mirrors, and both doors are similarly decorated with Neoclassical motifs, some of which, such as the guilloche border, closely resemble designs published by the engraver Jean Baptiste Fay (active 1780–90) in his *Cahiers d'arabesques*. The low-relief carving is characteristic of the work of a Bordeaux school of wood-carvers, and for stylistic reasons it has been attributed to the sculptor Barthélemy Cabirol (1732–1786) and his workshop. Born in Bordeaux, Cabirol is known to have undertaken the interior decoration of the

archepiscopal palace of the prince of Rohan, now the city hall, and of many private hôtels in the city.

The original wood floor, laid out in a radiating pattern that emphasized the circular shape of the room, as illustrated by Daly, has been lost. It has been replaced here by an eighteenth-century *parquet de Versailles,* which came from the Hôtel de Montmorency on the rue du Bac in Paris. A white marble chimney-piece, contemporary with the room, has been substituted for the original, and the lining of the fireplace was copied from eighteenth-century designs. The ceiling rosette was adapted from an engraving in Daly's book showing such an ornament from a hôtel in the rue Saint-Charles in Bordeaux. The room's plaster cornice was cast from an original fragment; new also are the molded panels beneath the two niches and beneath the mirror opposite the mantel, the plain pilasters flanking the overmantel mirror, and the window reveals. The room is furnished with pieces contemporary with the room. Its intimate ambience, with the table set as if for a private dinner party, resembles the decor of a similarly curved room depicted in *Le Souper interrompu,* a late eighteenth-century painting by an unknown artist.

The door frame and the frieze above display fine examples of Neoclassical ornament. The trophy above the lintel represents Architecture.

DANIËLLE O. KISLUK-GROSHEIDE

England

The Kirtlington Park Room

OXFORDSHIRE ◆ 1748

Before its removal in 1931, the dining room at Kirtlington Park, in Oxford-shire, was widely regarded as one of the most beautiful Rococo rooms in England. Recently it was described in *Country Life* as "arguably the most beautiful 18th century room in America," a comment that no one has challenged.

Sir James Dashwood (1715–1779), baronet, devoted much of his energy and most of his fortune to the building and furnishing of Kirtlington Park. He had inherited his title at the age of nineteen while on the Grand Tour. In 1738, two years after his return, he married an heiress, Elizabeth Spencer, and in 1740, he became a member of Parliament and prepared to build a house suitable for a family whose social status in Oxfordshire was second only to that of the duke of Marlborough at nearby Blenheim. Kirtlington Park was still unfinished in 1778, the year before Dashwood's death, when it was visited by the inveterate traveler and diarist Mrs. Lybbe Powys, who admired the owner as much as his house: "As to Sir James, we could not help saying at our return, that he was at sixty-three one of the finest men we ever saw."

The first plans, supplied by James Gibbs (1682–1754) in 1741, were fur-ther developed by William Smith of Warwick (1705–1747). The interiors were by the London architect John Sanderson (active 1730–74). Sanderson, whose career remains obscure, seems to have specialized in architectural decoration. His original designs, now in the Metropolitan Museum, show several variations

This portrait of Sir James Dashwood, second baronet, at the age of 23, painted in 1737 by Enoch Seeman the Younger (1694–1744), once hung in the saloon next to the dining room at Kirtlington Park.

LEFT:
The south front of Kirtlington Park. The grounds were landscaped by Lancelot "Capability" Brown between 1752 and 1756.

OPPOSITE:
The room from Kirtlington Park, designed by John Sanderson with plaster-work executed in 1744–45 by Thomas Roberts, was originally a dining room. The plaster frame on the end wall now contains one of a pair of pictures by François Boucher (1703–1770) painted in 1768 for the reception room of the duc de Richelieu's residence in Paris.

for an essentially Palladian room with pedimented door frames and chimneypiece and a compartmented ceiling strongly influenced by Inigo Jones's ban-
queting rooms of about 1620–35 at Whitehall and Greenwich, which were in
turn based on Palladio's prototypes.

What is not Palladian about the room is the stucco decoration, which
exhibits a combination of Italian Baroque and early French Rococo motifs:
masks, eagles, shells, scrolls, and trophies of fruit and flowers. Large-scale
stuccowork came into vogue in England in the 1720s, when a number of
particularly skilled *stuccadores* arrived from northern Italy. But the exuberant
plasterwork on the walls and ceiling at Kirtlington was done by a young
local artist from Oxford, Thomas Roberts (1711–71), who completed the job
in the period from November 1744 to January 1745. He had worked on the
Radcliffe Library at Oxford in the early 1740s, but Kirtlington Park was his
first independent commission. Roberts may have provided his own designs,
since the handling of ornament as well as the choice of motifs vary considerably from Sanderson's proposals. The oval pier glasses on the window wall,
with scrolls and garlands of flowers below female heads and swags of drapery,
suggest that Roberts's work was influenced by the contemporary London
cabinetmaker and ornamentalist Matthias Lock.

On the ceiling Roberts included the scheme of the Four Seasons.
Above the chimneypiece the festive god Bacchus represents Autumn opposite

The chimneypiece is carved with Dionysian motifs appropriate to a dining room. In the center of the mantel the bacchic goat is wreathed with grapevines by three festive putti.

RIGHT:
Stucco decoration on the window wall framing a built-in pier mirror

FAR RIGHT:
Stucco decoration on the chimney wall: an eagle perched atop a circle of foliage, scrolls, strapwork, a female mask, and a trophy of fruit and flowers

Spring in the person of Flora above the central window, while at either end are Winter (Hercules wreathed with berries and pinecones) and Summer (Ceres festooned with corn). An entry in the account book preserved at Kirtlington shows that the entire ceiling represented almost half of the £119 that Roberts billed for his work in the room: "Ornamenting to nine panels in cieling of dineing room: £63.0.0." The sculptural quality and naturalistic modeling of his plasterwork were admired by several of Dashwood's friends who later employed Roberts, including Lord Litchfield at Ditchley Park, Sir Charles Cottrell-Dormer at Rousham, and Lord Shrewsbury at Heythrop Hall.

At Kirtlington Park the large panels on the end walls, the four over-doors, and the overmantel were all intended for paintings, as can be seen in one of Sanderson's designs, but only the overmantel was completed: a genre scene set in the pastoral landscape of the Neapolitan Campania in the manner of Claude Lorrain, painted in 1748 by John Wooton (ca. 1686–1765). Why the other spaces remained unpainted is not known. Dashwood may have spent too much on the house at this point, or he could not find a suitable artist to complete the room. By the mid-1740s large-scale decorative painting was no longer fashionable in England, and most of the foreign painters who specialized in this work, such as the Italians Sebastiano Ricci and Jacopo Amigoni, had returned to the Continent. Two paintings by François Boucher, made in 1768 for the duc de Richelieu, now occupy the large plaster frames on the end walls.

The sculptors John Cheere (d. 1787) and his brother Sir Henry Cheere (1703–1781) are both named in the Kirtlington accounts. They worked in partnership in London, making statues, busts, and carved chimneypieces. One or the other—impossible to say which—supplied the elaborate marble chimneypiece for the dining room. Whether the carved wood overmantel with its figures of Summer and Autumn came from the same source is unclear, although the Cheere brothers did not normally work in wood.

The dining room, even in its unfinished state, was a splendid room, from which one looked out through the windows over a broad terrace to the verdant park splendidly landscaped by Lancelot "Capability" Brown (1716–83). There is no reason to think that it changed much over the next 150 years (other than the usual replacing of carpets and curtains), making the two watercolor views executed in 1876 and 1891 by Sir James's thrice great-granddaughter Susan Alice Dashwood of particular interest. Painted with perhaps more charm than skill, they are nonetheless very informative, especially about the furniture. For here we see the original hoop-backed ma-hogany dining-room chairs and, at the far end, a most extraordinary marble-topped side table with Homeric heads at the corners and heavy claw feet. Now in the Royal Ontario Museum in Toronto, it was probably one of a pair, possibly by the cabinetmaker who did most of the work at Kirtlington during the late 1740s, the celebrated William Hallett (ca. 1707–1781).

A watercolor of the dining room set for tea, as painted in 1876 by Susan Alice Dashwood, showing the original chairs and carved table at the end. At this date the ceiling was still its original yellow and cream colors, while the walls had been repainted a light green. A large Turkish carpet covers most of the floor.

Although the account book tells us only the amount he was paid (£545), both the dining-room chairs (which survive in a private collection in London) and the table are consistent with Hallett's sophisticated style and must have been executed by him, the table with the possible collaboration of Matthias Lock. Above the side table is Sir William Beechey's portrait of about 1790 (now in the Toledo Museum of Art) of four of the six children of Sir Henry Watkin Dashwood, third baronet, which then hung, somewhat uncomfortably, in the plaster frame originally intended for a larger and differently scaled painting.

In one of the watercolors the room is set for tea; in the other, without the table, is a grouping of the first nine of the eleven children of Sir George John Egerton Dashwood, sixth baronet, an evocative and poignant scene of happy times that were soon to end. High taxation, agricultural depressions, and the costs of a large family forced Sir George to sell Kirtlington in 1909. All six of his sons who played on the dining room carpet in 1891 served in World War I. Only three survived.

The house was purchased by the earl of Leven and Melville, but by 1922 it had been sold to Hubert Maitland Budgett, who decided in 1931 to sell the dining room. At this time the Metropolitan Museum was looking for English period rooms for a projected new wing, and the Kirtlington Park room "would represent the Chippendale period," according to the not-quite-accurate view held by Preston Remington, the curator of European Decorative Arts. In fact, the "Chippendale period" lasted until Thomas Chippendale's death in 1779 and encompassed both Rococo furniture from the 1750s and 1760s and his later Neoclassical furniture. Although the dining-room furniture appears to have been provided by William Hallett, the room itself does not "represent" either Hallett's or Chippendale's style. This neo-Palladian room with Rococo decoration is the unique result of the collaboration of John Sanderson and Thomas Roberts.

The stucco walls and ceiling were removed in about 250 sections still attached to the old wooden laths and timbers, and the floorboards were numbered and disassembled. The room remained in crates in the Museum

The children of Sir George Dashwood, sixth baronet, in the dining room in 1891, by Susan Alice Dashwood. The 18th-century custom of removing the table when not in use was still followed at Kirtlington Park. Sir William Beechey's portrait of the children of Sir Henry Dashwood, third baronet, hung on the end wall throughout the 19th century.

This chandelier, one of a pair supplied about 1715 for the state apartments at Holme Lacy, Herefordshire, is attributed to the court cabinetmakers James Moore and John Gumley. Made of gilt gesso on wood, it is embellished with gilt-metal masks and candle sockets.

basement until 1955, when it was erected in its present position. A team of skilled stucco workers assembled the sections and plastered the seams and flat areas, while carpenters relaid the floor. Based on a Museum study of the early paint layers, the room was given a uniform warm cream color. It was decided not to furnish it as a dining room because of the Lansdowne dining room nearby. The difficult question of how to install it was resolved with a selection of furniture of the period set out in one area of the room. The portrait of Sir James Dashwood by Enoch Seeman the Younger (1694–1744) was hung on one of the end walls.

When the English galleries were planned to be renovated in 1995, the room's color clearly needed to be reexamined. In the forty intervening years the technology of paint analysis had advanced considerably, and a new study revealed that the flat areas of walls and ceiling were originally covered with water-based distemper in a soft yellow straw color with the raised stuccowork in warm white. This scheme was re-created with casein paint that gives a subtly irregular effect similar to that of distemper. In order to allow access to the entire room, furniture is now displayed only around the sides.

The finest object in the room is the gilt-wood chandelier. One of a pair supplied in about 1715 to James, third viscount Scudamore, for the state apartments at Holme Lacy at Herefordshire, it is in the "French arabesque" manner of William III's architect Daniel Marot (ca. 1663–1752) and is attributed to the court cabinetmakers James Moore (d. 1726) and John Gumley (d. 1729), who specialized in finely carved gilt-gesso furniture. Holme Lacy later descended to the earl of Chesterfield, who, in 1910, moved many of the contents to Beningbrough Hall, Yorkshire, where the chandelier remained until 1958. Although earlier in date than the Kirtlington Park room, it seems to be a perfect complement to it and helps to illuminate what is unarguably a room of great beauty.

WILLIAM RIEDER

The Lansdowne Dining Room

LONDON ◆ 1766–69

Lansdowne House in Berkeley Square has the dubious distinction of belonging to two of the most unpopular British statesmen of the eighteenth century. It was begun about 1761 for the prime minister, John Stuart (1713–1792), third earl of Bute, who left office in 1763 in political disgrace. He sold the still-unfinished house in 1765 to William Petty Fitzmaurice (1737–1805), second earl of Shelbourne, who was created first marquess of Lansdowne in 1784. Following the twelve-year Tory ministry of Lord North, Shelburne was called in 1782 to form his own ministry. As foreign secretary, then first lord of the Treasury, and finally as prime minister for eight months in 1782–83, he favored free speech, free trade, and autonomy for the American colonies, but he accomplished little during his brief period in power. His enemies praised his knowledge and eloquence but were merciless about his shortcomings. Regarded as tactless, insincere, and devious, he was despised by George III, who called him "the jesuit of Berkeley Square." Henry Fox described him as a "perfidious and infamous liar." And Horace Walpole could find no redeeming qualities: "His falsehood was so constant and notorious that it was rather his profession than his instrument." He was thought to have benefited financially from the Peace of Versailles in 1783, which ended the war with the American colonies, as Bute was thought to have done from the Peace of Paris in 1763; hence a cynical view of the time held that Lansdowne House was constructed by one peace and paid for by another. However politically vilified Shelburne may have been in England, his efforts on behalf of the American colonies were appreciated abroad, as George Washington acknowledged when he wrote to him: "This Country has a grateful recollection of the Agency yur Lordship had in settling the dispute between Great Britian and it." And he was by no means without friends. Jeremy Bentham, Benjamin Franklin, David Garrick, Samuel Johnson, and Honoré de Mirabeau were only a few of the many who made Lansdowne House the center of the most liberal and cultivated society in London.

The house was designed by Robert Adam (1728–1792) and built on a large wedge-shaped plot of land at the southwest corner of Berkeley Square. Fronting spacious grounds, a situation unusual in crowded London, it was described in 1838 as "one of the few [houses] in London, which being situated in a garden surrounded with walls, unites the advantages of the most fashionable neighborhood with a certain retirement, and in the midst of pleasing

William Petty Fitzmaurice, second earl of Shelburne, is depicted in an engraving by H. Robinson after the portrait painted by Sir Joshua Reynolds (1723–1792) in 1764, the year before Shelburne bought the house in Berkeley Square. Shelburne served briefly as prime minister in 1782–83 and was created first marquess of Lansdowne in 1784.

OPPOSITE:
The grisaille painting from the gallery of Croome Court was inserted above the chimneypiece in place of a classical relief intended by Robert Adam but never installed. The original Turkey carpet was sold in 1806, together with all of the furniture from the room. The present Axminster carpet of about 1780–90 was probably intended for a drawing room.

This view of Lansdowne House, Berkeley Square, is from *The Repository of Art*, published in 1811. The house faced a large garden surrounded by a high wall at the south end of Berkeley Square. Designed by Robert Adam, the house was begun for the earl of Bute about 1761 and sold unfinished to the earl of Shelburne in 1765.

natural scenery." The architectural historian Nikolaus Pevsner thought of it as a country house in town. By any standards it was huge and often described by contemporaries as a palace. The central three-story block with a pediment supported by four Ionic columns was flanked by two-story pavilions. With its stately facade, handsomely proportioned rooms of varying shapes, and Neoclassical decoration of great refinement, it was regarded as Adam's finest London house.

Bute's decision to sell the structure half-finished was made under duress, with conditions that were guaranteed to lead to trouble for both principals and almost immediately did so. Shelburne managed to secure an agreement whereby Bute not only sold the house at a loss but also had to complete it for Shelburne to Adam's designs. In order to meet this obligation, Bute was forced to borrow money. A friend of Shelburne's who had visited Bute reported: "He is in worse humor than ever I saw him about the bargain of your house. He thinks it very hard to borrow money to build for you." Shelburne then began to request alterations, which were conveyed to the unhappy seller via the equally unhappy go-between, Robert Adam.

By the following year, 1766, the issue of alterations must have been resolved, and Adam submitted a number of new designs to Shelburne, including several for the dining room, which was also called the Great Eating Room. Located at the south end of the house, behind the three windows on the ground floor of the left wing, it was a large room, about forty-seven feet long, twenty-four feet wide, and eighteen feet high. Adam commented on its unusual size in the notes accompanying the plan of the principal floor in *The Works in Architecture of Robert and James Adam*, the folio publication that Robert and his brother James issued in installments during the 1770s. "The Scite of this house being more ample than usual in London, it has admitted of a noble suite of apartments. The eating-room, in particular, is of great dimensions." In fact, there was little space to spare, if it was to include nine niches for classical sculptures, as the drawing proposed. Two of the designs, which were executed with only minor changes, were billed to Shelburne in August 1766 as "a section of four sides for the dining room: £12 12s od" and "a ceiling for ditto: £10 10s od."

In the preface to *The Works in Architecture*, Adam discusses the function and decoration of the dining room: "The eating rooms are considered as the apartments of conversation, in which we are to pass a great part of our time. This renders it desirable to have them fitted up with elegance and splendor, but in a style different from that of other apartments. Instead of being hung with damask, tapestry & c. they are always finished with stucco, and adorned with statues and paintings, that they may not retain the smell of the victuals." The use of sculpture for decoration is one of several key aspects of his interiors in the 1760s. At Lansdowne House, as at Syon House in Middlesex, the room for eating and conversation became a combination dining room and sculpture gallery.

Classical sculpture was to play a prominent role in Lansdowne House. When the nineteenth-century art historian Adolf Michaelis catalogued the collection in his *Ancient Marbles in Great Britain* in 1882, he regarded it as one of the most beautiful and valuable in England. It was displayed in several rooms throughout the house. The entrance hall and anteroom adjacent to the dining room each had two sculpture niches. The vast tripartite library designed

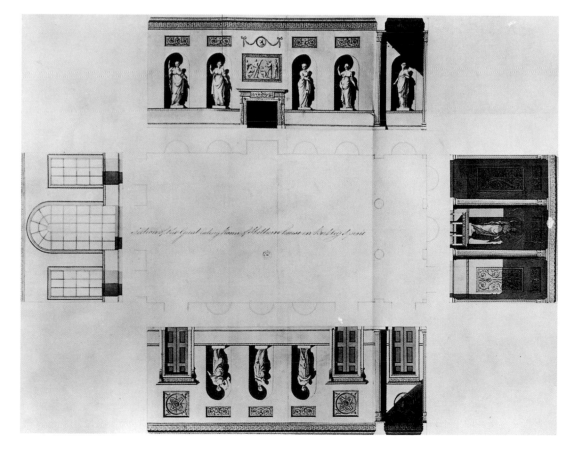

Robert Adam's pen-and-wash drawing *Section of the Great Eating Room for Shelburne house in Berkeley Square* dates from 1766 and is now in Sir John Soane's Museum, London. The opened-out wall plan shows the room as it was built with few alterations. In order to accommodate the room in the Metropolitan, the long walls were reversed.

by Adam went through many changes of architect before it was finally completed many years later as a sculpture gallery, by the third marquess of Lansdowne about 1815–19 to plans of Robert Smirke.

Adam's design for the dining room shows generic antique sculpture rather than specific figures, because Shelburne had only recently begun to buy ancient statuary. His request to James Adam in 1762 to find art of this sort for him in Italy bore fruit in 1765, when a shipment of marbles arrived in London from Civitavecchia. On a trip to Rome in 1771, he engaged the Scottish painter and antiquary Gavin Hamilton to buy sculpture for him, and it was Hamilton who assembled the major part of the collection during the next two years. Some of the sculpture that occupied the niches in the dining room came through Hamilton. Only one of Adam's designs for the room, an elevation of the wall opposite the windows, records a sculpture that was in situ in the 1760s: a statue of Dionysus, the deity most suitable for dining rooms. This Roman torso with eighteenth-century additions was a composite, about which later critics were unenthusiastic. "The merit of the sculpture is not in proportion to the size of the work," Michaelis commented diplomatically.

The serving end of the room with a sideboard recess was screened from the dining section by two tall columns. Adam used the Classical device of an area separated by columns to achieve spatial variety in a number of other houses during this period, most notably at Syon, Kenwood House, and Kedleston Hall. The plate in *The Works in Architecture* that illustrates details of the Lansdowne dining room identifies the ornament of columns and frieze as the "Composed Doric Order": "The capital is antique; the ornament in the frieze is new." Adam found the source for the fluted capital with overlaid leaves on the bottom half at Diocletian's palace at Split, in Croatia, which he visited in 1757 to study Roman domestic architecture. Together with the artist Charles-Louis Clérisseau, Adam viewed the ruins and made measured drawings, which he published in 1764 as *Ruins of the Palace of the Emperor Diocletian at Spalatro in Dalmatia*. He illustrated this particular capital in a detail of one plate and identified it as coming from a corner of the peristyle in the "Temple of Aesculapius."

Another feature of the dining room derived from Split is the pronounced cornice projecting over the frieze above the doors and supported at each end by a scrolled console, which he took from a door in the same temple. Adam's "new" ornament on the frieze, a ribbon weaving between husks and pendant leaves attached to rosettes, was executed on the doorways exactly as depicted in the engraving in *The Works in Architecture*, but, inexplicably, in the frieze below the ceiling, the same ornament is upside down. This reversal may have been an oversight on the part of the plasterer, Joseph Rose; or Adam and Lansdowne together may have simply decided that they liked it that way.

In the lengthy and largely inaccurate discourse on the historical evolution

of the compartmented ceiling in *The Works in Architecture*, Adam concludes, with typical self-congratulation, that he has finally perfected this element of interior decoration. The puff deserves consideration in regard to the dining-room ceiling, for it is a refined and successful design beautifully executed by Joseph Rose with only a few changes. The garland-carrying putti in the four corner compartments of the central section in the design became groups of figures emblematic of the Four Seasons in compositions showing that the architect also responded to eighteenth-century influence, in this case pottery from the Wedgwood factory.

The room is indeed a tour de force of Neoclassical stucco decoration, executed by the best and most expensive stuccoist in England. Joseph Rose's bill for this room amounted to almost £300, nearly one quarter of his charge for the entire house.

Other bills for Lansdowne House that record in fascinating detail every aspect of the work survive at the seat of the present earl of Shelburne, Bowood in Wiltshire, which was built concurrently by Adam. The carver John Gilbert was employed in the dining room from March 1767 to December 1768, and his invoice specifies the charges for every wood molding, shutter, and door, even the "fig leaves to figures to ye niches" (5 shillings each). Francis Pitsala's bill for the painting describes not only the colors ("pearl" with the ornament picked out in "dead white") but also the number of coats applied (ranging from four to five).

The marble chimneypiece was supplied in 1768 by the London firm of John Devall & Co., the chief masons for the royal palaces, the Tower of London, and the Royal Mews. Their work may have pleased the Crown, but

ABOVE LEFT:
Elevation of the serving end of the dining room, about 1764–68, by Robert Adam and his studio, now in the collection of the earl of Shelburne, the Bowood Estates, Wiltshire. In the niche a classical statue of Dionysus stands above a sideboard flanked by urns and pedestals designed by Adam and made by John Linnell.

ABOVE RIGHT:
This engraving from *The Works in Architecture of Robert and James Adam* (London, 1779) shows the entablature (executed with the leaf-and-rosette motif in the opposite direction), the "Composed Doric Order" of the columns, and a detail of entablature and console over a door.

This pen-and-wash drawing by Adam for the dining-room ceiling is in Sir John Soane's Museum. When executed, the Three Graces in the center were replaced by a rosette; the four figural rectangular compositions in the corners were changed to the Four Seasons.

it did not please Shelburne, who complained that the chimneypiece was not properly executed to Adam's design. Furthermore, he was annoyed at being charged £180 against an estimate of £150.

In 1768 the Shelburnes moved in, even though Lady Shelburne clearly thought it was premature to do so. She noted in her diary for August 20, 1768: "On the ground floor we have the Hall, Antechamber, and Dining Room, which are quite finished, except for the glasses, window curtains and chairs, which makes it very doubtful if we can ask the King of Denmark to dinner. . . . It is very noble, and I am much pleased with it, tho' perhaps few people wou'd have come to live in it, in so unfinished a state."

Indeed, it would have been very awkward to ask the king of Denmark to dinner, for there was as yet no furniture at all in the dining room. It arrived shortly thereafter, in late 1768 and 1769, and was provided by two of the leading cabinetmakers in London, John Linnell and Thomas Chippendale. Linnell supplied two dining tables and a breakfast table, which were brought in as the occasion required. It was not yet the custom in England to keep a large dining table permanently in the room. He also provided two sideboards with mahogany tops on white painted frames, which were probably placed on either side of the chimneypiece, and at the serving end a mahogany-topped sideboard flanked by a pair of pedestals and vases. The richly decorated pedestals with a carved frieze of rams' heads, paterae, and swags of husks, and the vases with scroll handles and carved acanthus also had a utilitarian function. The vases were lined with lead to hold water piped to taps in the pedestals. Adam sent Shelburne drawings for the sideboard and pair of pedestals and vases in 1765–66, and the elevation drawing for this end of the

One of two overdoor panels with a military trophy of shield, helmet, and quiver

room shows them in place below the niche and in front of the flanking pilasters. The architect believed in getting the most out of his furniture designs and often reused them with only slight variations for other clients. He had Linnell make virtually the same pedestals and vases in 1767 for the dining room in Osterley Park.

Chippendale billed Shelburne for the dining chairs in January 1769: "14 Mahogany Chairs with Antique backs and term feet very richly Carvd with hollow seats stuffd and coverd with Red Morocco Leather and double Brass naild £51 9 0." These were one of Chippendale's standard dining-room models, which he also supplied to Brocket Hall, Newby Hall, Harewood House, and Goldsborough Hall.

With the furniture in place, the dining room was complete, but the adjacent drawing room was still being painted in 1771, when Lady Shelburne died at the age of twenty-five, before giving any dinners in the new house. This was also the year that Lord Shelburne and Adam parted company over a disagreement regarding the latter's new development of houses, called The Adelphi, on the Thames. Adam was to have no further involvement at Lansdowne House.

Shelburne remarried in 1779 and continued to collect pictures, books, manuscripts, and furniture, most of which were sold after his death in 1805 by his son John (1765–1809), second marquess of Lansdowne. This "tall personable man, rather regardless of his dress" was at least able to retain the famous sculpture collection. The original dining-room furniture was sold in 1806, and none of it has been found.

During the first half of the nineteenth century, Henry (1780–1863), the third marquess, one of the great Whig hosts of his time, made the house once again a center of social and political activity. Among the many who dined there were Charles Dickens, the poet Thomas Moore, the historian Thomas Macaulay, the German philosopher Friedrich von Schlegel, and the very eccentric Lord Dudley, who as Moore recorded in his *Diary* sat at the table muttering to himself, "occasionally pushing about the meat with his fingers and uttering low-breathed criticisms upon it." Lady Eastlake describes many notable gatherings in the "cool, grand apartments." On one evening there was a concert at which two thousand guests, including several members of the royal family, "enjoyed that combination of the arts for which Lansdowne House has always been celebrated, and which was the dominant note in the character of the third Marquis."

The house remained in the family until 1929, when it was sold by the sixth marquess and partially demolished to make way for a new street at that end of Berkeley Square. The pavilions were removed, and the front of the main block was recessed about forty feet with the facade rebuilt on a smaller scale, to the horror of architectural historians such as James Lees-Milne, who called it "a shamefully hideous mess and muddle." During the demolition the dining room and the first drawing room were dismantled and acquired, respectively, by the Metropolitan Museum and the Philadelphia Museum of Art. The remnants of the house were remodeled and today form the Lansdowne Club at 9 Fitzmaurice Place.

The dining room remained in crates at the Metropolitan until space became available in 1954, when it was installed in its present position. In order to accommodate it in this area, the two long walls were reversed. The original sculpture from the room had been dispersed in the 1930 sale of the collection, so the niches were filled with plaster casts. However, in 1961 the Museum was able to acquire one figure from the dining room: Tyche, goddess of fortune, a Roman statue largely copied from a Greek original. Adam seems to have intended a classical relief to be placed in the plaster frame over the chimney-piece; but this was never done, and the frame remained unfilled. In 1959 a Neoclassical grisaille painting from the gallery of Croome Court was found to be almost exactly the right size and was placed in the frame. The room was furnished with Neoclassical Adam-style furniture, with the addition in 1970 of a set of dining chairs that would have greatly displeased Robert Adam, as they were made to a design of his rival, James Wyatt.

A study of the early paint layers in 1954 gave evidence for the gray-and-white scheme that was followed. In the 1995 reinstallation, a new color analysis revealed that Francis Pitsala's "pearl" was a lighter gray than previously thought, with a tinge of green that places it closer to celadon. The new scheme gives a much lighter cast to the room and will, no doubt, be the source of yet another study forty years hence.

With its many-layered references to the antique, handsome proportions, and refined decoration, the dining room from Lansdowne House is a fine example of Adam's mature manner. Immodest as he may have been, he was his own best critic. He described his accomplishment in *The Works in Architecture*: "The massive entablature, the ponderous compartment ceiling, the tabernacle frame, almost the only species of ornament formerly known,

in this country, are now universally exploded, and in their place, we have adopted a beautiful variety of light mouldings, gracefully formed, delicately enriched and arranged with propriety and skill. We have introduced a great diversity of ceilings, freezes, and decorated pilasters, and have added grace and beauty to the whole, by a mixture of grotesque stucco, and painted ornaments, together with the flowing rinceau, with its fanciful figures and winding foliage."

WILLIAM RIEDER

The figures in the niches of the wall opposite the chimneypiece are plaster casts. None of the Neoclassical furniture or silver is original to the room.

The Croome Court Tapestry Room

WORCESTERSHIRE ◆ 1771

Few houses in England have experienced a more checkered history than Croome Court in Worcestershire. In Richard Wilson's view of 1758, it stands in a bucolic landscape, bathed in sunlight. And for many years the sun continued to shine. King George III came to visit. As a girl, Queen Victoria spent summers there, as did George V when he was duke of York. Queen Juliana of the Netherlands and the Dutch royal family took shelter at Croome during World War II. But after 1948 things took rather a different turn. From 1950 to 1979 it was occupied by Saint Joseph's School for Boys. The dress code changed in the 1980s, when Chaitanya College moved in, and swaying children dressed in pale amber sang songs accompanied by small drums and cymbals to welcome visitors to the International Society for Krishna Consciousness and a museum of Vedic culture. Recently, much of the park was acquired by the National Trust, but the house, shuttered and empty, is at present on the market, perhaps to be converted by a new owner to a hotel or apartments.

OPPOSITE:
The tapestry room from Croome Court was the first of a series of rooms with tapestries woven at the Royal Gobelins Manufactory in Paris. It was begun in 1763 and completed in 1771. The Axminster carpet was woven in the 1770s for the library at Harewood House in Yorkshire.

Richard Wilson (1713–1782): *View of Croome Court* (Birmingham Museum and Art Gallery). As his first independent project, Lancelot "Capability" Brown built the Palladian-style house in 1750–52 and landscaped the grounds by creating a stream and bridge beside the broad lawn.

Allan Ramsay (1713–1784): *Portrait of George William, sixth earl of Coventry*, 1764 (Birmingham Museum and Art Gallery). The stand on the left and vase in the right background were carefully chosen to show Coventry's fashionable French taste.

Croome Court was built by George William (1721–1809), sixth earl of Coventry, a proud, argumentative, and not altogether attractive figure. His friend George Selwyn described Croome and its owner: "This house is full of tobacco, the yard is full of tenants, and the peer, with an important face, is telling us how much he pays to the land-tax." Opposition to the war with the American colonies ended his career in government. As described in his obituary notice in the *Gentleman's Magazine*, "He well understood the principles of the Constitution, and acted at all times in conformity with them, supporting the Government of the Country with zeal and integrity; but when, during the American War, he could no longer approve of the conduct of the then Minister Lord North, he resigned the place of one of the Lords of the Bedchamber, though contrary to his Majesty's wishes, resolving that no private consideration should shackle his public conduct." The earl's reputation for good taste was undermined by his predilection to talk about it, and he was more discriminating in matters of art and architecture than with people. His first wife, Maria Gunning, a legendary beauty, was mindless, silly, flirtatious and terminally vain. As she lay dying at the age of twenty-seven from consumption aggravated by the cosmetic use of white lead, her chief concern was, as ever, her appearance.

When Coventry inherited Croome in 1751, the marshy park was far from bucolic. "As hopeless a spot as any in the island," he wrote in a tribute to Lancelot "Capability" Brown (1716–1783), whom he had hired to improve both the grounds and the damp old Jacobean house. Demolishing everything but the chimneys, Brown built a rectangular block of Bath stone with corner turrets and a large tetrastyle Ionic portico. As his first major architectural work, it was a somewhat stiff exercise in the Palladian style that he had learned from William Kent. In rendering the elevation for *Vitruvius Brittanicus*, a publication of engravings of classical buildings in Britain, the authors tidied it up by deleting the old chimneys, something that the architect should have considered as well. However, Coventry was pleased. "Mr. Brown has done very well by me, and indeed I think has studied both my place and my pocket, which are not always conjunctively the objects of prospectors," he wrote to his friend the architect Sanderson Miller.

By 1760 he must have decided that his place and pocket could accommodate better interiors, and he changed architect, engaging the more fashionable Robert Adam (1728–1792) to design several of the principal rooms. Although Adam had only recently established his practice in London, his new Neoclassical style found a ready and eager audience with the nobility and gentry. At Croome Adam and Coventry worked together, if not always harmoniously, to create three splendid rooms: the gallery, the library, and the tapestry room, which were widely admired and greatly preferred to the sober exterior.

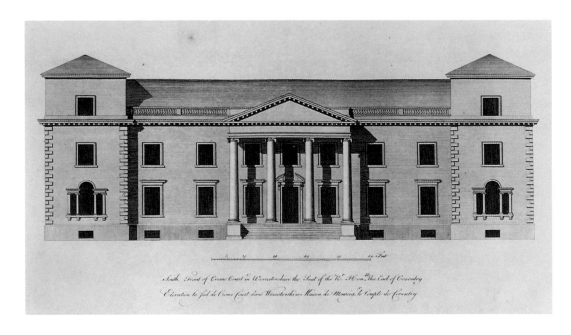

This elevation of the south front of Croome Court is from *Vitruvius Brittanicus*, a series of engravings of classical buildings in Britain published in 1715–17 and 1769–71. The tapestry room was located on the first floor behind the two windows to the right of the portico.

Richard Joseph Sullivan wrote in his travel journal in 1778: "The house, which, though heavy, has the look of a modern building, is large, but situated too low. The rooms are handsome and convenient; especially a drawing room, hung and furnished with Gobelins tapestry, the finest perhaps, in England."

There had been a long history in England of rooms hung with sets of tapestry. Coventry would have known the most recent example at nearby Hagley Hall in Worcestershire, where the tapestry drawing room was made in the 1750s, incorporating a set of floral tapestries that had been woven in the workshop of Joshua Morris in London during the 1720s. Rococo stuccowork and armchairs in the Louis XV style with new floral tapestry woven in London by Paul Saunders gave the room a decidedly French air. Coventry may have thought that he could improve on this decoration by having a tapestry room custom made in France, but travel there was almost impossible during the Seven Years War (1756–63).

After the Treaty of Paris in February 1763, frustrated Francophiles in England and Anglophiles in France could resume their respective shopping, and they did so in large numbers. As Horace Walpole noted: "Our passion for everything French is nothing to theirs for everything English. The two nations are crossing over and figuring in." Coventry shared his furnishing ideas with his friend "Gilly" Williams, who wrote to George Selwyn in Paris: "He talks of setting out next week for Paris, and is now hiring a French servant to pay his post-horses. Don't think of introducing him to any part of the great world, for he is determined to be as private as an upholsterer, and to pass his time in buying glasses [large plates of mirror glass] and tapestry."

The earl was very welcome indeed at the Royal Gobelins Manufactory, where business had not been going well. Under the supervision of the marquis de Marigny (brother of Mme de Pompadour and *Directeur des Bâtiments*) and the direction of Jean-Germain Soufflot (1713–1780) (*Contrôleur des Bâtiments* and the architect of the Panthéon), the manager, Jacques Neilson (1714–1788), had recently introduced horizontal (*basse-lisse*) looms in order to make tapestries more rapidly and at lower cost with no loss of quality. As the factory was receiving far too few royal commissions, the directors brought over the ever-popular François Boucher from the competing manufactory at Beauvais to execute paintings to serve as tapestry cartoons. "Whether their works are good or bad, the private individual, who is not much of a connoisseur, will always prefer novelty, and will be satisfied with subjects composed by, and showing taste of, Sieur Boucher," reads the internal memorandum, which would not have amused the earl of Coventry. Private orders were desperately needed and the English milords arrived just in time.

It appears to have been Soufflot who conceived of the new tapestry composition of medallions containing scenes by Boucher. This scheme was further elaborated in 1762 by the decorative painter Maurice Jacques (1712–1784), who placed the medallions on a crimson and dark pink ground patterned with

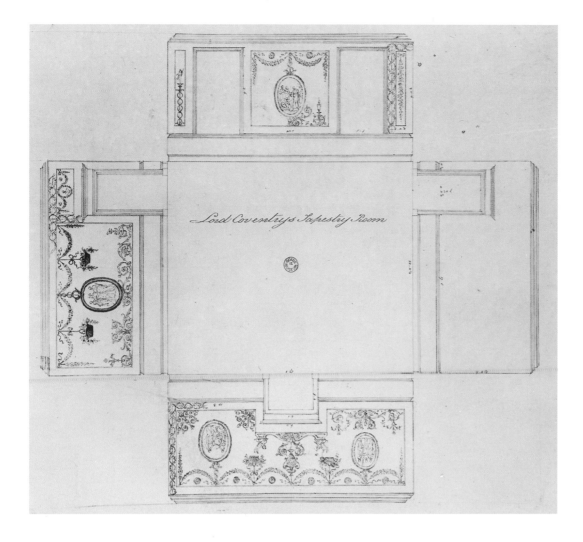

In his laid-out wall plan for "Lord Coventry's Tapestry Room," Robert Adam responded to the Gobelins designs with a more Neoclassical scheme.

flowers and leaves simulating silk damask and suspended them from a frame-like border resembling carved and gilded wood. This new design had a number of advantages: it could be adjusted to fit almost any size wall, allowed for endless variation of animals and flowers in the decorative surrounds, and could be complemented with matching furniture covers. Using tapestry almost like wallpaper to cover the walls from chair rail to cornice would so perfectly benefit the Gobelins that Neilson must have been responsible for the idea. Coventry was the first to see the new scheme and brought several sketches back to Croome to show Robert Adam.

The earl seems to have wanted Adam either to alter or further develop the French drawings. In his account to Coventry, Adam described one of the three drawings he produced at this time as "altering the French Designs of the Tapestry room in Colours." In this sketch, now in Sir John Soane's Museum in London, Adam took the basic idea of suspended medallions beneath garlands of flowers and added his own repertoire of sphinxes and linear acanthus scrolls in an attempt to translate the three-dimensional Rococo Gobelins concept into a flatter, more two-dimensional Neoclassical one. In doing so, he was showing Coventry, "Well, this is how *I* would design these tapestries," but it had no effect. If his patron took these designs back to Paris, which seems unlikely, when he returned there in 1764 to place the order, they were ignored

Ceiling for the Library at Croome

Janty 1763.

at the Gobelins and the set went into production.

For Adam, to have his designs rejected was bad enough; to have his bill for them questioned was simply unacceptable. When Coventry tried to cut ten pounds off the invoice, Adam responded: "I am extremely sorry your Lordship should have thought of deducting any part of the Money, as almost every person I have done designs for . . . have generally sent me a present over and above the Bill itself, and not long since upon delivering one of the seventy-five pounds, I received a Hundred, with this Compliment That he knew how many thousands I had spent in acquiring knowledge." The earl paid in full, and their bumpy working relationship continued.

Adam had given Coventry a ceiling design for the adjoining library in 1763, but his lordship changed his mind, as was his wont, and decided to use it for the tapestry room. The ceiling was executed by Joseph Rose, one of the most skilled plasterers of the time, in part from molds and the rest modeled and finished by hand. Through no fault of Rose, the result is not entirely successful, for the ceiling is both stylistically incompatible with the tapestries and overscaled for the room, problems that seem symptomatic of the difficulties possibly inherent in this Anglo-French venture.

In 1763 and the following year Boucher painted the subjects for the medallions, allegories of the Elements, which survive at the Louvre and the Grand Trianon, Versailles. Air (*Cephalus and Aurora*) and Earth (*Vertumnus and Pomona*) appear on the chimney wall, while Fire (*Venus Visiting Vulcan*) and Water

(*Neptune Rescuing Amymone*) are on the left and right walls, respectively. Maurice Jacques's bills in 1765 and 1766 for various motifs in the decorative surrounds indicate that the designs were still evolving. The floral cartoons for the furniture covers were executed by Jacques and the decorative artist Louis Tessier (1719/20–1781) from 1760 to 1767.

For some time one of the selling points at the Gobelins had been their custom of shipping wares for English clients to the French ambassador in London via the diplomatic bag to avoid import duty. In 1767 Neilson contacted the new French ambassador, indicating that he had some tapestries to send to "Monseigneur Coventry" and several others. "If the ambassador will cooperate he will be assisting the commerce of the kingdom and obliging the gentlemen who have no other means of receiving works they have ordered at great expense in a foreign country," he wrote. But the ambassador balked, so Neilson went higher up in the court for help. The ambassador was duly instructed, and the illicit commerce resumed.

Early accounts of the Croome tapestry room credit the design of the seat furniture to Robert Adam. Recent research, however, suggests that it must have originated at the Gobelins, perhaps by Soufflot, who had provided Neoclassical furniture for the marquis de Marigny. The chairs and settees were executed by the leading London cabinetmakers, John Mayhew and William Ince, who billed Coventry in 1769 for "6 Large Antique Elbow Chairs with oval Backs carv'd with Double husks and ribbon knot on top, Gilt in the Best Burnish'd Gold, Stuffed with Besthair, in Linen — Backt with Fine Crimson Tammy — proper for covering with Tapistry in the Country. . . £77 8s. od. 2 Settees for Each Side the Chimney, richly carv'd and Gilt Stuff'd and Cover'd to match the Chairs £56 10s od."

The large pier mirror appears on the same bill: "A large Architect Pier Frame, fluted, richly carv'd with shell on top, festoons and drops of double husks down the sides, goates head at bottom gilt in the very best Double Burnish'd Gold £35." It is called an "Architect Pier Frame" and may well have been designed by Adam, as the goat's head at the base and mask at the top have close affinities with his style.

One would expect the pier table below it to have been provided at the same time. However, the fine marble top was actually supplied ten years earlier, in 1759, by the sculptor and marble mason John Wildsmith (fl. 1757–69), whose bill noted: "To a Rich fine and Marble Table in squairs of all the curious sorts of marble No: 176 Sqrs. in Do. To 41 squairs cut out and others fixt in there places £42 10s od." There was a great interest in England and France at this period in slabs inlaid with specimen marbles, most of which were imported as finished tops from Italy. The wording of the invoice leaves unclear whether this example was made and then altered by Wildsmith or whether he replaced forty-one squares on an imported Italian top. The carved and gilt six-legged base may have been made together with the mirror frame and seat furniture in 1769 but damaged and replaced at a later date. The only bill in the Croome archives that seems to describe it was submitted by Ince and Mayhew much later, in 1794: "A large Frame for a Marble Slab, enrich'd with patteras &c. on turned legs, neatly carved and the whole gilt in burnished gold £17 10s."

In addition to supplying the top for the pier table, Wildsmith executed in the following year (1760) the chimneypiece with white-marble decorative elements on a ground of orange Veronese marble. The large tablet of lapis lazuli set in the center was provided by the sculptor Joseph Wilton, who specialized in richly ornamented chimneypieces and became in 1764 "Sculptor to His Majesty." One of the specimen squares in the tabletop, mentioned specifically in Wildsmith's bill, is also of lapis, suggesting that Coventry may have been particularly fond of this rare dark blue mineral flecked with brilliant pyrites.

By June 1771 all the pieces from the Gobelins had arrived, and Ince and

The pier mirror was made by the cabinetmakers John Mayhew and William Ince in 1769, probably after a design by Robert Adam. It is surrounded by a tapestry panel designed by Maurice Jacques (ca. 1712–1784). The specimen-marble tabletop was supplied by John Wildsmith in 1759. Mayhew and Ince replaced the original base with the present one in 1794.

Mayhew sent a crew to hang the tapestries and apply the seat covers. The earl was billed for "three men's time at Croome putting up the tapestry, making paper case hangings [covers for the tapestries] for ditto, stuffing and covering 2 settees and 6 chairs, fixing gilt borders and sundry other jobs." With this work the tapestry room was finished.

Nine sets of medallion tapestries, known as *Tentures de Boucher* at the Gobelins, were woven before the Revolution, with variations in iconography, design, and ground color; five of them went to England. In addition to Croome Court, tapestry rooms were commissioned by William Weddell for Newby Hall, Yorkshire; Sir Henry Bridgeman for Weston Park, Staffordshire; Sir Lawrence Dundas for Moor Park, Hertfordshire; and Robert Child for Osterley Park, Middlesex.

One of the most puzzling aspects of Robert Adam's career is the fact that he was the architect for each of these houses, where he had nothing to gain by covering walls with Rococo tapestry rather than his own Neoclassical stucco decoration. He cannot have been pleased by yet another client insisting on yet another tapestry room from the Gobelins, but he clearly recognized that it was in his interest to accommodate these rooms as best he could rather than to resist them.

The fashion in England of covering large areas of walls with tapestry, occasionally framed as though built in, in conjunction with the taste for things French during the second half of the eighteenth century may explain

One of the two settees and six armchairs made for the room in 1769 by Mayhew and Ince. The covers, en suite with the tapestries, were designed at the Gobelins by Maurice Jacques and Louis Tessier.

The marble chimneypiece by the sculptor and mason John Wildsmith was installed in 1760, when the room was described as a "breakfast room," four years before Coventry commissioned the tapestries. The tablet of lapis lazuli in the center was provided by the sculptor Joseph Wilton. The composition of a vase of flowers and putti with a shell, scrollwork, draped garlands, and birds was designed by Maurice Jacques.

why Gobelins tapestry rooms became fashionable. Why they did not become fashionable in France is less clear.

Museum visitors will be struck by the splendid colors of the tapestries. They have survived in this pristine state because the room, when not in use, was protected from the light by the "paper case hangings" and later by those of chamois. Through the visits of George III, Queen Victoria, and many others, it remained the favorite room at Croome until about 1902, when it was sold by the ninth earl of Coventry to a dealer in Paris. The covers were then removed from the seat furniture and placed on modern French frames in the Louis XV style so that those made by Mayhew and Ince could be sold separately. The ceiling, carved chair rail and door surrounds, mahogany doors, chimneypiece, and floor stayed at Croome until 1949, when the Samuel H. Kress Foundation decided to acquire and reconstitute the tapestry room, which was then given to the Metropolitan by the Foundation in 1958. The following year the wayward chair and sofa frames were found in Paris, purchased by the Foundation, brought to the Museum, and re-covered with their original tapestry seats, backs, and armrests, thus completing the move of this "drawing room, hung and furnished with Gobelins tapestry, the finest perhaps, in England," from Worcestershire to New York.

WILLIAM RIEDER

America

The Hart Room

IPSWICH, MASSACHUSETTS ◆ BEFORE 1674

In June 1635, when he arrived in this country on a ship named *Desire*, Thomas Hart (1611–1674) was a twenty-four-year-old servant to tailor John Browne from the village of Baddow in Essex, England. Hart settled in the Massachusetts Bay Colony at Ipswich and was listed as a landowner by 1639, when he may have begun to build the house that held this room, the earliest now installed in the American Wing. Initially, Thomas Hart's house was probably an extremely simple structure with one room, usually called a hall, on the first floor, and another, a hall chamber, on the second. A large chimney anchored one end of the house. In such a house the hall would have functioned as a multipurpose area, where all of the family activities—especially food preparation and eating but also sleeping—took place. The upstairs hall chamber served as an additional bedroom and storage space.

In November 1924, when the American Wing opened to the public, the curators wanted to include American rooms from the seventeenth through the early nineteenth century. Because no actual seventeenth-century examples were available at the time, it was decided to reproduce what was then called the parlor in the Hart house, which was well known to antiquarians. By 1924 the house had been much expanded and made into an inn. The reason cited in the 1924 *Handbook of the American Wing* for choosing this example to reproduce was that "it shows a more definite effort toward decorative effect than any contemporary room still in existence." When the actual room and the chamber above it were offered for sale by the owner in 1936, the Museum was delighted to have the opportunity to replace the reproduction with the original hall. The upstairs chamber was bought by H. F. du Pont and can be seen today at the Winterthur Museum in Delaware.

OPPOSITE:
The fireplace wall in the Hart room. A large oak court cupboard, made in the Plymouth, Massachusetts, area about 1670–1700, stands against the wall to the left of the fireplace. The cupboard's top is decorated with a display of imported ceramics of the type the Hart family might have owned.

The Hart house about 1890. The room currently installed in the Museum was on the first floor, to the left of the door. When it was built, the house consisted of only the left half of the structure in this photograph and did not include the small lean-to.

171

The decorative effect of this essentially medieval room, based on those in houses left behind by the Puritans in England, is found in the contrast of the massive, dark oak timbers against the whitewashed plaster ceiling and walls. The main timbers (the central ceiling summer beam and the wall girts) have been ornamented in a subtle manner. The beam edges have been chamfered, or smoothed, with a decorative plane, and the fireplace wall has been sheathed in vertical pine boards with bead-molded edges. This wall, though of the period, was taken from another Ipswich house in the first decade of the twentieth century and added to the Hart room. That the wall was not original to the Hart house was discovered about twenty years after its installation in the American Wing.

The small casement windows with their diamond-shaped leaded panes are accurate reproductions of the type found in New England in the mid-seventeenth century. Small windows were the norm because window glass, which was imported from England until well into the eighteenth century, was extremely expensive. They also helped retain the limited heat thrown into the room by the large but inefficient fireplace. Although the fireplace is missing its red-tile hearth, it is an accurate reproduction of the type built of local brick with clay mortar in seventeenth-century Ipswich. On average, a hall fireplace had an opening measuring seven to nine feet in width and, like this one, usually contained an oven. The floor in the Hart room was originally wide-plank pine; when the room was installed in the American Wing, an oak floor was substituted to withstand the wear caused by visitors walking through it.

At the end of his life, Thomas Hart, a tanner by trade, left a sizable estate worth £729.13.06, which included a fair amount of acreage as well as his "tan yard, dwelling house & homestead & barne." Although he bequeathed his house to his son Samuell, he stipulated that his wife, Alice, should continue in "the use of my parlor for her self & Rome [room] in the cellar & the other romes in my house." He also left her the bed in the parlor, clearly their marriage bed, valued at £8, by far the most expensive single item in the inventory taken of his "goods and chattells" after his death.

The reference to Alice's use of the parlor and the bed indicates that Thomas Hart's house had probably more than doubled in size by the time of his death in 1674. As New England settlers became more affluent, they would add a second back-to-back fireplace to the chimney mass, which opened into another pair of rooms across from the original hall and hall chamber. These new spaces, called the parlor and parlor chamber, would have alleviated the

Corner of the Hart room. The low bed dates from the early 19th century, but the sturdy cradle, made in eastern Massachusetts of wide oak panels held in place by a mortise-and-tenon frame, has survived more than three centuries of use.

This view of one of the corners in the room clearly shows the pegs that hold the tenoned ends of the heavy girts, or beams, in the mortised corner post. This type of post-and-beam construction is typical of the way houses were built by the early New England colonists.

crowded conditions that must have existed if Hart, his wife, and their four children had all been forced to live together in the hall and hall chamber. The parlor would then have functioned as the best room, where the parents also slept, freeing the hall to become more of a kitchen/dining area. However, the Museum's room has been installed as a multipurpose hall, as it may have been when Hart first built the house. The inventory does not indicate where the objects originally stood, so the Museum's Hart room has been furnished with the type of objects the family might have used in its hall.

The Harts owned three beds; the most expensive (or "best") bed, used by Thomas and Alice, was probably fully curtained to provide warmth and privacy for the couple. Because virtually no seventeenth-century bedsteads have survived, the best bed is represented here by an example of a later date; eventually a high-post curtained bed will be reproduced for the room. This latter type usually had a very simple joined bedstead but was considered valuable for its feather-filled mattress and expensive curtains and bedding. All but the most basic textiles were imported from Europe in the seventeenth century, and a fully draped bed could require at least eighty yards of the narrow-width fabric available at that time. The most popular fabrics for draping beds in the second half of the seventeenth century were made of wool, which was usually dyed red or green.

This room also held Hart's "grat [great] table with forms [benches]," at which the family dined. Because the room is now open to large groups of visitors, the center, where a table and benches of this type would have stood, has been left unfurnished. Two small English joined stools topped with red-wool cushions indicate the most common type of seating available at the time. Two chests are also mentioned in the inventory; the low-relief carved chest under the window (which is of the style associated with Ipswich join-ers William Searle and Thomas Dennis) is the type of object that Hart might have owned. The court cupboard standing to the left of the fireplace, which may have been used to store dishes and table linens, would probably have been beyond Hart's economic level. The multifunctional chair-table expresses the early settlers' need for versatile and space-saving furniture. Hart's inventory also listed a trundle bed, usually slept in by the children of the family and stored under the parents' bed during the day. Instead of a trundle bed, a rare paneled oak cradle ornamented with boldly turned finials is displayed here. In a busy hall such as the one we have imagined for the Hart family, the most recent baby in its cradle was never far from the warmth of the fire and the center of the family's activities.

AMELIA PECK

Furnishings in the room include this low-relief carved oak chest and the oak-and-pine chair-table of the late 17th century.

The Wentworth Room

PORTSMOUTH, NEW HAMPSHIRE ◆ 1695–1700

When the Museum acquired the Wentworth house in 1926, it belonged to a house-wrecking company. The once-grand Portsmouth home of John (1671–1730) and Sarah Hunking Wentworth (1673–1741) had been moved from its original site on a small inlet called Puddle Dock and was sitting on blocks in a junkyard. The massive chimney had been dismantled, its bricks thrown into the nearby bay. (Some of these were later recovered.) A local preservation organization asked the Museum to keep the house intact and move it to another site, either in Portsmouth or in New York City (Van Cortlandt Park in the Bronx was suggested), but when neither of these options proved viable, the Museum staff believed that the only way to ensure the preservation of at least some of the house was to have it painstakingly taken apart, carefully documenting the process with extensive photography. The pieces of the house were then stored for more than a decade in a Portsmouth barn.

In the years immediately preceding its demolition, the building had served as a rooming house; because of this use, as well as the changing needs over time of the various families who had lived in it, many of the rooms had been greatly altered. The first-story rooms had suffered the most, so in 1937 the Museum staff decided (after bringing the dismantled house to New York City) to install only one second-floor chamber and the house's main staircase in the American Wing.

Like the Hart house of about twenty-five years earlier, the Wentworth house was built of heavy oak timbers around a chimney core, but that is where the similarities between the two houses end. Thomas Hart was an immigrant craftsman who made his living by tanning leather, and his home was small and built to meet his family's everyday needs efficiently. John Wentworth's family had been in America for two generations and had acquired considerable wealth and standing in the community. Wentworth was a merchant and sea captain who served as lieutenant governor of New Hampshire from 1717 to 1730, and his brother Samuel was one of the leading merchants of Boston. John's wife, Sarah, was the only child of Mark Hunking, a man wealthy enough to purchase the land on which the Wentworth house was built as a gift for his daughter and son-in-law soon after they were married in 1693. The large house, which included two full stories and a garret,

ABOVE:
The Wentworth house on its original site on Manning Street. This photograph was taken May 16, 1925, shortly before the house was removed to a local junkyard. The front porch was a 19th-century addition.

OPPOSITE:
The furniture in the Wentworth room is in the William and Mary style, which was becoming fashionable at the time the house was built. The pieces are relatively light and vertical in form when compared to the late-17th-century furniture in the Hart room.

Several new furniture forms—such as the easy chair, oval dining table, high chest, dressing table, and daybed—were introduced at the beginning of the 18th century. These forms, which reflect an increased concern with personal comfort, demonstrate the use of specialized pieces of furniture in rooms set aside for specific functions.

was built between 1695 and 1701. Evidence found in the house when it was demolished revealed grand paneled rooms with ceiling heights of eight feet on both floors. The main staircase, with its spiral-turned balusters, is the earliest known New England staircase to include this type of turning. Although the original uses of all of the rooms in the house are unknown, the first floor most likely included a hall and a parlor that opened off to either side of the stair hall at the front of the house, with a kitchen to the rear flanked by a pantry to the north and a bedroom to the south. The second floor held the Museum's room on the north end; although the room was cut up into three sections when photographed in 1925, physical evidence seems to confirm that it originally ran the full depth of the house. On the south end of the second floor, there were at least two other rooms, including a chamber similar to the one seen here, but somewhat smaller, which was sold to H. F. du Pont in 1929 and is now installed in the Winterthur Museum in Delaware.

Apart from the scale of the Metropolitan's room—which at approximately twenty-nine feet long by eighteen feet wide makes it one of the largest domestic interiors surviving from the early colonial period—other notable features include the crisp quarter-round chamfering of two summer beams, as well as of the girts that run along the top of the long walls. Instead of leaving all the structural elements exposed, as they are in the Hart room, the builder of the Wentworth house boxed in the corner posts against the fireplace wall, in order to incorporate them into the wall's paneling, and plastered over the floor joists of the room above. Twelve-over-eight-pane double-hung sash windows with wooden muntins (bars between the panes of glass) are modern reproductions of typical windows of the period. Two additional windows once lighted the room from the short end walls, but these were changed into doorways to let visitors enter the space.

The fireplace wall, a harbinger of eighteenth-century interior fashion, is covered with raised paneling framed with bold moldings. Although the panels are irregularly spaced, the overall effect is certainly more elegant than the bead-molded sheathing of the fireplace wall in the Hart room. The pine paneling is painted dark red to match traces found beneath multiple layers of later paint. The fireplace opening is surrounded by a beautifully proportioned bolection molding, which is original to the room. However, the mantel shelf above the fireplace and the herringbone-patterned brickwork inside it are later additions; the curators who installed the room in 1937 based these details on a chamber fireplace from the Winslow house (1699) at Marshfield, Massachusetts. As in many of the Museum's period rooms, the original pine flooring has been replaced with more durable oak.

This grand space most likely functioned as the best chamber in the house. As such, it was used for both sleeping and informal entertaining.

The front door of the Wentworth house opened directly onto this small but beautifully detailed staircase. The massive center chimney was behind the stair, and the hall and parlor opened to either side.

OPPOSITE:
The wide fireplace was all that heated this large room during cold New Hampshire winters. For efficiency, the fireplace may have been outfitted with a cast-iron fireback, like the one shown here, which was probably made in New England about 1703. The low relief on the fireback is thought to depict Massachusetts governor Joseph Dudley atop a heavily defended fort. The brass-and-steel standing candlestick to the right of the fireplace could be moved from place to place, and the candles could be raised and lowered on the shaft.

Although it was probably John and Sarah Wentworth's bedroom, it may have been turned over to important visitors who stayed overnight. The Museum's installation omits a bed—which was surely a fine one, fully curtained and richly trimmed—because we have no appropriate bedstead in the collection. The beautifully veneered six-legged high chest, which would have held clothes, and the dressing table with a large imported English mirror above it indicate the activities that took place in the chamber.

The gateleg center table, on which refreshments could be served, is covered with a "Turkey carpitt." At the time Oriental rugs were such expensive luxuries that they were always used as table covers, never on the floor.

Most of the chairs in the room are lined up against the walls. Until the end of the nineteenth century, when furniture groupings came into fashion, it was customary to keep the center of a room uncluttered and to bring furniture to the area where it was needed. The English caned pieces in the William and Mary style seen here would have been typical possessions of a wealthy man such as Wentworth; it is documented that large suites of this type of seating were ordered from England at about this time. A caned daybed like the one seen here was often part of a suite. All these pieces are cushioned in green wool in the early-eighteenth-century manner. Inventories of the period often referred to rooms, especially chambers, by the color of the fabric used for the matching bed hangings, curtains, and cushions. Window curtains were uncommon this early in the century, but if they were used, it would have been in the bedchamber. The examples here are copied from a French engraving of about 1700 and are probably somewhat grander than the type the Wentworths would have had.

AMELIA PECK

This handsome high chest is one of the earliest versions of the highboy form, which would evolve over the next century in America. The vigorous carving of the legs and the use of fancy veneered surfaces are typical of the William and Mary style.

The Hewlett Room

WOODBURY, NEW YORK ♦ 1740–60

The fireplace wall paneling and the double door of the Hewlett room were the first colonial American architectural elements collected by the Metropolitan Museum. They were a gift in 1910 of Mrs. Robert W. de Forest, the wife of a vice president of the Museum's board of trustees. Robert de Forest later became president of the Museum, and in 1922 he and his wife donated the funds to build the American Wing. In his speech at the opening of the wing on November 10, 1924, de Forest described how he and his wife began to collect American decorative arts soon after their marriage almost fifty years earlier, and how they became convinced that what they termed "American domestic art" merited a place in the Museum.

Although many collectors became interested in American decorative arts and architecture in the decades following the 1876 Centennial Exposition in Philadelphia, the Colonial Revival wave reached its crest when the Metropolitan opened its American Wing. Many of the exhibits, including the Hewlett room, still bear the stamp of the Colonial Revival impulse, which tended to romanticize the lives and lifestyles of the American colonists. Although the writings and exhibits of the Colonial Revivalists did not convey a wholly accurate picture of pre-Revolutionary America, we are grateful to these early collectors, as they were responsible for raising the public's awareness of the objects and architecture that were too often discarded or demolished as America swiftly grew in the last decades of the nineteenth century and the beginning of the twentieth.

De Forest was aware that the practice of taking rooms out of standing houses was not universally condoned. He stated in his address, "Some of you when you see our original interiors . . . may be tempted to accuse us of vandalism. Not so; we have brought these rooms to our Museum to preserve them. There is not a single one of them which we would not have gladly left in place if there had been any reasonable chance of preserving it there . . . all would have been destroyed sooner or later unless we had given them a refuge." Although this may not have been precisely the case with all the rooms collected by the Museum in the early years of the century, it was true of the Hewlett room. The property had passed out of the Hewlett family by 1910, when the paneling was sold to Mrs. de Forest. Soon after that, the property was bought by the architect Philip Goodwin, who tore the old house down in 1916, replacing it with a grand French château.

ABOVE:
The Hewlett house, about 1910

OPPOSITE:
The Hewlett room. The grisaille-painted *kas,* with its sumptuous garlands of fruit, is thought to have once belonged to the Hewlett family. The New York-made table holds pieces of pewter and an English tin-glazed earthenware punch bowl. The looking glass is probably English.

ABOVE:

Dutch tin-glazed earthenware tile
of 1700–1750. This is one of many
tiles that surround the opening of
the Hewlett room fireplace. Most
are decorated with scenes from
the Bible; this tile depicts Noah
herding the animals onto the ark.
Stories from both the Old and the
New Testament are represented,
and some tiles even have inscriptions that refer to the verse they
illustrate.

RIGHT:

Fireplace wall. The rare leather-
covered cradle was made in New
York City for Rachel and Derick
Brinkerhoff just before the birth of
their first child, Isaac, in 1762.
Some of the other pieces of furniture in the room are also notable
for their original finishes and
coverings.

Unfortunately, no one adequately recorded the appearance of the interior of the Hewlett house before it was destroyed. The paneling appears to be from the parlor of a Dutch colonial-style house built for the John Hewlett family during the mid-eighteenth century. One of the few existing photographs of the exterior shows a five-bay-wide, one-and-a-half-story house on a raised stone basement. There is a chimney at each end, and a wide sweeping roof extends over a porch at the front of the house. In the May 1911 Museum *Bulletin* Norman Morrison Isham discussed the acquisition of the paneling and described the plan of the house as having four rooms on the main floor with our parlor and a hall at the front of the house and two additional rooms behind them at the rear. He wrote that houses like the Hewlett's had no center hall; the staircase to the second floor was placed "either in the corner of the smaller room or [was] a mere ladder to the loft, [which] appeared in a sort of rear entry partitioned off from the rest of the house." Isham did not claim to have seen the house, and the plan he described seems highly unusual (even unlikely) to architectural scholars today. If the house was set up in such a manner, the front door would have led directly into one of the formal front rooms.

The Museum's files reveal that an effort was made to reproduce the original wooden cornice and wainscot for installation in the room. There is no evidence that the windows were copied from the house (those that appear in the photograph are early nineteenth century in scale), and we do not know the original relationship of the fireplace wall to the windows or to the double door. Even the size of the original room is not known.

The fireplace wall itself seems mostly accurate. Some minor changes to the woodwork may have been made in the early nineteenth century, but on the whole the wall is a good example of the type of paneling found in the homes of well-established Long Islanders. It is an unsophisticated interpretation, probably by a local craftsman, of the type of classical design found in eighteenth-century English architectural pattern books. The two small

Detail of the paneled fireplace wall

pilasters, which in spite of their heavy entablatures rest on thin air, are a particularly amusing detail.

It is interesting that this English-influenced paneling was found in a Dutch colonial-style house. Long Island was settled by both the Dutch and the English. Originally, the Dutch from New Netherland (New York after 1664) settled in the western part of Long Island, and the English from the New England colonies settled in the eastern end of Long Island. By the eighteenth century the middle part of Long Island, where this house stood, was occupied by both groups. The Hewletts were an English family (and fiercely Loyalist during the American Revolution), yet they shared traditions with their Dutch neighbors, as can be seen in the exterior architecture of their house. The Hewletts are also said to have owned the *kas* that now stands in the room, a distinctive furniture form introduced by the Dutch and used as a storage cupboard for linens. This extremely practical object was adopted by many English families on Long Island, as well as by those in the Hudson River Valley, another area settled first by the Dutch. The grisaille-painted decoration simulated the carving found on the finest Dutch and Flemish *kasten*.

The paneled wall of the room is painted bright blue, based on a paint analysis done on the woodwork when the American Wing was reinstalled in 1980. This intense color was quite common at the time, as was the deep orange used in the china cupboard, a shade based on evidence found in a similar piece at the Obadiah Smith house in Kings Park, Long Island. The English and Dutch tin-glazed earthenware found in the china cupboard again illustrates the close relationship of the English and the Dutch in this part of Long Island. In keeping with the style of the times, New York-made pewter, continental brass, and tin-glazed earthenware are displayed on top of the kas. The tiles around the fireplace opening are also of Dutch tin-glazed earthenware and depict scenes from the Bible; these tiles are not original to the fireplace, but this type of tile was readily available in America after the 1720s. It is not known from what example the Hewlett room's fireplace opening and hearth were copied; if the opening was lined with expensive Dutch tiles, it is unlikely that they would have been placed four rows deep.

AMELIA PECK

Turned chairs of this type were made in great numbers in New York City and the Hudson River Valley beginning about 1750. This side chair is branded TVV for its owner, who may have been a member of the Van Vechten family. The chair's maker, Michael Smith, also proudly branded his own name on top of the front legs.

The Powel Room

PHILADELPHIA, PENNSYLVANIA ◆ 1765–66

The town house from which our room was taken stands today at 244 South Third Street in Philadelphia. It was built in 1765–66 for a Scottish shipmaster and merchant named Charles Stedman (1713–1784). He seems to have arrived in Philadelphia soon after 1746, joining in partnership with his older brother, Alexander. After about twenty years of success in a variety of businesses, including an ironworks and real estate, the brothers' fortunes began to decline. Stedman placed advertisements in *The Pennsylvania Gazette* in 1766, probably just after his house was completed, offering it for sale along with other real-estate holdings. The house was eventually sold, on August 2, 1769, to Samuel Powel (1738–1793) for £3150. Powel was married five days later to Elizabeth Willing, and he undoubtedly purchased the house for himself and his bride.

   Samuel Powel was a wealthy, privileged young man who came from one of the best-established families in Philadelphia. After graduating from the College of Philadelphia (later the University of Pennsylvania) in 1759, he embarked on a Grand Tour of Europe, a trip that had become, by the middle of the eighteenth century, an essential part of a gentleman's education. Powel's tour was unusually long: he stayed in Europe for seven years. During his travels he became interested in, among other things, what he called "the venerable remains of Antiquity," and in a portrait painted by the gifted

ABOVE:
The Powel house is a public museum today.

LEFT:
This punch bowl, unusual in that it has both a matching cover and a stand, is one of the most impressive forms of Chinese export porcelain whose ownership can be documented to colonial America. It belonged to Mary Brandford Bull of Charleston, South Carolina, at her death in 1772; in 1790 it was brought to Philadelphia by one of her descendants.

OPPOSITE:
The Powel room has been furnished as a parlor set up for an elegant tea. The portrait hanging above the fireplace is that of Mrs. Thomas Harwood; it was painted by the Philadelphia artist Charles Willson Peale (1741–1827).

ABOVE:
The fireplace wall before it was removed from the house in 1917

OPPOSITE LEFT:
This highly ornamental silver hot-water urn was crafted in 1766 by Louisa Courtauld (1729–1807) in London. It sits on a small but finely carved Philadelphia stand table. The mantel shelf is decorated with soft-paste porcelain figures from Derby, England, depicting John Wilkes and Mrs. Catharine Macaulay.

OPPOSITE RIGHT:
A marble-topped slab table sits against the wall between the two windows. Tables like this one were used for serving food and drink, since marble is impervious to heat and moisture. A looking glass was often hung between two windows to catch and reflect light. This gilded example was made in England between 1745 and 1780.

English artist Angelica Kauffmann (1741–1807), he holds in his hand an architectural plan for an unidentified building. It is not known if architecture was truly a passion of his; what is abundantly evident is that he was very interested in the appearance of the interiors of his house.

When the Powels took possession of Stedman's house, it was only four years old but clearly not as grand as they wished. They proceeded to hire many of the finest craftsmen in Philadelphia to embellish and elaborate on the rooms that Stedman had decorated in a relatively simple manner. They engaged carpenter-builder Robert Smith (ca. 1722–1777) to improve on the paneling and woodwork; Smith employed four different carvers—including Hercule Courtenay, partners Nicholas Bernard and Martin Jugiez, and James Reynolds—to make additional embellishments to the rooms. Records also reveal that craftsmen were hired for painting and "bordering" (the application of papier-mâché decorative motifs below the cornice), as well as marble workers to make the fireplace surrounds. The work of some of them can still be seen in the Museum's room.

During the Powels' residence in the house, it was one of the social centers of Philadelphia, and indeed of all the colonies. Samuel Powel served in many public capacities, most notably as the last mayor of Philadelphia under British rule and the first after the Revolution. His house was frequently visited by such luminaries as George Washington and John Adams, who called the house a "splendid seat." When the Metropolitan Museum bought the room in 1917, it was the association with these great men of the American Revolution, as well as the fine quality of the Georgian-style woodwork, that made it an attractive acquisition.

In order to illustrate the impact of the Colonial Revival on the way Americans view the past, the Powel room today remains much the same as it was when the American Wing opened in 1924. It is furnished as an ornate parlor, although its original function is still uncertain. The main part of Powels' town house, which held the formal rooms, was three bays wide and three stories high. A long narrow wing, which held the kitchens, additional bedrooms, and servants' quarters, was attached at the back. The first floor of the main part of the house contained two rooms with a passage to one side; the front was probably used as a parlor and the back for dining. The second floor held the grandest space in the house—a ballroom that ran the full width of the front of the building—which can now be seen at the Philadelphia Museum of Art. What is now the Metropolitan's parlor was located behind the ballroom; although it has been surmised that this was used for refreshments of some type, recent scholarship indicates that it may actually have served as the best chamber, or bedroom, in the house. The third floor held additional bedchambers.

When the Metropolitan acquired the room, the house had not belonged to the Powel family for over a hundred years. The owner in 1917 was

using the house as a manufactory and shop for horsehair products. The interior detailing of the first floor had been removed in the 1880s, and the second-floor ballroom was only partially intact. However, the Museum's acquisition, the back of the second floor, was for the most part complete. As installed, it is accurate in size and layout, except for a door that was added to allow Museum visitors to circulate. The paneled fireplace wall is clearly the main focus. The basic design of the mantel and overmantel (the paneling above the mantel) was commonly found in mid-eighteenth-century Philadelphia houses and was probably the work of Stedman's builders, but the richly carved ornamentation was most likely added in Powel's day. (When the room was acquired, some of the woodwork in the center tablet of the mantel had been lost; the twentieth-century reproduction now there lacks the crispness of what remains of the original carving on other parts of the mantel.) The carving has been highlighed in green; the evidence for this verdigris (copper acetate) glaze was found in a small rosette in the "ear" of one of the door frames. The light gray paint on the woodwork is appropriate to the period, but no evidence has been found to confirm an exact shade.

The Chinese wallpaper is of the period but not original; there is no evidence that the room was ever papered at all. The Powel house was saved from destruction in 1931 by the Philadelphia Society for the Preservation of Landmarks, which had been newly formed to save the house. One of the people most involved in its survival and subsequent restoration was Miss Frances A. Wister, who wrote to the Museum in 1949 that the plaster walls of the room had originally been painted a "beautiful blue." The Chinese wallpaper, however, has remained on the walls in order to illustrate the ideal colonial parlor in the eyes of the Museum's earlier curators.

The ceiling is another Colonial Revival confection. The Powel room originally had a plain ceiling, but the ballroom was decoratively stuccoed in 1770 by James Clow. In 1922–23 impressions were taken from that ceiling; the plaster elements were installed more closely together than their original design in order to fit into the considerably smaller Museum room.

The red damask draperies have a touch of the Colonial Revival in their pagodalike valances, undoubtedly designed to harmonize with the Chinese wallpaper. The English eighteenth-century needlework rug is a superb example, although it seems likely from bills for floor coverings found with the Powel family papers that the rooms were originally fitted out with less expensive types of carpets, laid over the original yellow-pine floors.

The pieces of furniture here are all high-style examples that might have been found in the parlor of one of Philadelphia's wealthiest families. They were all made in Philadelphia in the Rococo style popularized by Thomas Chippendale, and they feature the delicate, intricate carving and curving cabriole legs associated with Chippendale. None of the furniture was actually owned by the Powel family; no inventory of their house has ever been found, but other documents seem to confirm that the Powels furnished their home with a mixture of American-made pieces and English examples purchased by Samuel during his Grand Tour.

AMELIA PECK

This mahogany tilt-top tea table holds all the accoutrements for serving afternoon tea, a meal that had become a formal social ritual by the time the Powels furnished this room. The cross-stitched wool carpet was made in England in 1764; in addition to its floral and geometric motifs, it is inscribed with quotations from Edward Young's *Night Thoughts* (1742–45).

The Van Rensselaer Hall

ALBANY, NEW YORK ◆ 1765–69

This large entrance hall, one of the most magnificent domestic spaces built in pre-Revolutionary America, was originally part of the Van Rensselaer family manor house. The Van Rensselaers were a major power in the history of New York State from the time Dutch merchant Killiaen van Rensselaer began to purchase land around Albany in 1630. Killiaen was a member of the governing board of the Dutch West India Company, and, as a stockholder in the company, he had been given the opportunity to purchase land from the Indians if he could form a colony of at least fifty people over the age of fifteen on his property within four years. He did so and was given the title patroon (the Dutch equivalent of "lord of the manor") and the authority to govern almost all aspects of his tenants' lives. In this age-old feudal system, which lasted on these lands into the mid-nineteenth century, the tenants paid for the privilege of living on the patroon's land by providing him with crops and services.

Although there were other Dutch landowners in New Netherland in the 1630s, very few had holdings as large as the Van Rensselaer estate. At the

OPPOSITE:
Detail of the English wallpaper in the Van Rensselaer hall. This section of the paper, which was hand-painted in tempera, is copied from a French print depicting Spring, engraved by Nicolas de Larmessin (1684–1756) after a painting by Nicolas Lancret (1690–1745). All Four Seasons are represented in the room by paintings in Rococo-style cartouches.

BELOW:
This late-19th-century photograph shows the final appearance of the manor house after numerous remodelings. During the last campaign, in 1842–43, the wings and porch seen here were added to the house by noted New York City architect Richard Upjohn (1802–1878).

OVERLEAF:
The center of the Van Rensselaer hall is furnished with a large mahogany dining table made in New York City about 1760–90, surrounded by chairs from a set that descended in the Verplanck family. New York-made Rococo furniture is more compact in appearance and heavier in construction than 18th-century furniture made in Pennsylvania and New England.

This door, which now connects the Van Rensselaer hall with the Marmion room, once led into a parlor or dining room. A marble-topped slab table stands to the right of the door, and to the left is one of a pair of tassel-back side chairs that was originally owned by the Van Rensselaer family and may have once furnished the manor house. The large rectangular scene depicts Naples with Mount Vesuvius in the distance; a winter scene is within the cartouche.

time of its greatest size, the property extended forty miles from east to west, twenty-four miles north to south, and was bisected by the Hudson River. The original manor house (1651) and the two that succeeded it were built in what is today the city of Albany, an area approximately at the center of the Van Rensselaer lands.

The Museum's hall is from the third manor house, which was commissioned by Stephen Van Rensselaer II, a young man about whom very little is known. He was born in 1742, and by the time the house was begun, he had already married Catharine Livingston, daughter of Philip Livingston, a powerful New York City merchant and later one of the signers of the Declaration of Independence. Van Rensselaer died in 1769, soon after the house was finished.

The manor was started on May 13, 1765, a date known with precision because an account book for work done on the house between 1765 and about 1820 has survived. Unfortunately, no architect is mentioned in connection with the 1765–69 program. Because the house was remodeled a number of times during the nineteenth century, it is difficult to describe its exact eighteenth-century appearance. It seems to have been a dignified Georgian structure located on a site overlooking the Hudson River, similar to some of

the few great houses of the period that still stand, such as the Schuyler mansion (1761–62), also in Albany, and the Jeremiah Lee house (1768) in Marblehead, Massachusetts. Built of unusually large American-made bricks, the Van Rensselaer house had a seven-bay, two-story facade, with small dormer windows piercing the gently hipped roof. The three central bays were treated as a slightly projecting block capped with a pediment. After entering the front door, the visitors would find themselves in the great hall, which was twenty-three feet six inches wide by forty-six feet ten inches long and ran the full depth of the house. Four rooms opened off the entrance hall; although descriptions of their eighteenth-century functions have not survived, it is likely that there were two parlors, a dining room, and an office from which the estate's vast holdings were administered.

A beautifully carved archway, which once led to a narrower stair hall, pierces the center of one of the long walls. The carving on the spandrels of the archway was closely derived from Plate 12 in *A New Book of Ornaments, with Twelve Leaves,* by Matthias Lock and H. Copland, originally published in London in 1752 and reissued in 1768, when its Rococo designs were received with delight by a wider upper-middle-class audience. The quality of the

This ornate carved archway at the center of one of the room's long walls originally framed the entrance to the narrower stair hall. The cartouches on the wallpaper encircle scenes representing spring and summer.

carving is so exceptional that it is unlikely to have been produced by a local Albany craftsman. The spandrels were probably not carved on the site at all but in New York City by a skilled English-trained carver and then shipped upriver. Stephen and Catharine Van Rensselaer certainly had excellent connections to goods and services available in the city through her father. This is amply illustrated by the magnificent English hand-painted scenic wallpaper that graces the walls of the room, one of only three such sets known.

The Museum owns a fascinating letter that was sent by Philip Livingston in New York City to Stephen Van Rensselaer in Albany on October 12, 1768:

> I send You by Capt: Van Alen a Box Markd: P. which Contains 4 Marble slabs which I ordered for You from Holland the Cost of them is as pr: Accot: Inclosed £18.0.10 I Also send a small Case Marked P. which Contains paper for your Hall which Cost £38.12.8½ for both which sum I have debited Your Accot: I wish they may please You. the directions how to place the paper is in the Box & You must take special Care if You Open it to look at, that it be putt up as You found it, with the Letters on the outside I Opened it and think it very Handsome indeed.

On the back of the letter is a floor plan of the hall with all the openings for doors and windows carefully delineated. The plan had been sent to the maker of the wallpaper, who sold his wares through the London merchants Neate and Pigou, so that he might fit the paper panels exactly to the hall. The plan has been marked by the manufacturer with a letter key so that each scene or

The Marmion room, King George County, Virginia. Paneled about 1735–70 and painted 1770–80, this small parlor was taken from a plantation house on the northern neck of Virginia. It is displayed without furnishings in order to call attention to what may be the most ambitious painted decorative scheme to survive from 18th-century America. The wall design includes marbleized architectural detailing with large panels painted with imaginary landscapes and trompe-l'oeil stands overflowing with fruit. Both the adjacent Van Rensselaer hall and the Marmion room demonstrate the importance placed by well-to-do Americans of the 18th century on elegantly decorated wall surfaces.

decorative trophy could be installed in the right place.

The long walls are decorated with large painted views of classical Italian ruins based on engravings of paintings by such artists as Gian Paolo Pannini (1691–1764) and Joseph Vernet (1714–1789). These alternate with smaller representations of the Four Seasons after engravings of paintings by Nicolas Lancret (1690–1745). Trophies of the Four Elements, after engravings of paintings by Maurice Jacques (ca. 1712–1784), flank the front and back doors of the house. All of the scenes (which are surrounded with trompe-l'oeil Rococo-style frames) and trophies are painted in grisaille with tempera against a yellow background. This color was once a deep ocher, but in the nineteenth century it was overpainted with yellow calcimine. The reproduction of engravings in wallpaper, rather than the paintings on which they were based, reflects the great popularity of prints for use in decorating during the mid-eighteenth century.

The furniture is not original to the room, although several of the pieces were once owned by the Van Rensselaer family. In the eighteenth century, a hall usually contained utilitarian furniture that would not be harmed by wet or dusty clothes of people coming in from outdoors. As installed in the American Wing, the hall has been used as a gallery to show New York-made Rococo furniture.

The great Van Rensselaer estate was broken up by the late nineteenth century. The manor house was dismantled in 1893 after the Erie Canal, a series of railroad tracks, and the growing industrial city of Albany had totally hemmed in the property. The woodwork from the Museum's hall was installed in the dining room of a new house in Albany owned by a Van Rensselaer descendant. His widow gave the woodwork to the Museum in 1928, the same year the room's original wallpaper was donated by another member of the Van Rensselaer family. The four small doors that once led to other rooms were donated soon afterward from yet another source; more recently, research has confirmed that they were made during one of the house's later remodelings. Today, all of these elegant elements stand together as a reminder of the patroonships of old New York.

AMELIA PECK

The Verplanck Room

COLDENHAM, NEW YORK ♦ 1767

Although furnished with the eighteenth-century possessions of the well-to-do Verplanck family of New York City, this room was actually taken from the Orange County home of the Coldens, another family that figured prominently in the history of pre-Revolutionary New York. In 1939 the Verplancks offered to the Metropolitan Museum many possessions once owned by Samuel Verplanck (1739–1820). The primary condition of the gift was that the collection be exhibited in a room set aside for that purpose. To this end, the curators of the Museum purchased the paneling of the best parlor from the then-derelict, and since-destroyed, home of Cadwallader Colden Jr. (ca. 1721–1797). The room in Samuel Verplanck's home, where this furniture was originally placed, was probably more elegant and ornate than the one it occupies today, but no New York City parlors have survived from the eighteenth century. Therefore, when the Colden house room became available, it fit the Verplanck furniture in date and in New York associations, even if it did not reflect exactly the same level of sophistication and affluence.

When the Colden house was built in 1767, it stood within the three-

OPPOSITE:
The Verplanck room has a fully paneled fireplace wall. To the right of the fireplace, there is a small concealed closet, which contains hooks for hanging clothes.

THE COLDEN MANSION
Res. of LINDLEY M. FERRIS, Coldenham.

LEFT:
The Colden house, about 1855. This view appeared on a printed mid-19th-century map showing Orange and Rockland counties in New York State.

Samuel Verplanck's portrait by John Singleton Copley (1738–1815) was painted in 1771, when the sitter was about 33 years old. He is thought to have commissioned the suite of parlor furniture now displayed in the room.

Gulian Verplanck (1751–1815), Samuel's younger brother, was also painted by Copley. As many as six members of the Verplanck family may have been portrayed by Copley when the artist visited New York in 1771.

OPPOSITE:
The Verplanck suite of mahogany parlor furniture consists of a card table, six side chairs, and a high-backed settee. The suite is linked by the matching design of the cabriole legs on each piece.

thousand-acre family farm in Coldenham, a few miles west of Newburgh, New York. Cadwallader Colden Jr.'s father was a noted scientist and the lieutenant governor of New York State from 1760 until his death in 1776. His son David and daughter Jane pursued scholarly careers, but, according to family history, Cadwallader Jr. was always interested in farming, and so his father gave him title to five hundred acres of the family farm in 1744, when he was about twenty-three. He built a house and a barn on the land and soon after married Elizabeth Ellison, the daughter of a local merchant. About twenty years later, in 1767, Cadwallader and Elizabeth Colden built a second house on the property. Although no records have survived from the building of that house, it bore a date stone (now preserved at a local school) inscribed: "BUILT BY IW AND G MANY BRS 1767." The initials stand for James (a barred letter "I" was used instead of a "J" in the eighteenth century), Wines, and Gabriel Many, three brothers who, although born in New York City, probably lived in nearby Hamptonburgh.

No images of the 1767 house have survived, but from the physical evidence available in 1940, when the paneling was removed from the much-enlarged structure, the original rough stone house was two stories high, five bays wide, and only one room deep. The first floor consisted of two parlors, one on each side of the central hall. There were two chambers above the parlors and a basement kitchen below the east parlor. The Museum's paneling came from the west parlor. The room's fireplace wall has a simple yet elegant "earred" mantelpiece and overmantel, flanked by a narrow closet with hooks at the back for hanging clothing on the right and a china cupboard on the left decorated at the top with a very unusual shell. Instead of the usual rounded cove with fanning ribs (like that in the Hewlett room), the elements of the Colden house's shell are applied flat against the inside top of the cupboard, where its intricacies are difficult to view. This rather eccentric shell can also be found in the china cupboards of two other houses in the area; they are all undoubtedly the work of a rural carpenter who was not well acquainted with the accepted appearance of this type of cupboard. The other three walls of the room have a paneled dado under the chair rail, and a finely carved cornice runs around the room's perimeter.

When the room was installed in the Museum in 1941, the walls with the door and the single window were lengthened by about four feet to accommodate the Verplanck furniture. In the current installation, in order to allow visitors to enter, the placement of the door had to be switched with the window on the opposite wall. The plaster walls have been whitewashed, and the woodwork is painted a blue-gray color that was much used in this period. Recent paint analysis has revealed that the paneling originally may have been painted yellow. The vermilion color inside the china cabinet is the same as it was when the house was built.

The suite of Verplanck furniture in the Museum's installation is a

The William and Mary-style japanned secretary desk and the gilded Rococo looking glass are English. Their presence in the room is a reminder of the great quantity of imported furniture that originally graced fine colonial interiors.

This china cupboard displays a Chinese-export porcelain dinner service, which descended in the Verplanck family.

rare example of survival. Originally the property of merchant Samuel Verplanck (whose portrait by John Singleton Copley hangs in the room), the card table, six side chairs, and upholstered settee were all made in the same New York City shop. The treatment of the legs on all the pieces is identical—no other matching set of American Chippendale parlor furniture is known. The suite and many of the other objects here were originally used in Samuel Verplanck's substantial town house, which was built by Samuel's father, Gulian Verplanck Sr., sometime before 1750 and stood at no. 3 Wall Street in New York City. (Interestingly, the Verplanck house was demolished in 1822 to make way for the building of the Branch Bank of the United States. The facade of the bank became the front of the American Wing in 1924.) In 1763, soon after he returned from a trip to Amsterdam, during which he married his Dutch cousin Judith Crommelin, Samuel took possession of the house and most likely purchased the suite of furniture for his new home's parlor.

Another piece of furniture of particular note in the room is the red-and-gold japanned William and Mary secretary desk of about 1700–1720. This piece was brought from England in the early 1750s by Sir Danvers Osborn, the royal governor of New York, who committed suicide soon after taking up his post and whose effects were sold in Manhattan in 1753. The secretary was purchased by Lieutenant Governor James De Lancey, the grandfather of Mrs. Daniel Crommelin Verplanck, Samuel's daughter-in-law. The large, elaborately carved Rococo mirror that hangs between the two windows was also imported from England; mirrors of this scale and ambition were rarely made in America before the nineteenth century.

The pumpkin-colored wool damask used for the upholstery and window hangings is a reproduction of a fabric owned by the Verplancks. It was certainly imported from Europe (perhaps from Flanders), and the large scale of the pattern indicates that it was designed in the early part of the eighteenth century. When the room was installed in the American Wing in 1941, the period fabric (which had been sewn into curtains by the Verplanck family many years before it was donated) was used for upholstery. The window valances are reproductions of valances given by the family in 1939; all of the original fabric wore out after it was installed in the room and was replaced with a reproduction during the mid-1960s.

A major rift occurred in the Verplanck family during the Revolutionary War. Samuel, a fifth-generation New Yorker, was a supporter of the Revolutionary cause, while Judith, who had been born and bred under the monarchy of Holland, remained a Loyalist. When the British occupied Manhattan in 1776, Samuel retired to Fishkill, New York, where he remained until his death in 1820. Judith, however, chose to stay in the Wall Street house, where she maintained a friendship with Lord William Howe, commander-in-chief of the British forces. After being accused of setting a bad example due to "dissipation and high play," Howe was recalled to England. After he left New York, he sent Judith such presents as a set of French porcelain and two paintings by Angelica Kauffmann depicting Venus and Eros. Apparently, Judith never rejoined Samuel in Fishkill after the war. Following her death in 1803, the Wall Street house was closed and most of the furnishings were sent to Fishkill, where they remained until they found a new home at the Museum in 1939.

AMELIA PECK

One of a pair of 18th-century porcelain hearth jars made in China for the Western market. Although these jars descended in the Verplanck family, they came to the Museum 30 years after the room was first installed.

The Haverhill Room

HAVERHILL, MASSACHUSETTS ◆ ABOUT 1805

In the early years of the nineteenth century, James Duncan Jr. (1756–1822) and his wife, the former Rebekah White (1754–1838), built an elegant house for themselves on Main Street in Haverhill, a small but thriving town on the Merrimack River. The Duncan family had been merchants for two generations before James Jr. joined the family business; together with his father and brothers, he helped expand the business to encompass shipping, distilleries, real estate, and a chain of stores that followed the river upstream into New Hampshire.

The Duncans' new house, from which this room was taken, seems to have been typical of many homes of wealthy merchant families in Haverhill, as well as of those in the nearby centers of Newburyport, Massachusetts, and Portsmouth, New Hampshire. The building was greatly altered in the mid-nineteenth century, when it was expanded into a hotel, and it was torn down in 1910. Its original appearance has been determined by looking at other early-nineteenth-century houses in the area and at Duncan family documents.

We can assume that James Jr. and Rebekah built their new home in about 1805, because Duncan family descendants still possess invoices dated between 1805 and 1807 that pertain to its furnishing. Like many other houses along the North Shore of Massachusetts, it was three stories high, five bays wide, covered in clapboard, and topped by a low-pitched hipped roof. The main part was only one room deep, but an ell that ran behind it on the right contained a dining room and a kitchen. There were two parlors, one on either side of a center hall on the first floor, and two family bedrooms on

OPPOSITE:
The Haverhill room is furnished as a high-style bedroom and prominently features a Boston-made bed from about 1808–12 attributed to the workshop of Thomas Seymour. The bed's cornices, which are painted with bouquets of flowers and highlighted with gilding, are thought to be the work of painter John Penniman and picture-frame maker John Doggett.

In 1842 and again in 1852, the house from which the Museum's room was taken was expanded into Eagle House, the hotel seen in this turn-of-the-century photograph. The hotel used the two parlors from the original 1805 house as an office and reception room. The structure was demolished in 1910.

Many of the pieces of furniture in the Haverhill room, such as the dressing table and the dressing glass at the right, are inlaid with contrasting wood veneers, revealing a distinctive regional preference of Federal-period Boston and Salem cabinetmakers. Both objects are made of dark mahogany with birch veneer. The vase-back side chair, attributed to Samuel McIntire of Salem, sits in front of the dressing table. The dwarf tall clock in the corner is thought to have been made about 1780 by Samuel Mulliken of Newburyport.

both the second and third floors. The servants probably slept in attic bedrooms above the kichen ell. The Museum's room was originally one of the first-floor parlors, probably the more formal of the two, which would have been used for entertaining.

The interior of the house reflected the growing influence of the designs of the English brothers Robert and James Adam, two of architecture's greatest interpreters of Neoclassicism. Based on their knowledge of Greek and especially of Roman antiquities, their book *Works in Architecture* (1773–78) was well known in America by the end of the eighteenth century. The Adam brothers' elegant ornament and elaborate color schemes appealed to well-to-do families up and down the East Coast. The mantelpiece in the Museum's Haverhill room, with its delicate detached columns and urns and swags of molded composition, typifies the best of early Neoclassicism on the American continent. However, the design of the overmantel and the interwoven fret design of the frieze can be found in plates from William Pain's *The Practical Builder*, a simpler pattern book than the Adam brothers' volume, published first in London in 1774 but probably known in the Haverhill area through its fourth edition, which was printed and sold in Boston in 1792.

An inventory of the house made after James Jr.'s death in 1822 recorded in the best parlor: "2 Large Gilt frame Looking Glasses $140, Mirror $50, Sofa $30, 8 Chairs & 2 Settees $60, Brussels Carpet $100, 1 pair Card tables $30, 4 Glass Candle Sticks $10, fire Sett $12, 6 suits Window Curtains $60." The total value of these furnishings was $492, more than any other room.

This simple list provides us with many clues about the parlor's original architecture and decoration. The room had six windows to hold the "6 suits Window Curtains" (a "suit" probably indicating a multilayered window drapery, much like the ones seen in the present installation). One of the walls had a door that opened into the hall, and the fireplace wall stood opposite. The mantelpiece was flanked by two windows, as it is today, and two other windows pierced both the front and back walls of the house. Between each of these sets of windows, there stood a "Large Gilt frame Looking Glass," which must have reflected the light shed by the candles in the "4 Glass Candle Sticks." The mirror mentioned in the inventory was probably a girandole mirror like the one hanging over the mantel today. When guests arrived at the Duncan house for an evening's entertainment, the pair of card tables would have been pulled into the center of the room from their usual placement against the walls, and each table would have been surrounded by four chairs. The sofa and settees may also have been drawn into a grouping for guests who did not play cards, perhaps near the fireplace, where the brass "fire Sett" gleamed. A richly patterned Brussels (looped pile) carpet covered the floor from wall to wall.

Since so much information exists about the use of this room as a

Detail of a corner of a mantel

parlor, the question arises as to why it has been interpreted here as a bedroom. The answer lies in the history of its transfer to the Museum, which in 1912 bought from an antiques dealer the elements of both this room and another one (probably a bedroom) from the same house. When the dismantled rooms arrived at the Museum, it became clear that they were fragmentary, for some essential parts—such as doors and windows—were missing. Since the Duncan house had been razed two years earlier, the curators had no idea about the original size of the rooms or the location of window and door openings. When they were installed in the American Wing in 1924, the room we see today was interpreted as a best parlor, and the other was installed as a bedroom, holding a spectacular bed that had been purchased in 1918.

The bedroom, architecturally less interesting than the parlor, was removed from the wing in 1947 to make way for another period room, but the bed was deemed too important to be put into storage. Its frame has traditionally been attributed to the workshop of the great Boston cabinetmaker Thomas Seymour and its unusual gilded-and-painted cornices to framemaker John Doggett and decorative painter John Penniman. It was supposedly made for the daughter of merchant prince Elias Hasket Derby, a contemporary of James Duncan. The decision was made to convert the Haverhill parlor into a bedroom to hold this masterpiece. The 1822 Duncan inventory also contains a list for the master bedroom, which corresponds to the objects that are now on display. The list includes: "Bed Mattrass bedding bedstead Curtains & Cornish $100, 1 G [gilt?] Looking Glass $40, Easy Chair & Covering $8, 8 White flag [rush-seated] chairs $20, Toilet Table $3, Mahogany Bureau $20, 1 Carpet $30, Mahogany Wash Stand $10, 6 Window Curtains & Cornices $18, 1 G [gilt?] Brass Andiron $5." The room's contents were valued at $264. Although perhaps not quite as elaborate as the one in the room today, the Duncans' bed must have been quite grand; the average bed in the house was worth about twenty dollars.

The window and hangings give a good indication of the style of the period; white cotton fabrics were used extensively in decorating Federal-period bedrooms. The dressing table and mirror would have been draped as well. The flat-woven, or "ingrain," carpet is appropriate to a bedroom; this modern carpet was copied from that shown in a 1793 portrait by Joseph Steward of John Phillips in his New Hampshire home; however, that may have been a painted floor cloth rather than a carpet. Although nothing like them is mentioned in Duncan's inventory, the Massachusetts-carved figures of the Four Seasons on the mantel shelf add to the grace of the room.

AMELIA PECK

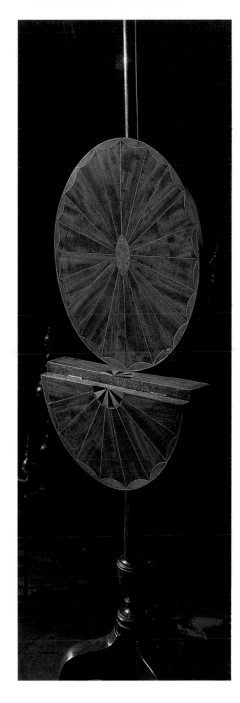

In the days when houses were warmed primarily by fires, screens were used in genteel homes to preserve a lady's delicate complexion by shielding her face from the direct heat. This exquisitely inlaid mahogany pole screen, with its unusual small hinged shelf meant for holding a candlestick, was made about 1785–95 and is attributed to cabinetmaker Samuel Phippen of Salem.

The Richmond Room

RICHMOND, VIRGINIA ◆ 1810

Richmond became the capital of Virginia in 1779. It was a small town, inhabited by only a few hundred people, but its location by the falls of the James River made it convenient for both trading and manufacturing. Tobacco, grain, and cotton brought from the western part of the state could be processed in Richmond before being shipped overseas to both Europe and South America. By 1810, when William Clayton Williams (d. 1817) built the house at 412 North Eighth Street from which our room was taken, the city's population had grown to almost ten thousand. Although we do not know how Williams became rich enough to build himself a grand house, it may be assumed that he was involved in some type of lucrative trade.

An inventory of Williams's goods taken after his death shows that he was wealthy enough to own seventeen slaves. The lot on which he built his house also held a stable and a brick office, from which he may have conducted his business. An 1811 tax assessment of these buildings was $12,800, a substantial sum at the time. One interesting fact known about Williams that seems most likely to unravel some of mysteries of this room is that his name appears on a committee involved with the furnishing of the newly built governor's mansion in 1813. His placement on this committee tells us that he was an important man in Richmond, probably a political insider, and was thought to have good taste, as well as the knowledge of what furnishings would be appropriate for the most important dwelling in the state.

OPPOSITE:
Although this elegant mahogany-and-rosewood pier table could be mistaken for a French example, the remnants of three labels from Charles-Honoré Lannuier (1779–1819) prove that it was made in New York City. The table's marble top is supported by two gilded swans, and its figured wood surface is further enlivened with gilt-bronze mounts and inlaid brass banding. A French gilt-bronze epergne and two English mahogany-and-glass candlesticks are on the table.

View of the Williams House, 412 North Eighth Street, in the 1920s. The columned porch and bracketed roof cornice were not original to the 1810 design; they were probably added after a fire destroyed the house's second story and roof. The building was demolished in 1936.

Upon closer study, we find many parallels between the Williams house and the governor's mansion. Built within three years of each other, they were close in size and have almost identical floor plans. A highly unusual feature of both plans is that the large central reception hall does not contain a staircase and has two doors at the rear. The very similar brick-clad exteriors of both were Federal in appearance, and each house was five bays wide and rose two full stories on a raised basement beneath a steeply pitched hipped roof. Both houses originally had fanlights above their front doors.

The architect of the governor's mansion, and perhaps also of the Williams house, was Alexander Parris (1780–1852), a native of Maine. In his later years Parris became known as one of the leading practitioners of the Greek Revival style; Quincy Market (1825) in Boston is one of his most famous buildings. When he arrived in Richmond to build a house for businessman John Bell, however, Parris's main inspiration was the work of Boston architect Charles Bulfinch (1763–1844), who worked in the Adamesque Neoclassical style. An early sketch for the governor's mansion bears a striking resemblance to Bulfinch's 1796 design for the first Harrison Gray Otis house in Boston.

Parris was paid fifty dollars to design the mansion. It is not known how much of the building's interior detailing he actually drew; it was common practice at the time for architects to be hired to design only the floor plan and four exterior elevations. Like the builder of the Haverhill house, the designers of the interiors at both the governor's mansion and the Williams house depended heavily on the works of William Pain. There are plates in Pain's *The Practical Builder* (first American edition, 1792) and *The Practical House Carpenter* (first American edition, 1796) that could have served as inspiration for the decorative detailing of both.

The signature of one "Theo. Nash" is carved into the top of a door frame in the room. Nash seems likely to have been the carpenter who worked on the interiors of the Williams house. All that is known about him to date is that his full first name was Theophilus; that he paid luxury tax on a watch in Richmond in 1815 and later lived in Petersburg, Virginia, where he worked on two houses in 1830; and that he lived in New Orleans between 1836 and 1854. It is not known if he served as a carpenter on the governor's mansion, although the quality of the woodwork in the Richmond room proves Nash was a very capable craftsman. Indeed, he was trusted with board upon board of imported Caribbean mahogany, a precious wood usually saved for fine cabinetmaking. It is the mahogany wainscoting and door and window surrounds that make the Richmond room so special; few other rooms of the period were finished in such expensive and beautiful wood. There was probably a mahogany mantelpiece in the room at one time as well; unfortunately, when the woodwork was given to the Museum in 1968, the mantel was not with it. (The Williams house was demolished in 1936; the woodwork for the

room was stored in a Pennsylvania barn for thirty years before it was presented to the Museum.) The marble caryatid mantelpiece here, although appropriate, probably dates from a few years later than the room.

Another striking feature of the present room is the scenic wallpaper. Entitled "The Monuments of Paris," the paper was designed in 1814 by Xavier Mader for the French manufacturer Joseph Dufour. It is not known if the original room was ever papered, but this pattern was offered for sale in Richmond during the period. It depicts the famous sites of Paris as if they stood together all in a row along the banks of the Seine. Since no complete set was available for the Museum to purchase, it was decided to reproduce the pattern, using existing wallpaper in a parlor in a house in Effingham, New Hampshire, as the primary model. More than two hundred color photographs were taken and spliced together to re-create the full panorama. Although the original was printed with handcut wood blocks, the reproduction wallpaper is silk-screened; more than one thousand screens were used for the complete series.

The room is furnished with some of the most high-style pieces in the American Wing's collection, including the work of New York City cabinet-makers Duncan Phyfe and Charles-Honoré Lannuier. Lannuier (1779–1819), who learned his trade in Paris before coming to New York in 1803, produced furniture based on the newest French Empire styles, while the Scottish-trained Phyfe (1768–1856) fashioned his work after English Regency models. It is likely that a man as wealthy as Williams would have purchased New York City furniture for his parlor; other Richmond gentlemen of the period, such as John Wickham, whose 1812 home is now part of the Valentine Museum, are known to have ordered pieces from Lannuier. The blue damask fabric used for both the window draperies and the upholstery is based on an eighteenth-century basket pattern that remains popular to this day.

AMELIA PECK

The floor in the Richmond room is covered with a French Aubusson carpet in the classical repeating-medallion design. The basket-pattern silk damask used to upholster the chairs and sofa is a copy of the fabric thought to be original to the suite of furniture. All the pieces are caned, with loose-cushion upholstery.

The Baltimore Dining Room

BALTIMORE, MARYLAND • ABOUT 1810

In the years just before and after the turn of the nineteenth century, Baltimore became a major Atlantic port. Its population almost tripled—from 13,500 in 1790 to 35,000 in 1800—and in 1797 it was officially designated a city. As the city grew around the harbor, street upon street of brick town houses were built. Many of these were constructed as attached row houses, in groupings of up to twenty. Freestanding structures like the one that originally contained our room were less common and were usually owned by relatively affluent citizens.

The town house at 913 East Pratt Street was substantial and basically typical of Baltimore. It was four bays wide and two and a half stories high; the half story at the top was a dormer-windowed attic. The house may have been built as an investment by the famous patriot and Declaration signer Charles Carroll of Carrollton, who, aside from owning immense estates totaling about eighty thousand acres, also had banking and real-estate interests. It is not known exactly when the house was built, but it existed by 1810, when it was sold by Carroll to Henry Craig (d. 1823), a merchant. Because Craig was not a famous man, only an incomplete record of his life can be pieced together. He seems to have been involved primarily in shipping goods, but he owned steamboats that conveyed passengers to and from Philadelphia as well.

Although the exterior of Craig's house was simple in appearance, the interior contained elegant rooms, which, while not overly ornate, were finely proportioned, following the new style of Neoclassicism popularized in Britain by the Adam brothers. It is not surprising that these designs were adopted by well-to-do Baltimorians, because the British were their primary trading partners. According to John Melish, an English visitor to Baltimore in 1806, "A great portion of the export trade is flour . . . and the citizens have a brisk trade in importing and reshipping foreign articles, particularly West India produce—rum, sugar, coffee. A great portion of the imports are manufactured goods from Britain." In addition to imported goods available at the time Henry Craig was moving into his home, Baltimore craftsmen, such as furniture makers John and Hugh Finlay, rose to the European challenge and began to produce highly sophisticated wares.

The first floor of Craig's town house held two formal rooms.

The Craig house, 913 East Pratt Street, in the early 20th century. The house was originally only two and a half stories high with a sloped roof and attic dormers; the third story and new cornice were added about 1875. The building was demolished in 1955.

OPPOSITE:
The use of elegantly simple geometric forms, such as the repeating ovals found in the mantel and wainscoting in the Baltimore dining room, characterizes the refinement of high-style Federal interiors. The room is decorated with American furniture from the Baltimore area, but, as would have been the case in the home of a well-to-do Baltimore merchant, many of the luxury items such as the English chandelier and matching candelabra that grace the mantel were imported. A 1796 portrait of William Kerin Constable by Gilbert Stuart (1755–1828) hangs over the fireplace..

One of a pair of looking glasses that hang in the niches flanking the fireplace. Made in Boston in about 1795–1810, the ornamented frames are of carved pine and wire coated with gilt gesso. A decorative *verre églomisé* tablet appears above the larger panel of plain mirrored glass.

RIGHT:
The mahogany dining table was made in Baltimore. It is not displayed with an appropriate tablecloth, since that would obscure the inlaid designs on the legs. The set of square-back chairs, which are upholstered in a durable cloth made of horsehair, were made in one of the southern or mid-Atlantic states. The floor cloth under the table is a modern reproduction.

This impressive mahogany sideboard is inlaid with satinwood, silver-coated copper, and *verre églomisé* panels. It is thought to have been made in either Baltimore or Philadelphia about 1815 for the Washington, D.C. home of General John P. Van Ness.

A side hall at the left ran straight through the house from front door to back, which opened to a yard. To the right of this hall, there was a parlor at the front and a narrower dining room behind overlooking a sliver of a side yard. Behind the dining room was a service area, and behind that the kitchen. While some grand Baltimore town houses were known to include formal drawing rooms on the second story that ran the full width of the front of the house, as in the Powel house (see page 191), Henry Craig was probably not high up enough on the social ladder to need a space of this type. His second floor most likely held only bedrooms, while the attic floor contained the servants' quarters.

Although the house was still occupied, in 1918 the Museum bought all the woodwork from the front parlor, including its original mantel, which had been moved into the dining room at some point; the carved archway from the hall; and a doorway that had been on the staircase landing. The archway and doorway were installed in 1924 in the central first-floor gallery of the American Wing, and the parlor was installed as one of the wing's original suite of period rooms. Although it had functioned as a parlor in the house, it was installed as a dining room in the Museum from the very beginning. One can assume that the Museum curators wished to display a dining room but chose to take the parlor from the house because it was larger and more architecturally decorative than the dining room, which, for example, had built-in cupboards on each side of the fireplace, while the parlor has arched niches. Few changes seem to have been made to the architecture of the parlor, except for the relocation of the doorway and the removal of a window that had once looked out on the side yard from the wall perpendicular to the left side of the fireplace.

This room illustrates how architects working in the early-nineteenth-century Neoclassical style preferred shallowly carved ornament that employed simple geometric forms. Although ornaments in this period were often molded out of compo, a mixture of plaster and other ingredients, all the decoration in this room was carved in pine. The oval motifs in the dado of the niches are repeated in the mantelpiece. Perhaps in reaction to the Rococo style, in which the mantel and the overmantel on its projecting chimney breast were dominant features, the architects of Neoclassical rooms often built the chimney flue deep into the wall and did away with the chimney breast entirely, as we see here. Lest these rooms seem too simple or austere, smooth plaster walls were often covered with painted decorations or, more commonly, with wallpaper. The first decades of the nineteenth century saw the perfecting of wallpaper manufacture in France by such firms as Zuber and Dufour and the establishment of an American wallpaper industry. When the woodwork seen here was scientifically analyzed in 1979, evidence was found that the room was originally wallpapered both above and below the chair rail.

A Baltimore-made dining table stands at the center of the room. Purchased in 1919, it may have been what inspired the American Wing's first curators to change the room from a parlor to a dining room. Its legs are inlaid with bellflowers in a carrot-shaped pendant, a motif often used by Baltimore cabinetmakers. The most imposing piece of furniture in the room is the highly decorated sideboard, a comparatively new form when the house was built. Until the nineteenth century, most Americans did not have formal rooms in their homes set aside just for dining. As more of them became wealthier, had more leisure time, and grew more interested in entertaining, dining rooms became more common. Sideboards were used for serving during a meal and for storing and displaying silverware (note the locking boxes on top). This sideboard was supposedly made for General John P. Van Ness, who in 1813 commissioned Benjamin Latrobe to build a large house for him in Washington, D.C. It is inlaid with silver and *verre églomisé* panels, with a marquetry griffin-and-swag design at center copied from Thomas Sheraton's *Drawing Book* (1793–94). A sideboard of this grandeur is unlikely to have been in Henry Craig's dining room.

The porcelain on the dining room table, which features the figure of Liberty, is part of an extremely rare French service made for the American market. A painted floor cloth has been laid under the table; a precursor of modern-day linoleum the easily cleaned floor cloth protected expensive carpeting or flooring from damage.

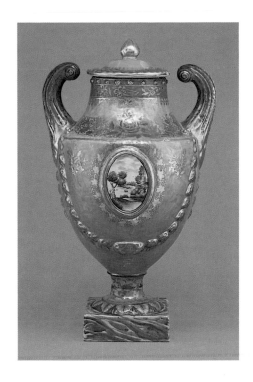

One of a pair of Chinese-made porcelain urns that sit on the pair of card tables in the niches on each side of the fireplace. Made for the Western market in about 1785–1815, they illustrate how Chinese craftsmen endeavored to create elegant wares based on European models. After 1785, when China entered into direct trade with America, many types of luxurious Chinese export objects, including lacquerware and silks, were proudly displayed in American homes.

AMELIA PECK

The Shaker Retiring Room

NEW LEBANON, NEW YORK • ABOUT 1830–40

In the years following the Revolutionary War, the practice of the Christian religion in America changed radically. As a direct aftermath of the fight for liberty against the British, the First Amendment to the Constitution was enacted on December 15, 1791, stating that "Congress shall make no law respecting an establishment of religion, or prohibiting the free exercise thereof." The official separation of church and state opened doors for far freer religious practices. The democratic and populist ideals that were formed in the wake of the Revolution fomented a religious revival that swept many Americans away from the established Protestant churches into less traditional religious groups. One of these was the United Society of Believers in Christ's Second Appearing, more commonly known as the Shakers, so called because of their unorthodox methods of communal worship, which often culminated in a frenzied dance.

Eight Shakers came to America from England in 1774, led by Mother Ann Lee (1736–1784), their prophet. Ann Lee was an unschooled woman from Manchester who preached that the only way to spiritual perfection was through open confession and complete celibacy. (Since Shakers were celibate, they were active in providing homes for orphans in order to add members to the flock.) She believed that Christ had revealed to her in a vision that she had become the embodiment of his spirit, and this revelation marked the beginning of the Millennium, a period of one thousand years of peace and harmony on earth.

Mother Ann's small band first settled in Niskeyuna, New York, about eight miles northwest of Albany. As the Shakers gained converts, nineteen communities sprang up between Maine and Kentucky. Truly communal in both spirit and action, the Shakers were one of the first groups to believe in full equality of the sexes. The brothers and sisters (as members were known) adhered to a rigid set of rules known as the Millennial Laws, which regulated all aspects of their lives, including correct methods of spiritual worship, proper deportment between the sexes, and suitable furnishings for their rooms.

During the middle decades of the nineteenth century, the Shakers thrived and at their peak had more than six thousand members. In order to support themselves, they developed various industries to make goods for sale to the outside world. The Shakers believed that labor for the benefit of the

The North Family Dwelling, New Lebanon Shaker community. The building was demolished in 1972.

OPPOSITE:
This desk and swivel chair were made by members of the New Lebanon community. The desk was built between 1825 and 1850 and was used by Sister Amelia Calver of the Church family. The chair dates from about 1860–70; innovative swivel chairs are thought to be the invention of the Shaker community at Enfield, Connecticut.

Many practical furniture and interior planning innovations can be noted in this typical Shaker room. The cast-iron stove was placed in the center of the room to distribute heat more evenly; the built-in cabinet provided a compact storage area. Shaker sisters may have done their sewing while sitting at a worktable or in a rocking chair such as the one shown here. The two-step footrest in front of the rocker enabled the sewer to put one foot above the other and thus elevate the stitchery on her lap to a convenient height. These sewing steps were so prized that they were inscribed by three consecutive owners.

community was labor for God; therefore, work was a form of worship. Although the Shakers were well known for their garden-seed business, brooms and brushes, and medicinal herbs, it is their simple, elegant furniture designs that are most admired today.

The New Lebanon community, which functioned between 1787 and 1947, was the central ministry of the sect, with approximately six hundred members living there at its height. Shaker communities were broken down into "families," who lived and worked together; New Lebanon had eight such families, each with its own dwellings and workshops. The Museum's Shaker retiring room is from the North Family Dwelling at New Lebanon. A retiring room served as both a bedroom and, as described in the Millennial Laws, a place to retire to "in silence, for the space of half an hour, and labor for a sense of the gospel, before attending meeting."

The North Family Dwelling was a large, unadorned frame building that stood five stories high. The basement floor held kitchens and dining rooms; the first floor had a large room, which served as a meeting room and chapel, as well as retiring rooms for the members. The floors above contained more retiring rooms, and the attic was used for storage. Most retiring rooms were shared by at least two people. The brothers and sisters lived on either end of the same floor of the dwelling, but they maintained separate hallways and staircases to their rooms, as well as separate entrances to the building.

The Museum acquired this retiring room in 1972, after the Darrow

ABOVE:
The Shakers' Millennial Laws specified that "bedsteads should be painted green—comfortables [bedcovers] should be of a modest color, not checked, striped, or flowered." This bed retains its large, nonpivoting wooden rollers, which enabled the sisters to pull it straight out from the wall for changing and cleaning. Most retiring rooms had two or more beds.

OPPOSITE:
The sisters who lived in this room would have washed themselves using furnishings like this white-pine washstand and towel rack, both of which were made in New Lebanon. The looking glass was specifically designed to hang from a pegboard.

Two bentwood oval boxes, a form associated with the Shakers, sit on the painted-pine blanket chest. One of a pair of ladder-back side chairs in the room hangs from the pegboard. These side chairs have ball-in-socket "tilters" inserted at the base of the back legs, so they could be tilted back without wear. The straw bonnet hanging next to the chair may have been made at the Enfield community.

After about 1850, Shakers began to manufacture furniture for sale outside their communities. Rocking chairs were particularly popular with customers. This chair cannot be attributed to a specific community, but its early date of about 1820–50 indicates that it was made for the Shakers' own use.

School, which today owns the buildings of the former Shaker community, was forced to take down the North Family Dwelling because of its deteriorated condition. The room reveals some of the most typical characteristics of Shaker design: utility, simplicity, and beauty. The Millennial Laws admonished that "beadings, mouldings and cornices, which are *merely for fancy*, may not be made by Believers. Odd or fanciful styles of architecture may not be used." This most unfanciful room has clean white plaster walls, a scrubbed pine floor, and simple stained woodwork that has been aged to a warm ocher. The room is furnished with objects that would have been found in a typical retiring room, although none of the pieces is original to the room and some were made at other northeastern Shaker communities. Some of the objects, such as the desk, are one of a kind, made for a specific Shaker user rather than for sale to the "outside world."

This useful spool stand, crafted in maple, still holds spools wound with thread that was most likely handspun and dyed by Shaker sisters.

As in many Shaker interiors, a pegboard runs around the room and holds various objects, including the light side chairs, which were lifted from the floor for day-to-day storage and to facilitate cleaning. The built-in drawers and cupboards at the end of the room are well designed and attractively proportioned. Much Shaker furniture was painted, although in the limited palette strictly dictated by the Millennial Laws. The unadorned bedside candlestand, with gently curving legs, typifies Shaker design at its best.

All the textiles in the room are reproductions, copied from existing Shaker examples. The pleated white-linen curtains are of particular note; a precursor of modern-day vertical blinds, their pleats allowed the fabric to lie flat against the window frame when pushed aside, yet be of enough fullness to cover the entire width of the window, thus affording privacy when drawn.

The decline of the Shaker communities after the Civil War has been attributed to a number of factors, including the waning of American religious revivalism. Perhaps the most important reason for the group's demise was the lure of the growing cities of newly industrialized America, which proved too tempting to young people. Children were educated and well cared for during the years they spent in Shaker communities, and at the age of twenty-one, they were given the choice of joining the group or seeking their fortunes elsewhere. In the later decades of the nineteenth century, fewer and fewer chose to stay. The highly regulated agrarian lifestyle must have seemed hopelessly outdated as the century came to an end.

Much of the furniture in the Museum's room was originally in the collection of Faith and Edward Deming Andrews, who in the 1930s began documenting the lives, beliefs, and crafts of the Shakers. As communities closed down, the Andrewses collected objects pertaining to the group, many given to them by, or purchased from, the few remaining Shakers. The Andrewses and other pioneering scholars helped to bring about our appreciation of the enduring nature and timeless quality of Shaker design.

AMELIA PECK

The Greek Revival Parlor

NEW YORK CITY ◆ ABOUT 1835

Installed in 1983 as part of the new American Wing, the Robert and Gloria Manney Greek Revival parlor is a re-creation of what the formal front parlor in a fashionable New York City town house of about 1835 might have looked like. The room was designed to showcase a rare suite of furniture made by Duncan Phyfe for New York lawyer Samuel A. Foote. The only period elements are the Ionic columnar screen at the entrance and the black marble mantelpiece, which once stood in Halsted, a Greek Revival house in Rye, New York. The rest was copied from existing parlors or based on designs found in some of the most popular architectural pattern books of the day.

Buildings in the Greek Revival style, America's first truly national architectural style, sprang up in the decades between 1820 and 1850. Although Neoclassicism had been popular since the end of the eighteenth century, designs of the Federal period were derived primarily from Roman models that had been filtered through the creative minds of such designers as the Adam brothers. The bolder, more robust Greek Revival, however, put a far higher premium on archaeological correctness. Architects studied actual Greek ruins, if not in person then through books, the most illuminating being Stuart and Revett's *The Antiquities of Athens* (1762). This volume was such an important source to nineteenth-century architects that one of the most famous, Alexander Jackson Davis (1803–1892), dated his beginnings as a practicing architect to the day in 1828 that he first studied it.

The Greek Revival style expressed many things about American ideals. During the 1820s the Greeks were battling the Ottoman Empire for independence, and Americans, like the citizens of many European countries, were strongly supportive of the Greeks' struggle. But, first and foremost, the Greek Revival style represented American optimism before the Civil War, at a time when the democratic system, adapted from the ancient Greek model, seemed to be flourishing. People who built houses, churches, and civic buildings based on Greek temple forms expressed their belief that America was becoming a great civilization, one that would rival the glories of the ancient past.

In rapidly growing New York City, Greek Revival town houses filled block after block in the area between Greenwich Village and Thirty-fourth Street. Designed for the expanding middle class, these structures were usually built on lots twenty to twenty-five feet wide and one hundred feet deep. A

OPPOSITE:
The Greek Revival parlor is a gallery of high-style decorative arts from about 1835. It is designed as a period room to give an appropriate context to an extraordinary suite of mahogany parlor furniture made by the workshop of Duncan Phyfe for New York City lawyer Samuel A. Foote. Before the second half of the 19th century, luxurious decorations, such as the glittering French chandelier that hangs in the center of the room were not manufactured in the United States and so were imported from Europe.

Argand lamp, one of a pair that sits on the mantelpiece. The lamp's burner tube bears the label of B. Gardiner, a well-known New York retailer.

typical house might be three full stories high, above a raised basement, often topped with a garret. It was usually only two rooms deep, with a stair hall on one side. The raised basement floor held the kitchen and perhaps the servants' dining room; the main, or first, floor contained the public rooms, while the second and third floors had the family bedrooms and the garret the servants' bedrooms. The main floor always had front and back parlors, which were invariably separated by a columnar screen with sliding doors like that in our Greek Revival parlor. The front parlor was saved for formal entertaining, while the back parlor was a family sitting room that was often used for dining.

The Museum's Ionic columnar screen is based almost exactly on Plate 60 of Minard Lafever's *The Modern Builder's Guide* (New York, 1833). We have no doubt that the screen was made in New York City soon after the publication of that book, but at the time it was donated to the Museum, the screen was installed in a Thirty-ninth Street town house that was not built until 1869. Obviously, it had been moved there from another location, but no one knows the house for which it was originally designed.

LEFT:
Desk attributed to the workshop of Duncan Phyfe. This very architectural piece is derived from a French Restoration form called *secrétaire à abattant* ("desk with a flap"), in reference to the fall-front writing surface. When closed, the desk presents an unornamented facade enlivened only by the rich grain of its mahogany veneer.

BELOW OPPOSITE:
This type of sofa, with its distinctive head and foot, is called a *meridienne*. A portrait of Mrs. Luman Reed, painted about 1835 by Charles Cromwell Ingham (1796–1863), hangs above the sofa. The curule-form stool next to the window is one of a pair from the Foote suite. It is interesting to compare Phyfe's more robust use of the curule design to the earlier curule furniture in the Richmond room.

Minard Lafever's books were some of the most popular American architectural pattern books published. His *Modern Builder's Guide* was reprinted six times, the last edition in 1855, and *The Beauties of Modern Architecture* (1835) had four reprintings, again ending with an 1855 edition. Published in New York City, the books had an especially strong influence there. Simply worded and clearly drawn, they addressed the "operative workman" (house builder) rather than the architect or scholar. The curator in charge of designing the Museum's Greek Revival parlor, perhaps more of a scholarly reader than Lafever intended, found his books to be an invaluable resource. The room was proportioned as Lafever advised: the deep plaster cornice was copied directly from Plate 58 of *The Modern Builder's Guide*, which shows a "Stucco Cornice For Story 12 Ft. to 14." Only the parlor floor in a typical town house would have had a ceiling as high as twelve to fourteen feet, so Lafever's drawing is undoubtedly meant for a parlor. The ceiling rosette was copied from *The Beauties of Modern Architecture*, where it appears in Plate 21 as "Design For A Centre Flower" and is described as "appropriate to parlors of the first class." The door surrounds were copied from an intact Greek Revival parlor in a house on East Eleventh Street; however, the top portions of those original surrounds can be traced to Plate 19 in *The Beauties* and the side panels to Plate 80 in *The Modern Builder's Guide*.

As was popular in the day, the walls are smoothly plastered and painted a warm beige. There are known Greek Revival parlors decoratively painted with trompe-l'oeil architectural detailing or even classical figures, but since this room was made to serve as a Museum gallery, such ornamentation did not seem appropriate. A modern reproduction of a wall-to-wall Brussels carpet, copied from an 1827 watercolor pattern found in the archives of an English carpet mill, has been laid on the floor. The curtains, with their unusual bullion-fringe valance, were copied from Plate 1979 of J. C. Loudon's *Encyclopedia of Cottage, Farm and Villa Architecture* (London, 1833), one of the nineteenth century's most popular books for house building and decorating. It was used extensively on both sides of the Atlantic.

The 1837 suite of furniture—couches, stools, benches, and side chairs—is an example of the late work of Duncan Phyfe and his workshop. The suite was made to furnish a town house at 678 Broadway, into which lawyer Samuel Foote moved his family in 1837. Phyfe is better known for his earlier style of English Regency-influenced furniture (see the Richmond room, pages 220–21). His later work, although quite different, is equally beautiful. More in keeping with the French Restoration designs that were being published in such journals as Pierre de La Mesangère's *Collection de meubles et objets de goût* (1802–35), these pieces feature luxuriously curving forms that highlight the beauty of their gleaming mahogany surfaces. The pair of armchairs in the room descended in Phyfe's own family, and the fall-front desk is almost certainly from his workshop. All of the seating furniture is upholstered with a reproduction fabric similar to that which originally covered the suite.

AMELIA PECK

The Rococo Revival Parlor

ASTORIA, NEW YORK ◆ ABOUT 1852

The architectural elements of the Rococo Revival parlor were once part of an Italianate villa that overlooked the East River from then-elegant Astoria in the borough of Queens, New York City. Astoria, incorporated in 1839, was named for John Jacob Astor. During the 1850s it was divided into large lots, upon which spacious family houses were built. The elements of our room were taken from a villa that stood at 4–17 Twenty-seventh Avenue. It was originally owned by Horace Whittemore, whose name first appeared in New York City business directories in 1851–52, when he began to work with his brother Albert, a fur merchant. (Horace later ran his own hat business.) His residence until his death in 1871 is listed as Astoria. By studying maps of the area, we can guess that Horace Whittemore went into business and bought or built a house in Astoria in the same year, about 1852.

In *The Architecture of Country Houses* (New York, 1850), the widely read architectural theorist Andrew Jackson Downing (1815–1852) defined a villa as a country house "where beauty, taste, and moral culture are at home." By the 1850s the city no longer seemed an acceptable place to raise a family, and the flight to suburbia began. This movement was a reaction to rapid urban industrialization and to the first great wave of Europeans who had come to America in the 1840s. Although many of these immigrants were poor and unskilled, some were immensely talented craftsmen who made furniture and other decorative objects for affluent customers building new homes in the suburbs.

OPPOSITE:
View of the Rococo Revival parlor. The lavishly carved white marble mantelpiece, with its original cast-iron grate, once stood in the Tweedy house in North Attleboro, Massachusetts. The gilded overmantel mirror probably comes from a New York City looking-glass maker; the prism-laden girandoles on the mantel may have been made by the New England Glass Company in East Cambridge, Massachusetts. The console table to the right of the fireplace holds an English Parian porcelain miniature version of Hiram Powers's famous sculpture of *The Greek Slave*. An American stereopticon viewer is next to the statuette.

The Whittemore house, 4–17 Twenty-seventh Avenue, Astoria, Queens. The building was demolished in 1965.

ABOVE:

This gas chandelier was probably made about 1850 by Henry N. Hooper and Company of Boston. Made of overlay glass, the top blue layer has been ground back in a decorative pattern to reveal the clear glass beneath.

RIGHT:

The Rococo Revival room show-cases a splendid rosewood parlor suite attributed to New York City cabinetmaker John Henry Belter, the foremost practitioner of the style. The suite consists of a sofa, two armchairs, two side chairs, and a *tête-à-tête*. Although not part of a suite, the firescreen to the left of the hearth is also attributed to Belter; a mid-19th-century needle-work depicting a parrot on a stand is stretched within the frame. Looking-glass maker John Knight of Brooklyn signed the pier mirror that stands between the windows. One of Belter's most elaborate works, the center table is covered with carved garlands of fruits and flowers. The blue overlay-glass lamp on the table was made about 1850 by Archer and Warner of Philadelphia.

Horace Whittemore's brick house stood three stories high on a raised basement and had column-lined verandas across both the front and the back facades. An inventory of its contents taken at Whittemore's death in 1871 gives a good indication of how its spaces were used. The dining room, kitchen, and pantries were all in the basement. The first floor held a pair of formal parlors on the south side of the central hall and a family living room as well as a billiards room on the north side of the hall. The second floor had five family bedrooms; the third floor probably contained servants' quarters.

The Metropolitan's curators re-created one of the formal parlors at the south side of the house, although a few structural modifications have been made. The plan was slightly widened, a window was removed from one of the long walls, and a chimney breast and mantel were added. Photographs taken when the rooms were removed from the house prior to its demolition in 1965 show the parlors without any fireplaces. There do appear to be floor vents, suggesting that the house may have depended upon central heating from the start, although this would have been unusual. However, a floor plan drawn in the 1920s indicates fireplaces in the parlors, so it was decided to add one to make this room accurately reflect a typical parlor of the period.

Objects made from Parian porcelain decorate the mantelpiece. The covered box at the left is modeled with a sleeping baby. An allegorical figure of Autumn is in the center, and a covered jar with applied grapes stands to the right. All are thought to have been made in Bennington, Vermont, in the mid-19th century .

Detail of the intricate cast plaster cornice that runs around the perimeter of the room. After precise molds were made from samples of the original plasterwork, a new cornice was cast for the room's installation.

The columnar screen, with its elaborate Corinthian capitals, originally separated two very similar rooms, which likely had matching sets of brocatelle draperies with lace undercurtains hung beneath gilt cornices, matching pier mirrors at either end of each room between the pairs of windows, and the same wall-to-wall carpeting throughout. The southwest parlor contained an abundance of seating furniture, while the southeast parlor had a piano, undoubtedly a useful possession when the young ladies of the family were asked to show off their accomplishments.

The room's parlor suite by John Henry Belter (1804–1863) is probably somewhat grander than the Whittemore family's furniture; in fact, it is among the most ornate produced by Belter, a German immigrant working in New York, who became famous after patenting a method of lamination that allowed wood to be bent into deep curves and then elaborately carved. His furniture was expensive, and pieces of this quality were found only in the homes of America's richest citizens. Belter worked in a style called "Rococo Revival" today, but at the time it was popular, it was usually described as "Modern French." The nineteenth-century designers working in the French style may have looked to eighteenth-century French furniture for inspiration, but in actuality Rococo Revival furniture is very different from those models. The forms are similar—both have graceful curves and cabriole legs—but Rococo Revival furniture is heavier, with deep, naturalistic carving and dramatically grained woods.

The entire parlor is decorated in what would have been called the "French taste," the accepted style for parlors during the middle decades of the nineteenth century. Downing, though not fond of it, admitted that "*Modern French furniture,* and especially that in the style of *Louis Quatorze,* stands much higher in general estimation in this country than any other. Its union of lightness, elegance, and grace renders it especially the favorite of

Detail of carved wood door surround

ladies. For country houses we would confine its use, chiefly, to the drawing-room or boudoir." The drawing room (or parlor) and boudoir were the parts of the house over which the ladies of the day reigned; they planned the activities that took place there and indeed were often allowed to decorate those rooms as they saw fit, while the men of the family usually chose the furnishings of the others.

The design of this Rococo Revival room follows Downing's suggestion that a parlor "...should always exhibit more beauty and elegance than any apartment in the house. In colour, it should be lighter, more cheerful and gay than any other room. The furniture should be richer and more delicate in design, and the colours of the walls decidedly light, so that brilliancy of effect is not lost in the evening." The wallpaper in the room is a reproduction of a period damask-patterned paper that has been separated into panels with trompe-l'oeil architectural molding. The four "pictures" in trompe-l'oeil frames are wallpaper views of Paris made by the French manufacturer Jules Desfosse in 1857. The upholstery fabric used for the draperies and furniture coverings reproduces a blue-and-gold silk brocatelle found on parlor furniture in Camden, a house in Port Royal, Virginia, built in 1856–59 for William Carter Pratt. The curtains are based on Plate 282 of *The Cabinet of Practical, Useful and Decorative Furniture Designs* by Henry Lawford, which, though undated, was most likely published sometime during the 1850s. The highly patterned English carpet is the type of floor covering referred to in the period as a "tapestry velvet." The ornately carved white marble mantel is from a house in North Attleboro, Massachusetts, built in 1853, and the

One of a pair of curvaceous tables. The tour-de-force carving of Belter's workshop can be noted in such details as the naturalism of the bouquet of flowers at the center of the base and the lacelike delicacy of the table's apron.

The shaped back of this robust armchair was created from multiple thin layers of wood that were steamed and bent into the desired curve.

beautiful blue overlay-glass chandelier was made about 1850 by the Boston company of Henry N. Hooper. Delicate vases and statuettes of Parian ware (a type of porcelain), much of it made in Bennington, Vermont, complete the room's ornamental scheme.

AMELIA PECK

The Gothic Revival Library

NEWBURGH, NEW YORK ◆ 1859

Frederick Clarke Withers (1828–1901), architect of the house from which the Gothic Revival library was removed, arrived in the booming Hudson River shipping town of Newburgh, New York, in early 1852. He had come from England to work for Andrew Jackson Downing (1815–1852), the great horticulturist, landscape designer, and architectural theoretician. Downing was well known for introducing the concept of the picturesque in architecture and landscaping to pre-Civil War America. Of all the picturesque architectural styles he popularized, Gothic Revival was the one he most vigorously promoted.

In 1850, after years of collaborating with the well-known architect Alexander Jackson Davis (1803–1892), Downing decided to set up his own

ABOVE:
The Deming house, which still stands in Newburgh, New York, as it looked in about 1885.

LEFT:
In addition to detailing taken from Gothic architecture, such as trefoils and clustered columns, Gothic Revival furniture is frequently embellished with oak-leaf motifs like those carved into the cornices of the library's two bookcases. The books date from the period when the room was built.

OPPOSITE:
The oak mirror above the carved walnut mantel was designed about 1840 by the architect Alexander Jackson Davis for Lyndhurst in Tarrytown, New York. The Gothic Revival cast-iron grate was probably made in New York State. The mantel is decorated with an English clock and two candlesticks attributed to William F. Shaw of Boston. The child's chair to the right of the hearth retains its original mid-19th-century upholstery and needlework cover.

253

practice at Highland Garden, his Newburgh home, although he was not in fact a trained architect. While traveling in England that summer, he asked English architect Calvert Vaux (1824–1895) to join him in his American enterprises, because he needed help with many projects, including the design of the grounds around the Capitol Building in Washington. The partnership was a success, and the following year Downing advertised in a London paper for an additional architectural assistant.

Downing looked to England for help because there were few trained architects in America before the later part of the nineteenth century (the first architecture school in America did not open until 1865) and because those who had trained in England were much more familiar with the design concepts Downing sought to popularize. The Gothic Revival style had been in fashion in England for decades before the first truly Gothic house was built in the United States.

Frederick Clarke Withers must have seemed a perfect candidate for Downing's purposes. A young man of twenty-four, he had worked in the architectural office of the Gothic Revival specialist Thomas Henry Wyatt. Withers arrived in Newburgh in February 1852 and was quickly put to work, but in July of that year, Downing was killed when the Hudson River steamboat on which he was a passenger caught fire. Withers and Vaux remained partners for four years and worked together on Vaux's 1857 book, *Villas and Cottages*. Withers drew most of the illustrations for designs by Vaux, although some of the projects were collaborations. When Vaux left Newburgh to

Detail of the hand-worked wool rug and striped oak-and-walnut floor. Oak and walnut were the two woods most commonly used to make Gothic Revival furniture and interiors.

help Frederick Law Olmsted plan Central Park, Withers set up a solo practice, working at first primarily on private houses, although later in his career he was known for his High Victorian Gothic churches and institutional buildings, such as the Jefferson Market Courthouse (1874), which still stands on lower Sixth Avenue in New York City.

The Museum's library came from the house designed by Withers in 1859 for banker Frederick Deming (1787–1860) and his family. In a pamphlet entitled *Wealth and Biography of the Wealthy Citizens of New York City* (1845), Deming was listed as "President of the Union Bank, and has long been rich by virtue of the laws of inheritance." His worth was listed at $300,000, an extraordinarily large sum for the time. In 1859, when the house was built for about $16,000, Deming was seventy-two. It may have been planned as a retirement home, but he died in 1860, soon after it was completed. His family continued to live there until 1868, when the property was sold.

Today the house still stands in the Balmville section of Newburgh, where, like its neighbors, it is situated on a large plot of land. The library's

Unlike the Greek and Rococo Revival rooms, the Gothic Revival library is not furnished with a suite of furniture. The pieces here were made by a number of different New York City cabinetmakers from the early 1850s through the mid-1860s and illustrate various interpretations of the style.

The library's bay window once looked out over the Hudson River. Paint analysis of the room revealed an original color scheme of rich earth tones of the type recommended for libraries by the architectural pattern books of the day. The plaster ceiling is decorated in imitation of medieval wood beams.

bay window originally overlooked the Hudson River. Although it had been abandoned for many years when, in 1977, the Museum was given permission to remove the room, the house has now been restored. It is a strongly massed yet graceful two-and-a-half-story red-brick structure. The sharply peaked roof line is decorated with boldly carved verge boards (a wide board fastened on edge below the slope of the roof on the gable end, often carved in ornamental patterns in Gothic Revival buildings), and Ruskinian stone-and-brick *voussoirs* (tapering or wedge-shaped pieces that form an arch or a vault) top the pointed-arch windows. The main floor held the library, a parlor, a dining room, and the kitchen area, and the upper stories contained bedrooms.

The curators in charge of acquiring a Gothic Revival room decided that the library from the house was the most aesthetically and historically interesting room to add to the Museum's collection. During the mid-nineteenth century the Gothic Revival style was thought to be particularly appropriate for libraries, and even houses that were not Gothic on the outside had libraries decorated in the style, which was intended to be reminiscent of scholarly preserves such as medieval monasteries and universities.

This octagonal walnut table was most likely made in New York City, but as with much Gothic Revival furniture a definite maker has not been identified. Questions have been raised about whether the luxurious Italian marble top was a later addition, but in studying the table's construction, the Museum staff has concluded that this unusual pairing occurred when the table was first crafted.

Before this time private libraries were the exclusive domain of wealthy gentlemen of an academic bent, but by the 1850s mechanized production of inexpensive cloth-bound books had brought the possession of a good library within reach of almost any middle-class family. Less formal than the best parlor, the library became the family sitting room, a place where relaxation and even coziness were encouraged.

The Museum's somewhat somberly designed library is enlivened by the play of the colors of contrasting woods. The floor is striped in alternating oak and walnut boards, and the room's wainscoting is walnut with chestnut panels. The original paint scheme is exactly replicated, as is the elaborate plaster medallion ceiling. The room as installed, however, differs in two ways from its original appearance. Visitors now enter through an enlarged archway, which has replaced a full-length window that opened onto the veranda. The space left for the room in the shell of the American Wing did not allow for an entrance through its interior doors. Also, the carved walnut mantel is a copy of the mantel from the library of a Newburgh house that Withers designed for David M. Clarkson in 1856. When the Deming room was acquired in 1977, all of the house's mantels had long since disappeared. A photograph of the library taken about 1885 shows that the mantel and overmantel mirror had already been changed to a later style.

The room is meant to illustrate how an upper-middle-class family library might have been furnished. Printed plates in contemporary design manuals by Downing and others guided the selection and placement of the pieces, none of which is original to the room. The majority are either oak or walnut and were most likely made in New York City between the early 1850s and the mid-1860s. A few English objects, such as the mantel clock, made about 1845 by H. Smith of York, and the bread plate designed by Augustus Welby Northmore Pugin and manufactured by Minton and Company in Stoke-on-Trent, serve as reminders of Withers's roots, as well as of the profound influence of English Gothic Revival on American design. The drapery and upholstery fabric, a wool-and-silk damask, was reproduced from a piece of English fabric woven in the period. The handmade needlepoint rug may be either English or American.

Directly outside the library, the entrance vestibule to the house has been replicated, although on a somewhat larger scale, complete with painted trompe-l'oeil panels. The floor of colorful Minton tiles now installed in the vestibule came from the center hall of the Deming house.

AMELIA PECK

The Renaissance Revival Parlor

MERIDEN, CONNECTICUT ◆ 1870

Today, at 816 Broad Street in Meriden, Connecticut, where once stood the "princely residence" of Jedediah Wilcox, there is a weed-covered vacant lot. The grand house was torn down in 1968, after a battle that pitted local preservationists against the Mobil Oil Corporation, which had bought the property intending to raze the house and build a gas station and a seventy-five-unit motel. The citizens of Meriden, led by their mayor, decided to try to preserve it as a museum, since much of the spectacular interior decoration and many of the original furnishings were still intact. Unfortunately, in the 1960s the preservation movement was still in its infancy, and many people did not see the value of saving America's architectural heritage. The local group failed to raise enough money to buy the property from Mobil, so the house was torn down, although nothing was ever built on the land.

When curators at the Metropolitan heard that the house was endangered, they asked to purchase some of its parts for installation in the

The Wilcox house at 816 Broad Street, Meriden, Connecticut, just before its demolition in 1968

The room's original rear parlor suite, which includes a sofa, two armchairs, two side chairs, an overmantel mirror and window cornices made of rosewood with medallions of carved mother-of-pearl, is attributed to John Jelliff & Co. of Newark, New Jersey. The original center table from the suite did not come to the Museum; in its place is an exotic Egyptian Revival center table of rosewood and walnut that was probably made by the New York City firm of Pottier and Stymus.

American Wing if the whole could not be saved. When all preservation efforts failed, the Museum acquired the house's front parlor, rear parlor, and formal front hall, including the magnificent staircase, as well as the rear parlor's suite of furniture. (The front parlor was later sold to Yale University, and the remaining architectural elements were sold at public auction.) Aside from their rich ornament, the rooms of the house were particularly desirable because they were among the first known nineteenth-century American examples that were clearly overseen by a single designer who had maintained a consistent idea in every aspect of their decoration. The fittings of each room were en suite, in that the overmantel mirror, window cornices, lighting fixtures, marble mantels, and furniture all matched. An account of the house published in the *Meriden Daily Republican* (November 28, 1870) attributes it to a somewhat obscure architect from Rockville, Connecticut, by the name of Augustus Truesdell, who both "designed and superintended" the building of the $125,000 home. (When completely furnished, it was valued at $200,000.) Whether he actually designed all aspects of the exterior and interior is not known.

The 1870 account describes the house as being built in the "Franco-Italian Villa style." Today, it might be called Second Empire—referring to the reign of Napoleon III in France (1852–70)—a style thought to indicate affluence and authority, as well as a cosmopolitan outlook, and one particularly popular both here and abroad for government and institutional buildings. The identifying features of the Second Empire style, which was inspired by the architecture of sixteenth-century France, were the mansard roof and the stepping out of the central block of the building to break up the elevation symmetrically. The Wilcox house deviated slightly from the style, in that the mass of the building to the right of the central tower was stepped out even farther than the center block. This asymmetry relates closely to the design of Italianate villas of the 1850s, so the newspaper reviewer was accurate in labeling the house "Franco-Italian."

The house was built between 1868 and 1870 for Wilcox, one of Meriden's most prominent citizens. He started his career in the 1840s as a manufacturer of carpetbags, but by the mid-1850s he had become more successful when he added ladies' hoop skirts and corsets to his line. By the mid-1860s he employed seven to eight hundred workers and made all sorts of woolen goods for ladies' apparel. The business failed in the early 1870s, and Wilcox declared bankruptcy in 1874. After selling his magnificent house with all of its furnishings for a mere $20,000 to Charles Parker, a hardware and firearms manufacturer, he disappeared.

The stately brick house was entered through a portico guarded by two stone lions. It was two full stories high, with a basement and a third-story-attic beneath the mansard roof. The first floor held a vestibule, the main hall, a reception room, front parlor, rear parlor (which was referred to as the "sitting room" in the newspaper account, suggesting that it was furnished more informally than the front parlor and used in a more casual fashion by the family), library, dining room, and pantry. The kitchen was in the basement. The second floor had bedrooms, including an entire suite for Wilcox. The attic contained bedrooms for the servants, a billiards room, and a storage area. The house was centrally heated with forced air and had many bathrooms with hot and cold running water, an unusual luxury at the time.

The Museum's 1985 installation re-creates the rear parlor, which the 1870 newspaper article noted as being "fitted up in the Marie Antoinette style of art." This description probably refers to the elegant suite of furniture and its matching overmantel mirror and window cornices.

Detail of the leg of the center table. While stylized motifs inspired by Egyptian art are evident throughout the design of the table, the most obvious tribute is the gilt-brass male head in Egyptian headdress that graces the top of each leg.

The white-marble mantel and rosewood overmantel mirror share similar decorative motifs and were clearly designed en suite. The mantel garniture, which includes an Egyptian Revival clock and two obelisks, was made by Tiffany and Company, New York, about 1875–85. Mitchell, Vance and Company of New York are thought to be the makers of the 12-arm gilt-brass chandelier and matching wall sconces. The center table holds a Parian porcelain figural group entitled *The Finding of Moses* (ca. 1870), attributed to the English sculptor William Beattie, and two examples of Connecticut-made silverplate, an ice-water pitcher from the Meriden Britannia Company (1868) and two goblets made by Roger Smith and Company, New Haven (ca. 1875).

Dating from about 1870, and not original to the room, this grand
Renaissance Revival cabinet, constructed of rosewood with light wood
inlays, was made by an unidentified New York City cabinetmaker of
great skill. On top of the cabinet is a pair of contemporaneous
porcelain vases with *pâte-sur-pâte* decoration designed by Marc Louis
Emanuel Solon for manufacture at the Minton factory, Stoke-on-
Trent, England.

Today the general term for pieces of this style is Renaissance Revival. Furniture makers of the day believed that they were following French models and reinterpreting designs fashionable during the reign of Louis XVI. The Wilcox furniture is attributed to John Jelliff & Co., a leading cabinetmaking firm based in Newark, New Jersey. Depending upon slight differences in detailing, Jelliff & Co. called its parlor suites by different names, all with French references, such as "Grand [*sic*] Duchesse," "Pompadour," and "Marie Antoinette." The Museum's furniture and the mirror and cornices are made of rosewood, which has been carved and decorated with incised and gilded designs and mounted with medallions of mother-of-pearl carved with classical heads in profile. The suite—which now consists of one sofa, two armchairs, and two side chairs—probably included at least two more side chairs and a matching center table. The center table in the room is in the Egyptian Revival style and is attributed to the New York City cabinetmaking firm of Pottier and Stymus.

This room is also notable for its beautifully painted ceiling, which features rosettes with trompe-l'oeil bouquets of flowers, all accurately copied from the original parlor (see detail on page 168). The newspaper account credits a local, Bela Carter, with all the painting in the house and notes that it "increases his well-earned reputation for superb work." Today decorative painting is, for the most part, a lost art, but in the second half of the nineteenth century, any sizable town could support a talented decorative painter to work on the homes of its wealthier citizens.

The Museum's parlor was also described in the same account as having "crimson curtains, [with the] sofas, lounges, chairs and furniture generally being covered with scarlet satin." Since none of the original textiles from the house has survived, modern fabric was used to replicate the furniture coverings and the heavily fringed and tasseled draperies, while the rug is a reproduction of a wall-to-wall carpet ordered from Paris in 1867 for the New York City home of the Tredwell family. The room's crowning touch, produced by the noted New York City lighting firm of Mitchell, Vance and Company, is the bold twelve-armed chandelier (with matching wall sconces), which picks up aspects of the design motifs found throughout this impressive room.

AMELIA PECK

Like this armchair, all the furniture from the original parlor suite is upholstered in a modern red satin in keeping with the 1870 newspaper account, which described the furniture as "generally being covered in scarlet satin."

The McKim, Mead and White Stair Hall

BUFFALO, NEW YORK • 1884

The Metropolitan Museum's stair hall was taken from the Metcalfe residence, which, when built in 1884, was probably considered an avant-garde addition to its suburban neighborhood. It was the first house the famous New York City architectural firm of McKim, Mead and White built in Buffalo, and a local journal, *Real Estate and Builder's Monthly*, called it "an example in domestic architecture unique, so far as we know, in this part of the state." The style of the house, which the same journal called "a somewhat conventionalized 'early colonial,'" was inspired by the architects' perceptions of the strengths of pre-Georgian American architecture. These included building with solid materials, employing steeply pitched roofs to guard against snowy northern winters, and using a minimum of exterior ornamentation. The interior planning of the house was also different from many of the more expensive homes of the day in that the architects attempted to design its rooms with "convenience, utility, and economy" in mind, three traits found in the interiors of early-eighteenth-century American homes.

OPPOSITE:
Detail of the carved oak screen and the Japanesque latticework that lines the staircase

View of the Metcalfe house, 125 North Street, Buffalo, soon after it was completed in 1884. The house was demolished in 1980.

Although the room functioned as a stair hall, its focus was the oak-and-Siena-marble fireplace within the inglenook. The door to the entry vestibule is to the left of the far built-in bench. The leaded-glass windows were made by the Decorative Stained Glass Company of New York City. The earthenware vase on the landing was crafted by artist M. Louise McLaughlin (1847–1939) in 1880. The plant stand is probably American.

The Metcalfe family held a prominent position in nineteenth-century Buffalo. James Harvey Metcalfe had come to Buffalo from Bath, New York, in 1855 and made his fortune in banking, railroading, and pork packing. When he died in 1879, he was president of Buffalo's First National Bank. Beginning in 1871 Metcalfe, his wife, Erzelia, and their children lived in an imposing Italianate villa next door to 125 North Street, the eventual site of the McKim, Mead and White house.

After her husband's death Mrs. Metcalfe decided to build a new house. Her daughter Frances was already married, and her three sons were either grown or very nearly so. It is thought that the somewhat radical choice of commissioning McKim, Mead and White to build the house came about

through Frances Metcalfe Wolcott's connections with the contemporaneous New York City art world; she was involved with a group of artists and writers that included such luminaries as sculptor Augustus Saint-Gaudens, artist John La Farge, architectural critic Mariana Griswold Van Rensselaer, and architects Charles Follen McKim, William R. Mead, and Stanford White.

The house's design reveals McKim, Mead and White's architectural ideals from the early years of their partnership, before they set aside the teachings of McKim's and White's mentor, the great Henry Hobson Richardson, in favor of designing the boldly Neoclassical buildings that brought them to the forefront of the architectural profession at the turn of the nineteenth century. Although the materials used to build the Metcalfe

The woodwork of the room displays an eclectic variety of decorative motifs. A late-colonial mahogany tall clock with works by Joseph Mulliken of Concord, Massachusetts, stands at the bottom of the stairs. A visitor entered the parlor of the Metcalfe house to the left of the clock through the doorway now curtained with a modern portiere.

house did not include wood shingles, it can still be considered Shingle style, which was the American response to the more ornate English Queen Anne-style architecture in favor during the previous decade. Soon after it was completed, the simply massed house was described as being "substantial, and plain almost to homeliness" and designed by architects who thought of "use, comfort and solidity" more than ornamentation.

The two-and-a-half-story house had rough-hewn red sandstone walls for the first story, pressed brick for the second, and red terracotta tiles for the attic gables and the roof. It was built both inside and out by local workmen. (The only decoration that is known to have been made in New York City is the leaded glass, which is the product of the Decorative Stained Glass Company, a firm formed by two of John La Farge's top glassmakers after his decorating business failed in the early 1880s.) Its interior was more ornamented than the exterior; the downstairs was paneled with oak and cherry, described as "very tastefully carved from designs of the architects." The entrance was through a porch and vestibule at the left of the front facade. One walked directly into the stair hall that is now installed in the Museum. Opposite the hall fireplace was the door to the library, and the public rooms on the first floor—a large dining room and small parlor—radiated from the hall. The family's bedrooms were on the second floor.

The notion of the stair hall, or living hall, as a room essential to a house was popular in the 1870s and 1880s. Late-nineteenth-century living halls were imagined to be versions of the late medieval halls that served as all-purpose living spaces in which people ate, slept, and performed myriad tasks. The Victorian living hall, however, with its cozy inglenook furnished with benches on either side of a glowing hearth, was a place meant for relaxation and leisure. Mariana Griswold Van Rensselaer described the perfect living hall as "a spacious yet cozy and informal lounging place."

A hall conceived of as cozy and welcoming represents a change from the planning of earlier Victorian houses. The Wilcox house of Meriden (see page 261), built a mere fourteen years earlier, had a formal hall and reception room meant to awe and perhaps even intimidate. Formal halls were designed to separate unwelcome visitors from the private family apartments. The Metcalfe family's stair hall drew guests right into the heart of their home. All the other major first-floor rooms opened off the stair hall through wide sliding doors, which resulted in a sense of spatial continuity rather than compartmentalization. This change in planning may be emblematic of the trend toward more informal social interactions and a less rigidly defined class structure that was taking place in society in the latter part of the nineteenth century.

The stair hall is paneled in quarter-sawn white oak. Most of the carved and turned decorative motifs were inspired by an eclectic range of sources, including Moorish, Japanese, and Italian Renaissance examples. One of the loveliest features of the room is the way the light (originally daylight) from the leaded-glass windows at the stair landing spills out across the first few steps and hall floor, giving dimension to the Japanesque latticework on the right of the staircase, and flows through the delicately turned balusters of the screen at the left.

The room is so carefully designed and ornamented that it needs few furnishings. The niches flanking the overmantel mirror hold ceramics by the Faience Manufacturing Company of Brooklyn, New York, and the massive deep-blue-glazed earthenware vase on the stair landing was made by M. Louise McLaughlin of Cincinnati in 1880. The brass andirons in the fireplace and the tall case clock at the base of the stairs both date from about the end of the eighteenth century; these types of late-colonial objects were popular for furnishing artistic houses of the late nineteenth century, when they served as romantic icons of a time thought of as simpler and perhaps better by Victorians faced with the impending twentieth century.

In 1980, despite efforts by local preservationists to save it, the Metcalfe house was torn down. However, in 1895 McKim, Mead and White had built another, much grander home next to it, on the site of the family's first Italianate villa. The 1895 structure was being remodeled for corporate offices of the Delaware North Company, Inc., and it needed parking space for employees' cars. To preserve at least a part of the 1884 Metcalfe house, an agreement was reached that the company would donate the stair hall to the Metropolitan Museum, the dining room and library to Buffalo State College, and architectural fragments to the Buffalo and Erie County Historical Society.

AMELIA PECK

The Frank Lloyd Wright Room

WAYZATA, MINNESOTA ◆ 1912–14

With the installation of the Frank Lloyd Wright room in 1982, the American Wing entered the twentieth century both chronologically and philosophically. The room completes the wing's survey of domestic spaces and aptly illustrates the changes that curatorial practices underwent between the first quarter of this century and the present. The earliest examples collected by the American Wing were often more prized for the historical associations they evoked—such as who had lived in the room, or at least had visited there—than for their excellence or authenticity as works of art. By the time the Museum acquired the Frank Lloyd Wright room in 1972, the criteria for collecting rooms had changed considerably.

Frank Lloyd Wright (1867–1959) can be counted among the truly great architects of the twentieth century. Our room provides Museum visitors with the opportunity to experience a Wright-designed domestic space, a pleasure rarely available to the general public. The room, installed as a freestanding pavilion in the Museum, much as it was on its original site, is a complete work of art designed by an artist with a highly individual aesthetic. Who lived in the room and what took place there are incidental, except to help tell the story of how this space came into being.

OPPOSITE:
This oak print table, finished with a dark stain, folds up into a narrow container for storing precious works of art on paper. One of four oak standing lamps, designed about 1913 for the Wayzata living room, is next to the print table. The bank of windows that once overlooked Lake Minnetonka now provides a view of Central Park.

BELOW LEFT:
Mr. and Mrs. Francis W. Little, about 1914, on the steps leading to their new home

BELOW:
The Little house soon after its completion in 1914. The living room is the large pavilion at the right. The structure was demolished in 1972.

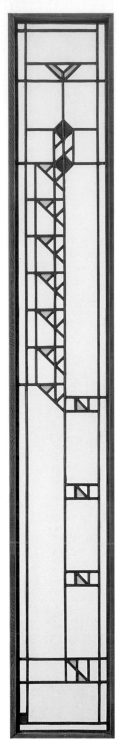

Narrow end panel from the lower bank of leaded-glass windows. In order to harmonize with the warm palette of the room, the leading in the windows was electroplated with a thin coating of copper.

RIGHT:
This photograph of the living room accurately illustrates the insistent horizontality of the space, emphasizing the visual interplay of the sweeping horizontal banks of the lower casement windows, the upper clerestory windows, and the hipped ceiling.

This was originally the living room in a house that Frank Lloyd Wright designed for Mr. and Mrs. Francis W. Little. He was a banker and she was an avid amateur musician. Wright had built them a home in Peoria, Illinois, in 1903; in 1908 they asked him to design their new country house in Wayzata, Minnesota. Wright counted the Littles among his favorite patrons; in addition to working with him on their Peoria house, they helped fund the first major publication of his designs in 1909.

The Wayzata house, however, tested the patience and loyalty of both the clients and the architect. As early as September 1908, the Littles were not sure that Wright could give them the building they wanted. He responded by writing that he would be hurt if they chose another architect for the job and that the "Littles can have anything I've got if they want it." One of the reasons for the continuing conflict over the design is revealed in Little's letter to Wright of November 5, 1913, when the building was well under way. He complained that "yours [of the] 3rd with revised glass designs for Living Room bays only reached me yesterday pm. You don't get what we want. Probably we have in mind at least in a vague way your designs of 8 or 10 years ago—the Thomas house [1901] or Miss Dana's [1903] say—While you are reaching for *something different.*"

Wright's ideas *had* changed between the years he built their first house and 1913, perhaps in part because of a trip he took to Europe in 1909. There he was exposed to the work of the European architectural community and saw that his own achievements had become celebrated. Wright also visited Japan in 1913, and the influence of Japanese art and architecture is evident in the design of the Little house.

In addition, the years between 1908, when the Littles first commissioned Wright, and 1912, when construction actually began, were personally tumultuous for the architect. In 1909 he left his wife, children, and Chicago practice to go to Berlin, where he wrote and produced a portfolio of his designs. He was joined there by Mamah Borthwick Cheney, the wife of a former client with whom he had fallen in love. The Littles disapproved of Wright's behavior, although they did not sever their ties with him, as many potential patrons did. Wright returned with Mrs. Cheney to the United States in 1910; the years that followed, before she died tragically in 1914, were some of the least productive of his early career. Clearly, Wright was distracted during this period, and Little wrote to him suggesting that he "wake up": "Have you lost interest in architecture or merely in the house? Something must be done soon or we must stop and wait for you to come to life."

In spite of these problems, the design was a resounding success. As with his other great Prairie-style houses, the Littles' was brilliantly integrated into its site. The series of pavilions that made up the building seemed to grow organically from the hilly landscape overlooking the nearby lake. The living

OPPOSITE:
One of two side chairs from 1912–14, stands next to the twelve-and-a-half-foot-long library table that Wright had made in 1902 for the Little's Peoria house. The active verticality of the plaster cast *Victory of Samothrace* (the original is in the Louvre) was used by Wright as a visual foil to balance the massive plane of the tabletop and to intersect with the horizontal lines of the windows and the oak trim.

room—the largest pavilion and the most important space in the house—was intended to serve both as a place for the family to gather and as an informal concert hall, where Mrs. Little could perform on the piano for guests.

The living room exemplifies one of Wright's most important contributions to modern architecture: the idea of dynamic spatial continuity. In the soaring glazed pavilion, the division between interior and exterior has been minimized. The room itself is not a single volume but a series of levels. The composition of the side walls—with their lower band of casement windows, long oak shelves, upper band of clerestory windows, and oak-trimmed panels

According to the furnishing plan Wright drew for the room, a sofa was supposed to face the fireplace. Although Wright may have designed a sofa for the room, it was probably never constructed. The example currently displayed was designed by Wright for the Frederick Robie House in Chicago about 1909. The four armchairs, which still retain their original wool-covered cushions, are thought to come from the Peoria house. The simple Japanesque forms of the four wall lamps reveal them to be later Wayzata designs.

that integrate the surface of the wall and ceiling—carries the viewer's eye upward to the leaded-glass ceiling light. The textured ocher-colored plaster walls blend harmoniously with the oak trim and floor and with the brick fireplace.

The furniture in the room is composed of two different sets: a group that Wright designed for the Peoria house and a number of pieces he designed specifically for the Wayzata room. All are of oak; the earlier pieces are stained dark brown and decorated with small square bands of trim, and the later pieces are the same light color as the room trim and are simpler and bolder in design.

281

The textiles in the room are either original or accurate reproductions.

The furniture and other objects in the room have been installed using a floor plan that Wright made for the room and a photograph of the interior that appeared in *In the Nature of Materials* (1942), a complete survey of Wright's work to date. Many years later the Littles' daughter explained to one of the Museum's curators that the family never used the room the way Wright had set it up for the photograph; in a 1981 letter she wrote, "This is a very old picture & was only arranged that way for a very few days. Mr. Wright turned up at the door with a group of students, when the authorities were looking for him. I think it was at the time when he was having his troubles with Miriam Noel Wright [a reference to the messy divorce battle Wright had with his second wife]. We didn't like his arrangement & put everything back where we were used to it." Nevertheless, the room has been installed as Wright envisioned it, as it is more important to show his conception than the way the family actually

In contrast to the earlier Peoria furniture in the room, this beautifully abstract table of 1913, composed of floating horizontal planes supported by narrow vertical uprights, is an exercise in pure geometric form.

lived. To the architect the exterior and interior design and the furnishings of a house were all part of an integrated whole.

In 1971 the Little house faced demolition because it was far too large for the needs of the Littles' descendants. The family wanted to build a smaller house on the property, but because of zoning laws, the Wright house would have to be torn down. In an effort to save as much of the building as possible, the Museum bought the entire house from the family, completely documented it, and, before installing the living room, managed to place many of the other rooms in other American museums. The Museum had come a long way from the early days of the American Wing, when it was a repository of inadequately documented, often incomplete rooms from houses that were sometimes more distinguished for their associations than for their architecture.

AMELIA PECK

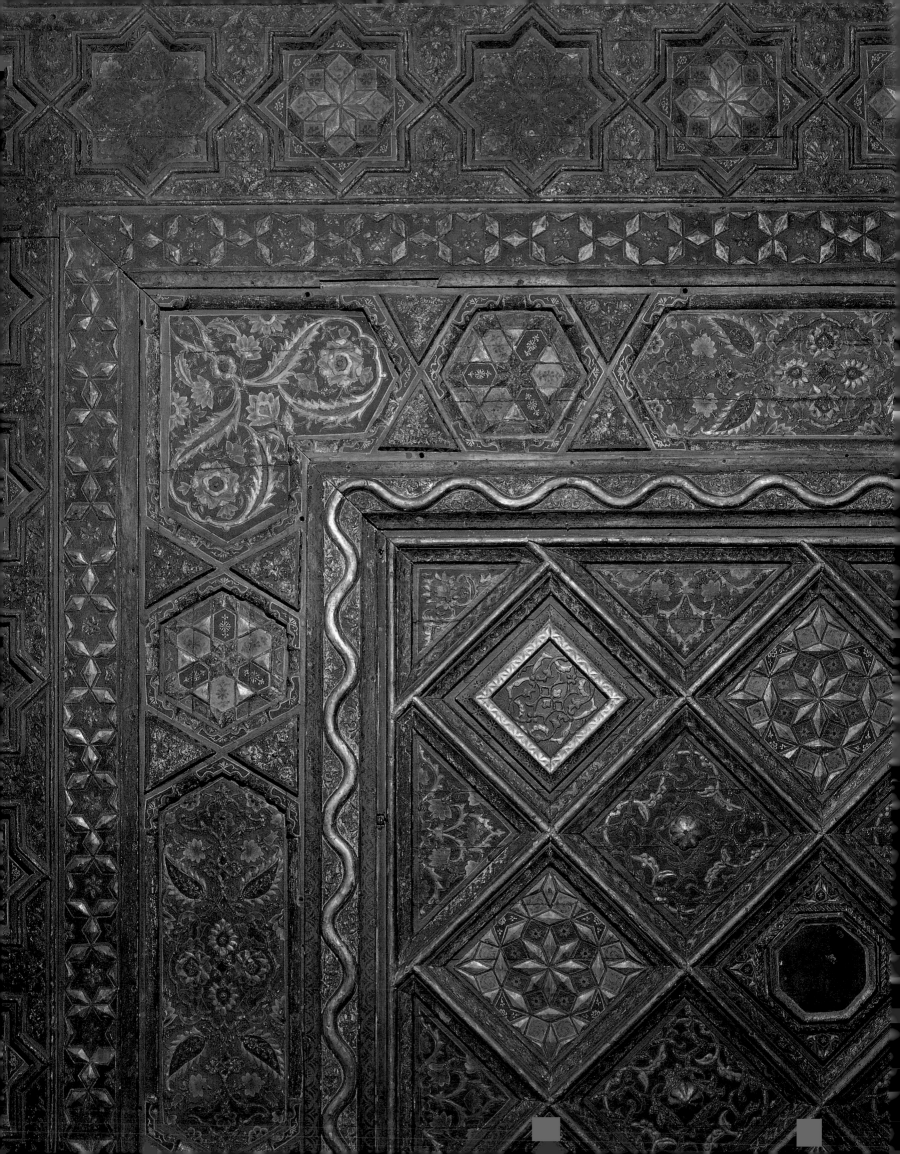

Near
and Far
East

The Nur al-Din Room

DAMASCUS ◆ 1707

In the Islamic collection of the Museum is a splendid work of art called the Nur al-din room, an appellation it received for lack of the real owner's name. The disassembled room arrived in this country from Syria in the 1930s and remained in storage until it was donated in 1969 to the Metropolitan by Hagop Kevorkian. After approximately three years, the time needed for its installation, research had not produced any precise information as to its provenance. Thus, the rather incongruous name of the famous thirteenth-century Syrian conqueror Nur al-Din was attached to it, although the room clearly belonged to a much later period. For this reason, it is preferable to call it the "Damascus room," for the city of its origin.

Anonymous though it may be, the room is a valuable document that can reveal some, if not all, of its history. Its approximate dimensions are twenty-two feet high, twenty-six feet long, and sixteen feet wide. The room's lavishly decorated wood ceiling and wall paneling soar above an inlaid-marble

The overdoor panel features a large fruit bowl flanked by two fruit trees and two identical halves of a mosque.

floor. Unlike most Western domestic interiors, Islamic reception halls were often embellished with calligraphy. The Damascus room has three registers of lobed cartouches bearing the verses of two poems and a single couplet. The poetry is inscribed in gold against a black background strewn with extremely fine wildflowers. One of the panels gives a date, A.H. 1119 (A.D. 1707), thereby establishing this room as the earliest surviving example of a nearly complete Damascus reception chamber.

OPPOSITE:
Over the vestibule section, or 'ataba, are exposed-beam ceilings, typical of those used in houses in Damascus.

In the early eighteenth century the typical house of a wealthy man in Damascus would have offered a plain and undifferentiated facade to the street, with windows only on the upper floors. The entrance door would have opened onto a long, not always straight corridor leading to an inner courtyard. Admittance to the private domain could thus be carefully controlled. Having stepped past the threshold, the visitor making his or her way through the dark, unadorned passageway could leave behind the dust and tumult of the street and begin to anticipate the comfort and luxury within. Very prominent households would have as many as four courtyards, usually decorated with fountains, flowers, and fruit trees (trees were a measure of a person's prosperity). If the visitor was female, she would be ushered to the women's apartments, either on another side of the house or upstairs. If the caller was a man, he would, depending on the season, be escorted either to a lofty summer hall, known as the *iwan* (or *liwan*), on the south side of the principal courtyard, or to its winter counterpart on the north, which benefited from a warm southern exposure.

The iwan, closed on three sides and open on the fourth, would have a marble floor, walls inlaid with a mixture of colored powder and glue, and a high wooden ceiling. With one side completely open to the courtyard and availing of northerly breezes, the iwan's purpose was to provide a cool space for summer entertaining.

Although most middle-class houses had both an iwan and some kind of winter salon, only palaces or very large houses revealed their status by having a very formal winter reception room, known as the *qu'a*. The exquisite quality and the quantity of the decoration in the Museum's room attest to its having been one such exalted *salle d'apparat*. This interior would have had the distinction of being the house's showpiece, displaying the finest workmanship and the master's most prized possessions. And, as movable furnishings were few in the traditional Islamic household, the walls, ceiling, and floors of these rooms served principally to convey their owner's social prestige.

The guest invited into the qu'a would first step into its antechamber, known as the *'ataba*, a kind of vestibule at the same floor level as the courtyard. To conform to the available gallery space in the Museum, the room's doorway had to be switched; originally the entrance was through the left-hand wall (in place of the present second window), where it connected with

Inscription panels in the wainscoting
above the overdoor panel

View into the 'ataba. To the right is
the entrance door as reconstructed for
the Museum's installation; to the left is
the masab, a decorative niche that would
have held a vase and a set of ornate
coffee or sherbet cups.

the courtyard. In the 'ataba the visitor would be greeted by the host. After removing his shoes, he would be invited to ascend to the reception area proper, the *tazar*. The tazar is always attained by a high riser and is set off by an imposing arch. While servants in the 'ataba busied themselves with the preparation of water pipes, braziers, and refreshments (coffee, sherbet, sweets), the visitor would cross the tazar's heavy carpets and take his place next to the host on comfortable cushions and divans. The degree of the guest's importance determined his place in the so-called bosom, or *sadr*, of the tazar. Seats were classified by their height (achieved by the thickness of the cushions) and by their location in the sadr; the most honored guest would occupy the highest and innermost spot. Once the visitor was seated, the spectacle of the room's decoration would begin to unfold. The architectural ornamentation, spreading over the floor, walls, and ceiling like an intricate tapestry inviting prolonged contemplation, would soon exclude the outer world from the viewer's mind and begin to evoke thoughts of God's infinite nature, the eternal patterns of creation, and the rhythmical process of growth and decline of this transient world.

The floor of the 'ataba below was paved in a marble grid and dominated by a small fountain. The room's fountain is decorated in opus-sectile and mosaic-inlay techniques. Its main design follows a seventeenth-century style inspired to a large degree by even earlier Mamluk (fourteenth–fifteenth century) fountains with octagonal basins enclosing "arcades," laid out flat with arrowlike *voussoirs*. Another striking feature of the 'ataba is the niche known as the *masab*. In the Museum's room this niche is located on the right-hand side, just before the spring of the great arch. Originally it faced the entrance door and would have been the first thing seen by the visitor. Its function was simply decorative, intended to hold an objet d'art, a flower vase, a water jar, or a precious set of cups. As installed, this masab is a pastiche of elements from the room and from other interiors dating to the early eighteenth century. The upper part, which came with the room, is fitted with a wooden trilobed vault called a *muqarnas* filled with the characteristically Islamic ornament resembling a honeycomb. Below is a Syrian tile panel from the Museum's collection that is a typical example of those produced in Damascus in the first half of the eighteenth century. Around its design of arches, trees, and flowers are inscribed the names of God, the prophet Muhammad, and the four orthodox caliphs Abu Bakr, 'Omar, 'Othman, and 'Ali. In the center a cartouche reads, "Trust in God." Because this masab was missing its topmost ornamental panel, it was installed incorrectly to begin at floor level, when it should have started at the same height as all the other arched openings in the room. The single panel bearing the room's date should be at its topmost limit, just below the cornice.

As would any Islamic room of this significance, the Museum's qu'a is enveloped in an ensemble of wood paneling featuring several arched openings

ABOVE:
The fountain in the center of the 'ataba floor. Decorated with inlaid colored marbles and stones, this rare example features a design inspired by much earlier fountains.

OPPOSITE:
The Museum's *masab* comprises an original wooden vault, or *muqarnas*, and a typical 18th-century Damascene tile panel.

springing from the same level: shuttered windows facing the courtyard, open niches with shelves exhibiting objects of value or leather-bound books, and large cupboards with double doors either holding furnishings, such as cushions and rugs, or serving as "treasure" cabinets. The large cupboard in the middle of the tazar's right wall, known as a *semandara*, would have served in the latter capacity. In the center of each of its doors is a gold medallion enclosing a star motif. Around it revolves an inscription that repeats "Oh, Glorious!" eight times. The room's paneling is circumscribed at its upper limit by a concave cornice that runs uninterrupted around the entire space. It features more inscribed cartouches alternating with gilded muqarnas segments.

Between the wainscoting and the ceiling, both ornamented in rich colors and gilding, is a zone of white wall punctuated only by windows of a jewellike quality. The wall's basic function is to frame and accentuate the woodwork and to increase the height of the room. Light entering through the windows' pierced-stucco grilles, inlaid with pieces of colored glass, would have created a kaleidoscopic effect below. The finely tuned aesthetic of Islamic interiors such as this one makes provision for areas of simplicity to be counterbalanced by others of visual excitement. Water and light are also integral to the decorative scheme.

Detail of a golden vase with a
bouquet of naturalistic flowers set
in a gilded medallion. Series of
similar motifs are employed on
a number of long vertical panels.

In the Museum's installation the decorated panels are affixed to a
modern wooden armature. The ceiling over the 'ataba has exposed beams,
whereas the tazar ceiling is composed of suspended boarding, with beams
and other elements concealed. In Damascene interiors wood was both local
and imported, poplar and walnut being the most common. The decorative
motifs of all the woodwork were executed in various specialized techniques,
and the patterns were transferred by paper stencils. A sense of textures in
relief was sought in several areas, and gesso served as the actual base for the
polychrome decoration. Areas of gold or silver were painted in fine leaves
of gold sheet or tinfoil.

The owner of the Metropolitan's qu'a clearly aimed at an interior
firmly embedded in the local Syrian-Arab tradition of such grand reception
rooms: spatial divisions, materials, techniques, small floral and geometric
ornamentation, and inscriptions that at least in part eulogize the Prophet
Muhammad. On the other hand, he seems to have been cognizant of certain
new elements that were just beginning to make their mark in the interiors
of Istanbul, the Ottoman capital. These imported motifs—bowls of lush
fruit, architectural vignettes, curiously shaped cornucopias, and naturalistic
bouquets of tulips, carnations, wild roses, and hyacinths emerging from
golden vases—were incorporated into the overall decorative fabric as novelty
"punctuation marks" that would have had considerable impact on visitors.

The Damascus room originated in the period when Turkey became
fascinated with European, in particular French, elements of decoration, leading to a phenomenon commonly termed Turkish rococo. This corresponded
to the vogue for things Oriental, especially Turkish, among the European
upper classes. Perhaps the central figure of this new aesthetic was the Ottoman
sultan Ahmed III, who ushered in the so-called Tulip Era (1703–30), an
epoch of rarefied extravagance and pleasures whose emblem was the tulip.
The remarkable presence of these motifs at such an early date in the Museum's
room indicates the cosmopolitan milieu of its owner. Interesting parallels
can be drawn with Sultan Ahmed III's Fruit Room and Library, built
between 1705 and 1720 in the Topkapı Palace, which feature whole series of
flower vases and fruit bowls. Both of these rooms evoked the ambience of
garden pavilions. Similarly, the Museum's Syrian qu'a originally would have
resembled a kind of garden pavilion, for its countless blooms and fruit bowls
would have been set off by the fresh, apple-green color of their background,
today obscured by a brownish layer of overpainting. Thus, it seems that the
Metropolitan's room was in the vanguard of contemporary interior decoration.

More direct European influence can be ascribed to the walls' cornucopias, as well as to the architectural vignettes on the doors of the semandara
and on the overdoor panel. These paintings stem from the late-seventeenth-
and early-eighteenth-century Ottoman vogue for interior decoration that had
been the combined result of the *vedute* of European interiors, of Western

engravings, and of Turkish miniature painting with its pronounced love of topographical and architectural detail.

Finally, a guest could turn to the poetic verses that figure prominently on the paneling, its cornice, and the cornice of the tazar. It is here that the host's intellectual achievements could best be evidenced, because similar inscriptions were a long-established genre in the Islamic world, and poetry was a major part of any soirée of cultivated gentlemen. The more subtle the poetic allusions and the finer the versification on the walls of the qu'a, the more the room could "speak" of its master's erudition. A number of Damascene salons had inscriptions eulogizing the Prophet, being frequently inspired by the famous "Ode on the Prophet's Mantle" by the seventeenth-century poet Busiri. The poetry in the Damascus room comprises two poems and an independent couplet. The poem inscribed on the paneling is interrupted by the couplet exhorting the Prophet and placed precisely over the sadr of the tazar, in the center of the far wall, where the host and his honored guests would have sat. The poem at this level extols the virtues of the house and its owner and makes veiled reference to "feasts of rejoicing," possibly indicating that, as was often the custom, the room was decorated on the occasion of some auspicious event such as a wedding or a circumcision. The other poem runs around the cornice of the paneling and that of the tazar ceiling. It appeals to God, praises and describes the Prophet, and draws the image of daybreak and morning rain in a flower garden, an appropriate theme for a qu'a replete with floral motifs and the produce of a garden's fruit trees.

Even though the Museum's room still guards the mystery of its owner, its special magic can touch any visitor who stands at the threshold and contemplates the decorative vocabulary, bearing in mind the following lines from its inscriptions:

> House of praises, glorious deeds and magnanimity,
> [May] feasts of rejoicing remain with you eternally.
> Noble hands erected you in highest dignity;
> . . . .
> In [your] towers are assembled splendor and generosity!

ANNIE-CHRISTINE DASKALAKIS MATHEWS

Detail of the unusual cornucopias found on parts of the paneling

The Astor Garden Court and Ming Room

SUZHOU ♦ 1634

In the early 1970s the Metropolitan Museum embarked on a program of reinstalling the permanent galleries for Asian art. Brooke Russell Astor, a trustee of the Museum who had spent part of her childhood in Peking, suggested that a garden court could provide a place of repose in the midst of conventional galleries. In 1977 a team of Chinese experts was assigned the task of creating an authentic Chinese garden court, using traditional materials and methods, and in the spring of 1981, the Astor court and the adjacent Ming room opened to the public.

The design of the Astor court is based on a small courtyard within a scholar's garden called Wang Shi Yuan, the Garden of the Master of the Fishing Nets, in Suzhou, a city west of Shanghai that experienced a flourishing garden culture during the Ming period. The courtyard was first built in the twelfth century by a government official, who named his residence Yu Yin, the Fisherman's Retreat, in admiration for the pure and uncomplicated life of the fisherman. (The retreat was far from modest, however, as it contained an extensive personal library, the Studio of Ten Thousand Scrolls.) By the fifteenth century the garden had fallen into disrepair, but during the eighteenth century it was rebuilt twice, with further alterations made by subsequent owners, in the tradition of the great Chinese scholar-officials.

Scholars in Chinese society were held in the highest regard, second only to members of the imperial family. After years of education and a series of difficult examinations, a scholar might be given an appointment in the

The pavilion in the courtyard in the Garden of the Master of the Fishing Nets in Suzhou, China, which was used as the model for the Astor Court. Architecture and nature are interwoven here; the wall is a backdrop for the fantastic rocks and luxuriant plants, while the pavilion is both a place from which to view the garden and a showcase for the exhibition of a fine rock.

From the moon-viewing terrace one looks south along the covered walkway to the moon-gate entrance and the south wall, which is dominated by a spectacular Taihu rock and four latticed windows, which were based on those in a 1634 Chinese garden manual.

civil government. While such positions brought considerable prestige, they also required scholars to uphold the Confucian ideal of unswerving loyalty to their sovereign, a responsibility that brought with it the need to speak frankly, even to criticize other officials. Such acts were sometimes viewed as treason, and as a consequence the careers of many scholars were short. The punishment might be mild or severe, but often the scholar saved face by retiring into exile, to write or teach, or to build a garden.

The Chinese garden was a symbol of cultural and artistic achievement, and it was not unusual for retired scholars to design their own gardens, a task that posed an interesting creative challenge as well as providing a place for contemplation. Ji Cheng, author of *Yuan Ye*, a treatise on gardens written in 1634, wrote that the purpose of having a garden in the city was "to live as a hermit even in the middle of the marketplace, enjoying a better view than you would have from nesting in the trees. In a well-planned urban garden, even if the neighborhood is somewhat vulgar, all noise is shut out when the gates are closed."

The Garden of the Master of the Fishing Nets is densely but harmoniously arranged on one and a third acres in the center of the bustling provincial city of Suzhou. Besides the residence and some dozen smaller buildings, there is a spacious central pond, with handsomely proportioned courtyards flanking the east and west sides of the main garden, and ten tiny gardens tucked in among the buildings. The vast expanse of whitewashed exterior walls gives little hint of the delicacy and beauty that lie behind them.

Originally the Garden of the Master of the Fishing Nets was entered through the formal entrance and public rooms on the first floor, which led eventually to the garden beyond. Buildings virtually ring the pond, carefully positioned with respect for the landscape. Water is an indispensable visual and symbolic element in Chinese gardens, often representing that which is pure and noble and, beyond all else, true to its own nature. Water brings immediately to mind the yin-yang duality so fundamental to Chinese thought. The yin-yang complementary polarities of dark and light, soft and hard, void

The main entrance to the Astor Court is the moon gate in the south wall. Looking through the gate to the north, one sees only parts of the garden and primarily zones of darkness and brightness, a manifestation of the complementary pairs of yin and yang. The eye moves from the white wall to the dark vestibule, to the sunlit garden, to the dark Ming room, and on to the bright windows at the far end. The contrasts create a sense of rhythm, distance, and space.

and mass can be seen everywhere in Chinese gardens; if the design is successful, the contrasts will be infinite and subtle, with neither aspect predominating.

Past the central pond, over a small zigzag stone bridge and through a gate, one comes to a modest courtyard in front of a room called the Late Spring Studio. Because of its appropriate size, harmonious proportions, and utter simplicity, this courtyard was adapted for the Astor court, which incorporates a simple plan in keeping with the yin-yang principle of alternation. Similar elements, such as plaster walls, wood structures, or rocks, do not face each other. Viewed from outside the entrance at the south end, a circular moon gate frames a rectangular doorway, through which successive spaces defined by colonnades and an alternating pattern of light and dark may be seen. The complexity of space is achieved through an orderly use of

At the north end of the garden court lie the moon-viewing terrace and the Ming Room. As in its model courtyard in the Garden of the Master of the Fishing Nets, the tall lattice doors and windows can be completely opened to merge the exterior and interior spaces.

yin and yang opposites: the circle versus the rectangle, the small dark vestibule leading to the sunlit courtyard, which in turn leads to the dark main hall with backlighted windows suggesting deeper spaces beyond. The symmetry of the main hall is broken by the pillars of the walkway on one side; the straight line of the walkway is interrupted by a jog from the wall, and the hard lines of architecture contrast with the soft lines of rocks and plants.

At the north end of the Astor court are the moon-viewing terrace and the Ming room. As in the Garden of the Master of the Fishing Nets, the tall lattice doors and windows can be opened completely to merge the garden and interior spaces. The high wall with a roof ridge of terracotta tiles suggests that the Ming room is part of a larger building complex. The bricks of the courtyard floor, placed in alternating squares of four, were made at the imperial kiln at Lumu, not far from Suzhou.

The west wall of the courtyard is crowned by a half pavilion with exuberant upturned eaves. The gracefully curved bench back is called the Beautiful Lady Balustrade after the women who delicately leaned against it. In contrast to the walkway on the opposite wall, which encourages a moving survey of the garden, the pavilion provides a place for the visitor to contemplate it from a fixed point of view. The half pavilion takes its name—the Cold Spring Pavilion—from the little spring that bubbles up out of the rocks and flows into a pool to the left of the structure.

An important element in Chinese garden design, the covered walkway guides the visitor to the most interesting views, while providing a pleasant refuge from the rain or sun. In large gardens covered walkways often rise and fall, winding around hills; in the Astor Court garden the jog in the walkway creates an alcove for a tall sleek rock called a bamboo shoot, a visual pun on the surrounding bamboo.

The covered walkway on the east wall of the courtyard jogs so that the view changes with each step.

301

From the moon-viewing terrace one looks along the covered walkway to the moon-gate entrance and the south wall, which is dominated by a spectacular Taihu rock and four latticed windows. The lattice patterns—each different lest the eye become bored with the repetition of one design—were taken from the 1634 garden manual *Yuan Ye.*

The small hall at the north end of the garden was designed for the display of the Museum's collection of Ming-dynasty hardwood furniture. Although the Late Spring Studio dates from the late nineteenth century, the engineers who supervised the creation and execution of the construction took great care to carry out all the architectural designs in an appropriate Ming style, using the best available Chinese woods. In traditional fashion, the Ming room faces south, and the furniture is formally arranged for receiving guests and viewing the garden.

The hallmark of Chinese wood construction is its supremely accomplished joinery. To join two pieces of wood, carpenters carved projecting tenons for insertion into correspondingly shaped holes, or mortises. Glue was used only sparingly and nails not at all. Mitering, a handsome way to abut pieces of wood, was also used in both architecture and furniture. Such elements as the balustrades are built-in furniture, while the lattice patterns of the windows find clear echoes in the designs of the best Ming pieces.

Fine Chinese furniture can stand on its own aesthetic merit in any setting, but placing it in an authentic architectural setting allows a better understanding of its function and cultural significance. The pieces share materials, techniques, and design patterns with architecture, and the arrangement also reflects the basic architectural principle of north-south orientation, with the most important seat facing south. The large clothes cupboard dates to the fifteenth or sixteenth century and is made of Indian rosewood. The early-sixteenth-century Indian rosewood side table and the set of four red sandalwood armchairs are masterpieces of functional simplicity and elegance.

ALFREDA MURCK and WEN FONG

ABOVE:
The brass hardware on the tall lattice doors of the Ming room has small handles that depict a pair of fish, a symbol of harmony and freedom and an evil-averting charm. Like the other materials in the Astor Court, the brass fittings were made in Suzhou.

OPPOSITE:
Views of the Ming room, in which the pillars, rafters, and wall panels were interlocked by craftsmen with the precision of a Chinese puzzle, sliding together with only the tap of a wooden mallet

GLOSSARY

ACANTHUS: a classical ornament based on the scalloped leaf of the acanthus plant

ARCADE: a series of arches on columns or pilasters; also a covered passageway or shopping street

AXMINSTER CARPET: hand-knotted-pile carpets produced at a factory in Axminster, Devonshire, from 1755 to 1835

BALUSTER: a short post; often refers to a furniture or vase support. A series of balusters support a rail to form a balustrade.

BERGÈRE: a type of armchair with a rounded back and wide seat, with upholstery between the arms and seat

BOISERIE: a French term that usually describes wood paneling of the 17th and 18th centuries elaborately decorated with low-relief carvings of foliage and often painted white with the carved sections picked out in gold or other colors

BOLECTION MOLDING: convex molding used to cover the joint between two beams or other members that are at different levels

BRÈCHE D'ALEP: a brecciated, or fragmented, marble found in France and Italy

BROCATELLE: a silk textile similar to damask but in which, because of added filling threads, the pattern woven into the fabric stands out in relief

BRUSSELS CARPET: a loop-pile carpet woven in narrow strips that are matched for pattern and sewn together to make room-size rugs

CABRIOLE LEG: a furniture leg curving out at the knee and tapering in below, ending in a shaped foot (club, paw, claw-and-ball, or scroll); popular on furniture during the first half of the 18th century

CARTOUCHE: an ornamental panel shaped like a scroll or piece of paper, usually bearing an inscription; an oval or oblong enclosing a sovereign's name

CARYATID: a sculpted female figure that supports an entablature in the place of a column; often seen as decorative bronze mounts on furniture

CHAIR RAIL: a molding installed around the walls of a room to prevent chairs when pushed back from damaging the surface of the walls

CHAMFER: the surface made when the sharp edge of a piece of wood is cut away, usually at a 45-degree angle to the other two surfaces

CHIMNEYPIECE: also mantelpiece; the ornamental frame around a fireplace recess

CHIMNEY BREAST: the masonry structure that projects into the room and that contains the fireplace and flues

CHINOISERIE: European imitations or adaptations of Chinese art

COFFER: a small chest or strongbox; also a recessed panel in a vault ceiling, or soffit

COMMODE-EN-CONSOLE: a console table with a drawer

CONSOLE: a curving carved ornamental bracket

CONSOLE TABLE: a side table, usually with a marble top supported by a carved wooden base consisting of two or more legs, often fastened to the wall with screws

CORNICE: the upper section of an entablature; also, any projecting molding, often decorated

COROMANDEL LACQUER: a type of lacquer with incised designs made in China beginning in the 17th century

COUCH: a long lounge chair, usually upholstered; also called a chaise longue or day bed

COVE: a large concave molding usually found between a room's wall and ceiling surfaces

CUPOLA: a small structure with a round dome built over a circular base that crowns the roof of a building

DADO: part of the base of a column; also, a decorated section of the lower part of a wall from floor to waist height

DISTEMPER: a type of paint used for murals, scenery, or plaster walls and ceiling in which the pigments are mixed in an emulsion containing egg yolk or egg white

ÉBÉNISTE: French for cabinetmaker or furniture maker who specializes in veneered pieces (see *menuisier*)

EN SUITE: a term meaning that all parts of a room's decoration are matched, belong to the same series, or are part of the same set

ENTABLATURE: in the classical orders, the group of horizontal members supported by a column and consisting of the architrave, frieze, and cornice

EPERGNE: a type of centerpiece, usually tiered and made of silver, popular in the 18th and 19th centuries

FASCES: an ornament derived from a bundle of rods tied up with an ax, symbolizing authority in ancient Rome

FLEUR DE PÊCHE (peach flower): an Italian brown-and-white marble found in Tuscany and formerly in Greece

FLUTING: shallow concave grooves running vertically on the shaft of a column or pilaster

FRESCO PAINTING: the art of painting with water-based paint pigments on a damp, fresh lime plaster; a popular technique in Minoan to Roman civilizations, perfected during the Italian Renaissance

GALLOON: a woven ribbon or braid of gold, silver, or silk thread, used as a trimming

GARTH: a small enclosed garden area

GILT-BRONZE: usually bronze gilded by the mercury-gilding process

GIRT: the main horizontal support at the front, back, and sides of a heavy timber-frame house

GRISAILLE: painting in various shades of one color, usually gray, to create a trompe-l'oeil effect in imitation of sculptural relief

GROTESQUE: fanciful decoration composed of small animal and human forms, often interwoven with foliage motifs; derived from ancient Roman decorations discovered during the Renaissance

GUILLOCHE: an architectural scroll pattern of interlacing bands used to ornament moldings

HERM: three-quarter-length figure on a pedestal, used in furniture and metalwork, particularly during the Renaissance and Baroque periods

HÔTEL: town house

INGLENOOK: a small recess, usually with a bench, flanking a fireplace

INGRAIN CARPET: a double-cloth carpet in which the same pattern appears on the front and back but in reversed colors

INLAY: a decorative pattern composed of different types or colors of wood or other materials set into a base of solid wood

INTARSIA: Italian term for inlay, especially of wood pieces

JAPANNING: name given to several methods of imitating oriental lacquer in Europe and America, in which shellac or another substance was substituted for true lacquer

JOINT STOOL: a wooden stool in which the frame is fitted together with mortise-and-tenon joints

LACQUER: an Asian varnish made from the sap of a tree indigenous to China and later Japan; another type of lacquer is made from the secretion of an insect native to India

LANCET WINDOW: a high narrow window with a sharply pointed arch at the top

LOGGIA: a covered colonnade open-air on one or more sides

MARQUETRY: decoration in which pieces of shaped wood are applied to a base to form a mosaic

MENUISIER: French for joiner, or furniture maker, who specializes in small pieces, such as chairs made of solid wood (see *ébéniste*). In the 18th century several craftsmen, such as joiners and woodcarvers, might collaborate on a single chair.

MITER: the diagonal joint formed by the meeting of two pieces of molding at a right angle

MORTISE AND TENON: a method of joining two pieces of wood. The tenon (projection) is cut out of the end of one piece and inserted into the mortise (hole) hollowed out of the other.

MOUNT: a cast-metal ornament attached to furniture or other objects; also a jewelry setting

MUNTIN: the vertical member in the framework of a door, screen, or paneling, which bolts into the horizontal rails

OPUS SECTILE: ornamental paving or wall covering made of marble slabs cut in generally geometric shapes

ORTHOGONALS: lines intersecting at right angles

OVERDOOR: a decorative panel set above a door, usually carved, painted, or cast

OVERMANTEL: decorative panel above a mantelpiece

PALLADIAN: style of architecture inspired by the work of the Italian Renaissance architect Andrea Palladio (1508–1580), especially popular in England in the 18th century

PALMETTE: a decorative, fan-shaped motif based on a conventionalized palm leaf

PARQUET DE VERSAILLES: compartmented oak squares used mainly for French 17th- and 18th-century floors

PATERAE: flat circular or oval ornaments, often decorated with acanthus leaves; popular decoration on late-18th- and early-19th-century architecture and decorative arts

PÂTE-SUR-PÂTE: a method of decorating porcelain with slip, which is applied in many successive layers, allowed to dry, and then modeled before the vessel is glazed and fired

PAVILION: a pleasure house in a park or garden; also the parts projecting from the center or ends of a building

PERISTYLE: colonnade around a building or court; also the open space enclosed by a colonnade

PIANO NOBILE: the main floor of a building, usually the second or third floor

PILASTER: a shallow rectangular pier attached to a wall

PILASTRE: a narrow undecorated panel used as a filler in a paneled room

PORTICO: a colonnaded porch, usually an entrance

PYLON: a gateway, usually of monumental proportions

RINCEAU: French for a motif of scrolling decorative foliage, often painted or carved

SAVONNERIE CARPET: hand-knotted-pile carpets produced at the Savonnerie factory in Paris from the 17th to the 19th century

SEGMENTAL ARCH: an arch that is a segment of a circle drawn from a center below the springing line

SETTEE: a seat with a back wide enough to hold two or more people; more formal and less comfortable than a sofa

SHAGREEN: sharkskin; also a type of granulated untanned leather, usually dyed green

STRAPWORK: a type of ornament using interlaced bands, which resemble leather straps or carved fretwork

STUCCO: a fine plaster used for modeling or molding

SUMMER BEAM (from the Anglo-French word sumer, meaning burden bearer): the horizontal support beam in a heavy timber-frame house that spanned the middle of each room

SURROUNDS (as in door surrounds): the wooden border of a window or door

TERRAZZO: a floor of marble chips mixed with mortar, ground smooth, and polished

TETRASTYLE: building or portico with four columns in front

THYRSUS: a staff, usually with a pinecone finial, originally a wild fennel stalk; an attribute of Dionysus, god of wine

TRESTLE TABLE: a table supported by a braced wood framework

TROPHY: originally a victory monument of arms and armor and other spoils taken from the enemy; also refers to painted or carved groups of various motifs, such as musical instruments and allegorical figures

TURNING: carving wood pieces on a lathe

VERRE ÉGLOMISÉ: glass decorated on the back by gilding or painting

VOLUTE: a spiral scroll on an Ionic capital

VOUSSOIR: a wedge-shaped stone or brick forming part of an arch

WAINSCOT: wood wall paneling that usually covers only the lower three or four feet of a wall

FURTHER READING

CONTINENTAL EUROPE

Anderson, Maxwell L. *Pompeian Frescoes in The Metropolitan Museum of Art.* The Metropolitan Museum of Art Bulletin, New York, 1987.

de Bellaigue, Geoffrey. *The James A. de Rothschild Collection at Waddesdon Manor: Furniture, Clocks, and Gilt Bronzes.* 2 volumes. London, 1974.

Dauterman, Carl Christian. *The Wrightsman Collection.* Volume 4, *Porcelain.* New York, 1970.

Dell, Theodore. *The Frick Collection: An Illustrated Catalogue.* Volume 4, *Furniture and Gilt Bronzes, French.* New York, 1992.

Dubon, David, and Theodore Dell. *The Frick Collection: An Illustrated Catalogue.* Volume 5, *Furniture, Italian and French.* New York, 1992.

Fahy, Everett, and Sir Francis Watson. *The Wrightsman Collection.* Volume 5, *Paintings, Drawings, Sculpture.* New York, 1973.

Fleming, John, and Hugh Honour. *The Penguin Dictionary of Decorative Arts.* Revised edition. New York, 1989.

Hughes, Peter. *The Wallace Collection: Catalogue of Furniture.* 3 volumes. London, 1996.

Little, Charles T., and Timothy B. Husband. *The Metropolitan Museum of Art: Europe in the Middle Ages.* New York, 1990.

Parker, James, and Clare Le Corbeiller. *A Guide to the Wrightsman Galleries at The Metropolitan Museum of Art.* New York, 1979.

Pons, Bruno. *French Period Rooms, 1650–1800: Rebuilt in England, France, and the Americas.* Dijon, 1995.

Pradère, Alexandre. *French Furniture Makers: The Art of the Ébéniste from Louis XIV to the Revolution.* Malibu, 1989.

Raggio, Olga, and Antoine M. Wilmerding. *The Liberal Arts Studiolo from the Ducal Palace at Gubbio.* The Metropolitan Museum of Art Bulletin. New York, 1996.

Verlet, Pierre. *The Eighteenth Century in France: Society, Decoration, Furniture.* Rutland, Vt., 1967.

———. *French Furniture of the Eighteenth Century.* Charlottesville, Va., 1991.

———. *French Royal Furniture.* New York, 1963.

———. *The James A. de Rothschild Collection at Waddesdon Manor: The Savonnerie, Its History. The Waddesdon Collection.* London, 1982.

Watson, F. J. B. *Louis XVI Furniture.* New York, 1960.

———. *The Wrightsman Collection.* Volumes 1 and 2, *Furniture, Gilt Bronze and Mounted Porcelain, Carpets.* New York, 1966.

Watson, F. J. B., and Carl Christian Dauterman. *The Wrightsman Collection.* Volume 3, *Furniture, Gold Boxes, Porcelain Boxes, Silver.* New York, 1970.

Young, Bonnie. *A Walk Through the Cloisters.* New York, 1979.

ENGLAND

Adam, Robert, and James Adam. *The Works in Architecture of Robert and James Adam.* Reprinted. London, 1959.

Bolton, Arthur T. *The Architecture of Robert and James Adam.* London, 1922.

Hayward, Helena, and Pat Kirkham. *William and John Linnell.* New York, 1980.

Hussey, Christopher. *English Country Houses: Early Georgian.* London, 1955.

Parker, James, Edith Appleton Standen, and Carl Christian

Dauterman. *Decorative Art from the Samuel H. Kress Collection at the Metropolitan Museum of Art.* New York, 1964.

Standen, Edith. *European Post-Medieval Tapestries and Related Hangings in The Metropolitan Museum of Art.* 2 volumes. New York, 1985.

Stillman, Damie. *The Decorative Work of Robert Adam.* New York, 1966.

Stroud, Dorothy. *Capability Brown.* London, 1975.

AMERICA

Aslet, Clive. *The American Country House.* New Haven, 1990.

Bolger Burke, Doreen, et al. *In Pursuit of Beauty: Americans and the Aesthetic Movement.* Exhibition catalogue, The Metropolitan Museum of Art. New York, 1986.

Cooper, Wendy A. *Classical Taste in America, 1800–1840.* New York, 1993.

Cummings, Abbott Lowell. *The Framed Houses of Massachusetts Bay, 1625–1725.* Cambridge, Mass., 1979.

Fowler, John, and John Cornforth. *English Decoration in the 18th Century.* London, 1974.

Garrett, Elisabeth Donaghy. *At Home: The American Family, 1750–1870.* New York, 1989.

Gere, Charlotte. *Nineteenth-Century Decoration: The Art of the Interior.* New York, 1989.

Heckscher, Morrison H., and Leslie Greene Bowman. *American Rococo, 1750–1775: Elegance in Ornament.* Exhibition catalogue, The Metropolitan Museum of Art, Los Angeles County Museum of Art. New York, 1992.

Howe, Katherine S., and David B. Warren. *The Gothic Style in America, 1830–1870.* Houston, 1976.

Kaufman, Edgar, Jr. *Frank Lloyd Wright at The Metropolitan Museum of Art.* The Metropolitan Museum of Art Bulletin. New York, 1982.

Mayhew, Edgar de N., and Minor Myers Jr. *A Documentary History of American Interiors: From the Colonial Era to 1915.* New York, 1980.

Nylander, Jane C. *Fabrics for Historic Buildings: A Guide to Selecting Reproduction Fabrics.* Washington, 1983.

———. *Our Own Snug Fireside: Images of the New England Home, 1780–1860.* New York, 1993.

Peterson, Harold L. *Americans at Home: From the Colonists to the Late Victorians.* New York, 1971.

Seale, William. *Recreating the Historic House Interior.* Nashville, 1979.

———. *The Tasteful Interlude: American Interiors through the Camera's Eye, 1860–1910.* American Decorative Arts Series. New York, 1975.

Thornton, Peter. *Authentic Decor: The Domestic Interior, 1620–1920.* New York, 1984.

———. *Seventeenth-Century Interior Decoration in England, France and Holland.* New Haven, 1978.

NEAR AND FAR EAST

Burns, Ross. *Monuments of Syria: An Historical Guide.* London and New York, 1992.

Murck, Alfreda, and Wen Fong. *A Chinese Garden Court: The Astor Court at The Metropolitan Museum of Art.* The Metropolitan Museum of Art Bulletin. New York, 1994.

Welch, Stuart Cary. *The Metropolitan Museum of Art: The Islamic World.* New York, 1987.

CREDITS

Henry-Pierre Danloux, *Peintre de Portraits, et son Journal durant l'Émigration* (Paris, 1910). Engraving: from César Daly, *Décorations Intérieures Empruntées à des Édifices Français* (Paris, 1880)

Page 129. Wall lights: Gift of Bernice Chrysler Garbisch, 1952 (52.206.7,8). Carpet: Gift of Mr. and Mrs. Charles Wrightsman, 1976 (1976.155.102)

Page 130. French school, *Le Souper Interrompu* (location unknown)

ENGLAND

Page 134. Detail of the Kirtlington Park Room (see page 137)

THE KIRTLINGTON PARK ROOM
Text by William Rieder, Curator and Administrator, European Sculpture and Decorative Arts

Page 136. Room: Fletcher Fund, 1931 (32.53.1)

Page 137. Enoch Seeman the Younger, *Sir James Dashwood, Second Baronet*: Victor Wilbour Memorial Fund, 1956 (56.190). Photograph from European Sculpture and Decorative Arts archives

Page 138. John Sanderson, Design: Rogers Fund, 1970 (1970.764)

Page 139. John Wootton, *Hunting Scene*: Fletcher Fund, 1931 (32.53.2)

Page 142. Susan Alice Dashwood, *The Dining Room Set for Tea*: Edward Pearce Casey Fund, 1993 (1993.28)

Page 143. Susan Alice Dashwood, *Children of Sir George John Egerton Dashwood, Sixth Baronet*: Private Collection

Page 144. Chandelier: Purchase, Wrightsman Fund, and Mrs. Charles Wrightman Gift, by exchange, 1995 (1995.141)

THE LANSDOWNE DINING ROOM
Text by William Rieder

Page 146. Room: Rogers Fund, 1931 (32.12)

Page 147. Joshua Reynolds, *William, First Marquess of Lansdowne*: National Portrait Gallery, London. Overmantel painting: Fletcher Fund, 1960 (60.50a). Carpet: Funds from various donors, 1957 (57.162)

Page 148. View of Lansdowne House from *The Repository of Art* (London, 1811)

Page 149. Robert Adam, Drawing: Sir John Soane's Museum, London

Page 151. Left: Robert Adam and studio, Elevation of Serving End: The Bowood Estates, Wilshire. Right: Engraving from *The Works in Architecture of Robert and James Adam* (London, 1779)

Page 152. Robert Adam, Drawing: Sir John Soane's Museum, London

THE CROOME COURT TAPESTRY ROOM
Text by William Rieder

Page 156. Room: Gift of Samuel H. Kress Foundation, 1958 (58.75.1). Carpet: Harris Brisbane Dick Fund, 1970 (1970.141)

Page 157. Richard Wilson, *View of Croome Court*: Birmingham Museum and Art Gallery, Birmingham, England

Page 158. Allen Ramsay, *George William, Sixth Earl of Coventry*: Birmingham Museum and Art Gallery

Page 159. Elevation from *Vitruvius Brittanicus* (London, 1771)

Page 161. Robert Adam, Drawing: Sir John Soane's Museum, London

Page 162. Left: Robert Adam, Drawing: Sir John Soane's Museum, London

Page 163. Above: François Boucher: *Water (Neptune Rescuing Amymone)*: Grand Trianon, Versailles

Page 165. Pier mirror: Gift of Samuel H. Kress Foundation, 1958 (58.75.18). Pier table: Gift of Samuel H. Kress Foundation, 1958 (58.75.130)

Page 166. Settee: Gift of Samuel H. Kress Foundation, 1958 (58.75.18)

AMERICA

Page 168. Detail of the Renaissance Revival parlor (see page 261)

THE HART ROOM
Text by Amelia Peck, Associate Curator, American Decorative Arts

Page 170. Room: Munsey Fund, 1936 (36.127). Court cupboard: Gift of Mrs. Russell Sage, 1909 (10.125.48)

Page 171. Photograph from the American Wing departmental archives

Page 173. Bed: Gift of Joseph Downs, 1953 (53.14). Cradle: Gift of Mrs. Russell Sage, 1909 (10.125.67)

Page 175. Chest: Gift of Mrs. Russell Sage, 1909 (10.125.24). Chair-table: Gift of Mrs. Russell Sage, 1909 (10.125.697)

THE WENTWORTH ROOM
Text by Amelia Peck

Page 176. Room: Sage Fund, 1926 (26.290)

Page 177. Photograph from the American Wing departmental archives

Pages 178–179. Easy chair: Harris Brisbane Dick Fund, 1935 (35.117). Dining table: Gift of Mrs. Russell Sage, 1909 (10.125.133). High chest: Gift of Mrs. Russell Sage, 1909 (10.125.704). Dressing table: Gift of Mrs. Russell Sage, 1909 (10.125.66). Daybed: Gift of Mrs. Russell Sage, 1909 (10.125.175)

Page 180. Fireback: Gift of Mrs. J. Insley Blair, 1947 (47.103.15). Candlestick: Bequest of Sarah Williams, 1944 (44.12.13)

Page 181. Photograph from the American Wing departmental archives

Page 182. Daybed: Gift of Mrs. Russell Sage, 1909 (10.125.175)

Page 183. High chest: Gift of Mrs. Russell Sage, 1909 (10.125.704)

THE HEWLETT ROOM
Text by Amelia Peck

Page 184. Room: Gift of Mrs. Robert W. de Forest, 1910 (10.183). *Kas*: Gift of Sarah Elizabeth Jones, 1923 (23.171). Table: Gift of Mrs. Russell Sage, 1909 (10.125.110). Punch bowl: Rogers Fund, 1935 (35.14). Looking glass: Gift of Mrs. Russell Sage, 1909 (10.125.357)

Page 185. Photograph from the American Wing departmental archives

Page 186. Tile: Gift of Mrs. Frederick Allien, in memory of her mother, Julia Taber Martin, 1924 (24.122.1–102)

Page 187. Cradle: Gift of Cecilia E. Brinckerhoff, 1924 (24.143)

Page 188. Photograph from the American Wing departmental archives

Page 189. Side chair: Rogers Fund, 1933 (33.121.1)

THE POWEL ROOM
Text by Amelia Peck

Page 190. Room: Rogers Fund, 1918 (18.87.1–4). Charles Willson Peale, *Mrs. Thomas Harwood*: Morris K. Jesup Fund, 1933 (33.24)

Page 191. Above: Photograph from the American Wing departmental archives. Below: Punch bowl: Purchase, Joseph Pulitzer Bequest, 1940 (40.133.1ab)

Page 192. Photograph from the American Wing departmental archives

Page 193. Left: Urn: Gift of Lilliana Teruzzi, 1966 (66.192.1). Table: John Stewart Kennedy Fund, 1918 (18.110.44). Porcelain figures: Fletcher Fund, 1944 (44.89.1,2). Right: Table: Purchase, Rogers Fund; The Sylmaris Collection, Gift of George Coe Graves, and Gift of Mrs. Russell Sage, by exchange; and funds from various donors, 1961 (61.84). Looking glass: Rogers Fund, 1935 (35.22)

Page 195. Tea table: John Stewart Kennedy Fund, 1918 (18.110.13). Carpet: Purchase, Clara L. S. Weber Gift, 1980 (1980.1)

THE VAN RENSSELAER HALL
Text by Amelia Peck

Page 196. Wallpaper: Gift of Dr. Howard Van Rensselaer, 1928 (28.224)

Page 197. Photograph from the American Wing departmental archives

Pages 198–199. Hall: Gift of Mrs. William Bayard Van Rensselaer, in memory of her husband, 1928 (28.143).

Dining table: Purchase, Ella Elizabeth Russell Bequest, in loving memory of Salem Towne Russell, 1933 (33.142.1)

Page 200. Slab table: Purchase, Joseph Pulitzer Bequest, 1946 (46.154). Side chair: Purchase, The Sylmaris Collection, Gift of George Coe Graves, by exchange, 1957 (57.158.1)

Page 202. Marmion room: Rogers Fund, 1916 (16.112)

THE VERPLANCK ROOM
Text by Amelia Peck

Page 204. Room: Purchase, The Sylmaris Collection, Gift of George Coe Graves, by exchange, 1940 (40.127)

Page 205. Print from the American Wing departmental archives

Page 206. John Singleton Copley, *Samuel Verplanck*: Gift of James DeLancey Verplanck, 1939 (39.173). Copley, *Gulian Verplanck*: Gift of Mrs. Bayard Verplanck, 1949 (49.13)

Page 207. Card table: Gift of James DeLancey Verplanck and John Bayard Rodgers Verplanck, 1939 (39.184.12). Side chairs: Gift of James DeLancey Verplanck and John Bayard Rodgers Verplanck, 1939 (39.184.3–8). Settee: Gift of James DeLancey Verplanck and John Bayard Rodgers Verplanck, 1939 (39.184.2)

Pages 208–209. Secretary desk: Gift of James DeLancey Verplanck and John Bayard Rodgers Verplanck, 1939 (39.184.1). Looking glass: Gift of James DeLancey Verplanck and John Bayard Rodgers Verplanck, 1939 (39.184.13)

Page 210. Dinner service: Gift of James DeLancey Verplanck and John Bayard Rodgers Verplanck, 1939 (39.184.22, 27–39). Bequest of Mrs. Samuel Verplanck, 1942 (42.37.1, 3–6)

Page 211. Jar: Rogers Fund and Gift of Mrs. Russell Sage, by exchange, 1971 (1971.140.1)

THE HAVERHILL ROOM
Text by Amelia Peck

Page 212. Room: Rogers Fund, 1912 (12.121). Bed: John Stewart Kennedy Fund, 1918 (18.110.64)

Page 213. Photograph from the American Wing departmental archives

Pages 214–215. Dressing table: Gift of Mrs. Russell Sage, 1909 (10.125.153). Dressing glass: Gift of Mrs. Russell Sage, 1909 (10.125.384). Side chair: Samuel D. Lee Fund, 1937 (37.81.1). Clock: Gift of Mr. and Mrs. Perry Ausschnitt, 1989 (1989.360)

Page 217. Pole screen: Gift of Mrs. A. Goodwin Cooke, in memory of her mother, Mrs. Frederic C. Munroe, and Purchase, Clara Lloyd-Smith Weber Gift and Friends of the American Wing Fund, 1977 (1977.425)

THE RICHMOND ROOM
Text by Amelia Peck

Page 218. Room: Gift of Joe Kindig Jr., 1968 (68.137). Pier table: Friends of the American Wing Fund, 1968 (68.43). Epergne: Rogers Fund, 1954 (54.172.3). Candlesticks: Gift of Mrs. Screven Lorillard, 1952 (52.195.15ab,16ab)

Page 219. Photograph from the American Wing departmental archives

Page 220. Card table: Funds from various donors, 1966 (66.170)

Page 221. Furniture suite: Gift of C. Ruxton Love Jr., 1960 (60.4.1–15)

Page 223. Carpet: Gift of Frederic R. King, 1952 (52.59)

THE BALTIMORE DINING ROOM
Text by Amelia Peck

Page 224. Room: Rogers Fund, 1918 (18.101.1). Gilbert Stuart, *William Kerin Constable*: Bequest of Richard De Wolfe Brixy, 1943 (43.86.2)

Page 225. Photograph from the American Wing departmental archives

Page 226. Looking glass: Sansbury-Mills Fund, 1956 (56.46.1)

Page 227. Dining table: Rogers Fund, 1919 (19.13.1,2)

Page 228. Sideboard: Purchase, Joseph Pulitzer Bequest and Mitcbel Taradash Gift, 1945 (45.77)

INDEX